of related interest

Dramatherapy for People with Learning Disabilities
A World of Difference
Anna Chesner
ISBN 1 85302 208 X

Dramatic Approaches to Brief Therapy
Edited by Alida Gersie
ISBN 1 85302 271 3

Movement in Drama and Therapy
2nd edition
Audrey Wethered
ISBN 1 85302 199 7

Dramatherapy
Clinical Studies
Edited by Steve Mitchell
ISBN 1 85302 304 3

Arts Approaches to Conflict
Edited by Marian Liebmann
ISBN 1 85302 293 4

Essays in Drama Therapy
The Double Life
Robert Landy
ISBN 1 85302 322 1

Persona and Performance
The Meaning of Role in Drama, Therapy and Everyday Life
Robert J Landy
ISBN 1 85302 229 2 hb
ISBN 1 85302 230 6 pb

Dramatherapy with Families, Groups and Individuals
Waiting in the Wings
Sue Jennings
ISBN 1 85302 014 1 hb
ISBN 1 85302 144 X pb

Art Therapy and Dramatherapy
Masks of the Soul
Sue Jennings and Åse Minde
ISBN 1 85302 027 3 hb
ISBN 1 85302 181 4 pb

Discovering the Self
Through Drama and Movement

Edited by Jenny Pearson

Foreword by Anthony Stevens

Jessica Kingsley Publishers
London and Bristol, Pennsylvania

First published in the United Kingdom in 1996 by
Jessica Kingsley Publishers Ltd
116 Pentonville Road
London N1 9JB, England
and
1900 Frost Road, Suite 101
Bristol, PA 19007, U S A

Copyright © 1996 Jessica Kingsley Publishers
Foreword Copyright © 1996 Anthony Stevens
Cover photograph: Pablo Picasso's *The Flute Player* (1959)
Copyright © 1996 Succession Picasso/DACS

Library of Congress Cataloging in Publication Data
Discovering the self through drama and movement : the Sesame approach
/ edited by Jenny Pearson.
p.   cm.
Includes bibliographical references and index.
ISBN 1-85302-384-1 (pbk.)
1. Psychodrama. 2. Movement therapy. I. Pearson, Jenny, 1936-
RC489.P7D57   1996
616.89'1523--dc20   96-13400
                                                          CIP

British Library Cataloguing in Publication Data
Discovering the self through drama and movement : the
Sesame approach
1. Psychodrama 2. Arts - Therapeutic use 3. Recreational
therapy
I. Pearson, Jenny
616.8'91523

ISBN 1-85302-384-1

Printed and Bound in Great Britain by
Athenaeum Press, Gateshead, Tyne and Wear

Contents

Figures

To Marian Lindkvist, known as Billy, who followed her dream.
With love and gratitude from us all.

Acknowledgements

Our first thanks are to the Wates Foundation for their generous support to the Sesame Institute over the years and especially for the grant which made this book possible.

We would all like to thank our clients in every setting for sharing of themselves and of their energies in the Sesame drama of imagination, which is as much their creation as ours.

As Editor, I would like to thank everyone who has given their time, energy and thought to the book in all its stages, and particularly the contributors who have worked hard at the challenging task of putting the experiential into words. The fact that we have been able to weave this intricately interconnecting web of evidence together bears witness to the degree of mutual trust engendered in the training which remains with us. The book is an achievement of the spirit of Sesame.

My personal thanks to the Founder, Marian Lindkvist, and the Council of the Sesame Institute for entrusting me with the task of creating the book and especially to Mary Smail, Di Cooper, Jo James, Kharis Dekker and Graham Suter for their unfailing support; to Ian Fenton for encouraging the book in the first place; to Charles Rycroft, Ann Syz and Eleanore Armstrong-Perlman for reading and encouraging; to James Roose-Evans for inspiration; to Jessica Kingsley for her creative listening; and to Molly Pearson, my mother, and Ti Green, my daughter, for their patience with my enthusiasms.

Foreword

This is an important book. It demonstrates how Billy Lindkvist and the valuable people who have gathered round her have extended the boundaries of therapy beyond the limitations of Freud's 'talking treatment' to the active use of deeper, more emotive and more ancient modes of communication which Western society, to our great misfortune, has increasingly tended to ignore. In this sense, Sesame has been responsible for developing imaginative means for healing not only the individual but the culture we all share. Many writers in this volume describe what our secular century has jettisoned and the bereavement which this loss has inflicted on what Jung called 'the two-million-year-old human being in us all' – the dance and song, the myths and legends, the rites and rituals designed to connect us with eternal values, the ultimate meanings of existence.

Therapy demands engagement of the *whole* person at a level much deeper than speech. It is a question of mobilising the healing powers inherent in the human psyche. Therapy, Jung declared, is less a matter of treatment than of developing the creative possibilities latent in the patient him or herself. We are all creative in the sense that every one of us possesses in some degree the capacity to bring something new into existence. Inner processes which are invisible, silent, and intangible can be rendered visible, audible and tangible in images, sounds, physical gestures and movements. Something previously occult and private becomes manifest and public, something potential becomes actual; and, as many writers in this book testify, the uprush of energy that this self-actualisation generates can inaugurate a new sense of life affirmation which is itself experienced as healing.

The virtue of this book is that it is immensely practical as well as theoretical, describing in detail how richly symbolic work can be achieved not only in studios specially designed for the purpose but in prisons and acute psychiatric wards, as well as schools, community day centres and homes for the elderly. In these diverse and unlikely settings, Sesame has provided us with the means 'to experiment with our own nature', to discover new forms of understanding and communication, to enter new modes of experience, and to grow beyond our stereotyped ways of living. It is no mean achievement.

Anthony Stevens

Introducing Sesame

Jenny Pearson

> Ali Baba climbed down from the tree and went up to the mysterious rock. Finding the surface as smooth and solid as before, he marvelled at the magic that had forced it open. 'What priceless treasures must lie within it!' he reflected and, remembering the Captain's words, decided to try uttering them himself.
>
> 'Open Sesame!' he shouted.
>
> The rock opened, just as it had done before, and Ali Baba walked in... He found himself in a huge cave piled up with rich ornaments, chests brimful with gold and silver coins, and great bags bursting with precious stones – which must have taken hundreds of years to accumulate. (Traditional)

Introductions usually begin with a name. This one begins with the source of a name: the story of 'Ali Baba and the Forty Thieves' from *The Arabian Nights*. The image of the cave yielding its treasure to the words 'Open Sesame!' was chosen as a symbol when Marian Lindkvist was pioneering drama and movement therapy in the early 1960s. It reflects an experience people often have when they take part in sessions: they may wander in expecting very little and suddenly the art form takes over, opening up a place they didn't know was there. Like Ali Baba, they are amazed: they have discovered the inner world, the theatre of the imagination, where anything can happen and be experienced as real. How is it done? What is the secret of the Sesame magic?

A Sesame session in action is very simple. People move or dance to the sound of music – sometimes from a cassette player, sometimes played on simple musical instruments; a circle is formed and a story is told; people take on parts, enact the story, become absorbed in a scene; they improvise like actors in rehearsal, using their voices; they sing, chant, call out words; they try on hats and use them as a starting point for role play. The content varies but the basic form of a session is always the same: it begins with a physical warm-up leading into the Main Event, the place where the real action is. It concludes with a 'grounding', returning people from the shared 'Land of Imagination' to their own, everyday selves. All the work of the session is done within the art form, with no attempt at 'interpretation' of personal material, reflecting Jung's emphasis on the importance of symbol. Because Sesame doesn't interpret personal material, there is no conflict involved in people taking part in the session work when they are in psychotherapy: indeed, the medium of drama has been known to 'unblock' a problem that has been eluding a client in psychotherapy.

While Sesame doesn't interpret what goes on in sessions, it does address the needs of those taking part at a very deep level. How and why the art form is able to do this is the subject addressed in the pages that follow. This book is the first full account of this unique form of dramatherapy – which has movement as an essential component in its way of working. The theoretical base of the Sesame training, which grew organically around its clinical work over a period of 30 years, rests on three distinct theories: the psychology of CG Jung, Rudolf Laban's Art of Movement and Peter Slade's Child Drama.

Sesame drama and movement therapists tend to work across a wide range of clinical settings – as the list of contributors to this book will show. This is because we do not 'treat' people, as a doctor does, for specific diseases or conditions: our concern is with the person behind the disease, behind the outward circumstances of age, condition or disability. Whether the client group is in a hospital, in a prison, or taking part in a weekend of personal growth, what we are about is enabling them, through the medium of drama and movement, to make contact with one another and with themselves.

Being able to create a session that flows in an easy, comfortable way depends on feeling comfortable with the medium and with people, having some insight into what may be going on in the client group. In Sesame work this insight leans partly on an understanding of Jungian psychology and the healing work of symbol and partly on a technical training in Laban's analysis of movement – learning to work with people's movement patterns from an understanding of how they can express underlying feelings and attitudes. These two different ways of looking at human experience combine and complement one another surprisingly well, one speaking in verbal and imagistic terms of the psyche while the other is about body language and the language of physical movement. Slade isn't taught as a subject in the training but is present within the Sesame art form. The crucial factor in the training that enables the therapist to work from him/herself and be present in the moment is its experiential nature. The theoretical learning is supported by a huge amount of studio work, in which students take turns to run sessions and the rest of the group becomes the 'client group'. In this way those who are not in charge experience what it is like to be at the receiving end. Everyone learns to work on their feet, getting feedback from the group and the tutor afterwards. This experiential learning is extended into clinical placements in the second and third terms of the academic year. Sesame is the only drama therapy training in which tutors, who are practising drama and movement therapists, accompany and teach the students on their clinical placements.

The full-time Sesame training was first established in Kingsway Princeton College, London in 1976 and moved to the Central School of Speech and Drama in 1986. It is recognized by the Department of Health, the Department of Education and the British Association of Dramatherapists, and was validated as a Postgraduate Diploma by the Open University in 1995. Sesame is a member of the European Consortium for Arts Therapies in Education (ECARTE).

Putting this book together was a bit like collecting coloured pieces for a patchwork quilt and then looking to see how they combine. Though commissioned by the Sesame Institute, our parent body, it was not created, as the camel is said to have been, by a committee. It has been more like a research project: talking, over a period of nearly four years, with people who teach or have taught the different theoretical components of the Sesame Course, with people in clinical practice, and with others who have insight into the broad fields of drama and therapy. Many of them agreed to write or, in some cases, to talk on cassette. The result is quite a full and detailed account of Sesame drama and movement therapy as it is practised today.

It will be seen from PART 1: MAINLY THEORY that the work of Sesame rests on having experienced the rite of passage, known as the Sesame Course, which takes students into the depths of themselves, beginning a process of inquiry and reflection which goes on for years afterwards, if not for ever. The capacity to work with troubled people stems from these insights and the way the individual therapist is able to address and use them. How the work itself connects with the theory and draws inspiration from it emerges in PART 2: MAINLY PRACTICE, in which Sesame practitioners write about working in different clinical settings. The section also contains chapters reflecting on the training itself and contributions from individual clients in clinical settings.

In all that we do, Sesame remains very close to Jung. He told stories to his patients and understood the healing power of imagination. Laurens van

...uer Post gave a lovely example in a recent lecture on *Africa's Literature of the Living Word* at the Temenos academy:

> There was a girl who was sent to Jung by a doctor in the country as being totally alienated and at the end of the day Jung sent her back, apparently cured. He met the doctor at a conference and the doctor said 'What miracle cure did you perform in her?' because she had come back completely cured and gave no trouble again. And Jung said 'Well, I started talking to her and I found she was just homesick for the things she had left behind.' And he said 'I sang with her a bit, I danced with her a bit and we told stories to each other.' And he said 'I even rocked her to sleep with a lullaby she taught me. And that's all that she wanted. She wanted a recognition, a confirmation of the pattern of the stories which had been suppressed and not fed to her for so long a time.'[1]

Throughout this book the names and other details of clients in clinical work have been altered to protect confidentiality. Some locations have also been changed.

---

1   Quoted with kind permission of Sir Laurens van der Post.

Part 1

Mainly Theory

CHAPTER 1

Discovering the Self

Jenny Pearson

...This body memory conveys memories of our earliest existence. It is a form of knowledge which has yet to be thought, and constitutes part of the unthought known. (Bollas 1987, p.46)

The task of defining Sesame and laying bare our unique approach to working with drama and movement in therapeutic settings is daunting for a number of reasons. The most obvious of these applies to all endeavours in the field of mental health since all systems of working with the mind, with the invisible essence of what it means to be a person, are, of necessity, based on constructs – as compared with those areas of medicine which have a solid base in anatomy and physiology. However careful the research upon which any treatment of the mind is based, there is no way of applying a scalpel and opening up the area in question for physical examination. The mind is not accessible to the scalpel, being impossible to locate within the body. Mind (meaning the invisible part of me that thinks and makes me uniquely myself) is an indecipherable combination of qualities that range from inherited factors encoded in the cells of the body since birth to the way these have combined with physical development and the impact of the individual experience and history up to the present moment. Some of these details may be recorded in the brain, but there is no kind of x-ray or surgical operation that can bring them to view and demonstrate beyond doubt that a particular treatment has or has not solved a problem of mental functioning.

Because there is no conclusive way of demonstrating how the mind works, theories of the mind abound. This has always been the case, but it seems there has never been such intense and widespread interest in finding a viable theory of mind upon which to base the treatment of mental illness as there has been over the past century. As a result, we now have a vast body

7

of observations and theories, supported by the medical profession, which we call Psychiatry and another vast body of observations and theories, initiated by the work of Sigmund Freud, which we call, variously, Psychoanalysis, Analytical Psychology and Psychotherapy.

The approach to working with mind and body that we call Sesame is, essentially, just another way of engaging with human beings in the pursuit of healing. What makes it difficult to talk about is not only the elusiveness of the whole subject of mind, but the fact that Sesame seems to need a different kind of language from either psychiatry or psychoanalysis/psychotherapy to convey what it is about. This is because its work with the psyche is done through an art form and mainly at a non-verbal level. Not only this, but it is taught to its practitioners through a training that is mainly experiential – relying a great deal on non-verbal communication within the training group.

Something of the difference between Sesame and more verbally based therapies may be felt if you first try speaking the words of Hamlet's soliloquy 'To be or not to be' and then picture how it would look and feel if some of the images were conveyed in gesture and movement by a dancer:

> ...to suffer
> The slings and arrows of outrageous fortune
> Or to take arms against a sea of troubles
> And by opposing end them. (*Hamlet* III.1.58–60)

When expressive communication is separated from the verbal language in this way it becomes difficult to recognize that they are saying the same thing. It isn't that one is superior or inferior to the other; they are just different and distinct from one another, taking the mind on to different, divergent planes of communication.

Dance movement and mime, which rely on gesture, non-verbal sound and touch, form the basic language of Sesame session work and the prime means of communication between therapist and clients. Using the example of the Hamlet speech, our way of working would be much closer to the dancer conveying the images in a series of movements and gestures than to the person speaking the words. For anyone who has not worked in the medium this is very hard to imagine, describe, or convey other than by example and sharing. The only satisfactory way to know what it is about is to experience it 'in the doing' – a phrase that comes up over and over again in the training. This is one important reason why so much of the training has to be experiential. It also makes Sesame difficult to write about.

Marian Lindkvist, the founder of Sesame (known to all of us by the familiar name of Billy), was aware from the earliest days of difficulties about communicating what she was she was doing by verbal means. When doctors, psychiatrists, psychologists, occupational therapists and others became interested in her work and asked questions about it, she would invariably invite them to take part in a demonstration session so that they could experience the work at the receiving end – an approach that is still used to good effect by Sesame practitioners promoting their work. In order to demonstrate the effectiveness of her new therapy in clinical settings she set up research projects under scientific control with psychologists observing and noting results so that it was proved to work 'in the doing' and so, when a formal training was eventually set up, the inherent difficulty of translating Sesame into words was successfully overcome by means of experiential teaching – the main reason for the large number of tutor hours that is still a feature on the present training at the Central School of Speech and Drama.

It is characteristic of Billy that her life's work should have been set in motion by a dream and that, from the moment of dreaming it, she set about making it come true (see Chapter 7). The dream, in which she observed some people in a hospital ward communicating with one another in a happy, animated way and recognized that they were taking part in drama, had a quality which Jung would call 'numinous' – partly because it sprang from her own personal experience of drama as a life-giver in difficult circumstances. It is also characteristic of Billy, and of Sesame, that its creation sprang directly from a feeling rather than from an intellectual concept or a theory. From this deep impulse her drama therapy evolved into a way of working that enables people to connect with their innermost feelings through the art form and through the body, using that connection to find a path towards health and wholeness.

Sesame trainees today still begin, as Billy did, with experiencing and doing – discovering the medium at first hand – before they start to learn about the more formal disciplines that support and extend its scope. The central thrust of the training is to enable people to discover and experience, like Ali Baba, the magic and the riches that are to be found 'within'. A faith that the riches are there to be found in *everyone* is axiomatic to all Sesame work. Personal experience in the training and observation of others in the student group leads to an awareness of every human being's innate capacity for aliveness and self expression through movement, song, music and symbolic representation of the self in drama – a recognition that Sesame shares with Jung. Once this basic fact is recognized and taken on board it becomes possible to find a dynamic connecting with the three bodies of theory upon which the Sesame approach is securely based: Rudolf Laban's Mastery of Movement, Peter Slade's Child Drama and the psychology of C.G. Jung.

The difficulty when it comes to writing about Sesame is that what we know, we know with our whole selves, body and soul, and any theories we may have about the way it works are secondary. As Sesame practitioners, whether in the studio or in clinical settings, we work primarily from this non-verbal knowledge. The knowledge resides partly in a connectedness with our physical energy as it flows from the centre of our being, by which I mean not only the physical centre of the body but also the psychic and spiritual centre. The very term 'free flow', which Laban uses to describe those flowing, lyrical dance movements that seem to emerge from a place deep within us, has implications about the way a Sesame therapist works from a place within. Having consciously experienced what it is to move and work from one's true centre, one is strengthened by the knowledge that it is there to be connected with any time. There is no way this can be taught verbally but it can be learnt in an experiential way within the training group and by working in clinical placements with a tutor on hand to encourage and ground the experience.

There is a common feeling among people familiar with Sesame, whether as practitioners or as clients, that something at the heart of it is in danger of getting lost when you try to put it into words. Let me give an example from a rather unlikely source. When I first began to look for material for this book, Bernie Spivack, who did session work and directed plays in Wormwood Scrubs prison for eight years, said 'Why don't you ask Colin to write something? He's editor of the Annexe magazine and came to Sesame a lot at one time!' The Annexe at Wormwood Scrubs is a treatment centre where prisoners can choose to serve their sentences getting therapy of various kinds to help them change their lives. This man, Colin, had initially come to the Annexe with a history of crime and violence and had made big changes. As well as doing a lot with Sesame, he edited the prison magazine and began to write poetry and meditate. However, having said he would like to write about Sesame, he eventually got in touch with me to say he was having difficulties though he couldn't understand why. I made my way to Wormwood Scrubs, across the wide exercise yard with its tall wire fences, to the Annexe where I asked him about it. He said 'It's impossible to write about Sesame. I've tried and tried.' In the end he was able to talk very clearly about Sesame and how the sessions had helped him to calm down and find himself, but only after he had talked through his block about finding words for experiences which had been emotional and physical rather than verbal in quality (see Chapter 15).

This episode took place quite early on in the process of collecting material for this book, but it wasn't the only instance of people having problems putting their experience into words. Several chapters by Sesame practitioners were written by me from recorded interviews after taking people through a comparable barrier. The process of finding words for an experience that is essentially non-verbal seemed not only difficult but also, in some way, painful. It has even been so for me as a lifelong writer. I am still trying to work out why this is. Once the translation has been made, it feels satisfying to have the verbal accounts of what we do. The moment of 'unpleasure' seems to come at the point of squaring up to the task of defining what is felt to be undefinable, verbalizing that which it feels more natural to dance or sing or express in a gesture shaped from within. Perhaps it is the difficulty of making the transition from 'right brain' to 'left brain' functioning.

Another clue to the difficulty in putting Sesame into words may lie in an equation psychoanalysis sometimes makes between the non-verbal and the pre-verbal. The patient on the analyst's couch sometimes lapses into non-verbal states, which often seem to be happy experiences without any obvious reason for this. The analytical interpretation may be that, lying there beside the analyst, the patient has regressed within the transference to a state of infantile dependence and trust which rightly belongs to a very early stage of life. The non-verbal patient is sometimes felt to be, symbolically, re-experiencing some kind of pre-lapsarian paradise – possibly the paradise of symbiotic relatedness with the mother. When a patient reaches this regressed place there are, typically, silences – not of resistance or withdrawal but coming from a feeling that in this place there is no need for speech: enough just to be there, to notice the pattern of.sunlight on the window frame, the quiet presence of the analyst beside the couch. People report feelings of being wrapped around with warmth and of being physically held, a feeling that comes from way back in infancy to manifest itself in an almost physical way within the peace and quiet of the consulting room. There is no actual touching, no actual holding, but there is an almost palpable sense of having recovered a holding that once was.

These regressed states in analysis are often felt as healing and potentially creative in the sense that they return the patient to a place where there is a chance to start again, a place where growth and repair become a possibility. The psychoanalyst Michael Balint (1952) wrote about this as a good experience which he felt to be of central importance to the patient's recovery and growth. His term for it was 'the new beginning'. It feels to me as if the non-verbal place people sometimes get to in Sesame movement and drama may have something in common with this aspect of the analytic experience.

The analyst whose writings seem to me to reflect most vividly what happens in a Sesame session is Winnicott (1971) with his concept of the 'potential space' held by the mother while the infant goes through a process of not only discovering but 'creating' the world within the protective illusion that the world is an extension of himself. The infant 'creates' the mother and the 'good enough' mother is able to anticipate and collude with this creative experience by simply being there and anticipating the infant's needs. The infant is protected from intolerable disillusion up to the point where he/she has developed enough ego strength to begin to recognize that there is another person out there, a separate being with autonomy. Because it lies deep within our experience, a psychic space and time usually remembered with varying degrees of pleasure and excitement, this 'potential space' can turn into an area where it is possible to get away from the 'false self' that people produce in order to survive the demands and insults of the 'real' world outside and rediscover the vulnerable, playful, creative 'true self' that may have been hidden away for years as a defence against hurt and fear of annihilation by the powerful and rejecting Other.

The form and content of a Sesame session are designed first of all to create a sense of safety, of being 'held', and second to open up the possibility for people to 'play' – that is, to engage with the art form and with one another in activities which have no practical purpose beyond what happens in the moment. The space is held by the session leader who is responsible for bringing people into the inner space by way of some kind of warm-up and bridging activity, being firmly present and in charge while the group experiences the symbolic reality of the shared inner space, and then bringing them back to a sense of the here and now at the end of sessions. As a Sesame group works over time, there also is a sense in which the group itself takes on some of the functions of the Mother, mediating the experience of its individual members.

The fact that people sometimes have bad experiences in sessions is fully recognized and worked with, just as it is in analysis. The difference from analysis is that the good and the bad are met strictly in the terms of the art form and not, ever, by verbal interpretation. Here again I am aware of deep correlations with early experience in the Mother/Infant dyad. When a small baby falls into a fit of terror and rage, crying and shaking and turning red in the face, the mother doesn't talk to the baby about what it is feeling, or if she does it isn't the meaning of the words but the sound of her voice that soothes baby, together with the firmness of the mother's holding and her acceptance of the baby's rage as something she can deal with. In a similar way, a Sesame session can allow room for the worst feelings you can have and express, without any sense of judgement or ruling them out of order. Away from the need to masquerade as 'good' and 'civilized' and 'in charge of the situation', the person who comes to play in Sesame is thus helped to recover those unacceptable aspects of the self that get repressed in the course of creating the 'false self' that the world seems to require of us. The choice to take on angry, negative roles in the drama, or to engage in strong, slashing movement with the body, provides an outlet for these dark, negative feelings within the holding of the story or the dance form. Very real and potent feelings can emerge in this symbolic way, to be held within the sense of physical connection through hands in the circle and in the warming-up and grounding exercises. So the feelings that emerge and discharge themselves non-verbally are met, interacted with, and held in the physically-based, non-verbal medium. I have often observed how the feeling tone that people bring in from the depths of themselves, feelings which they have felt to be so horrible they would never want to show them to anyone, will bring a chosen role alive in the drama with such power and authenticity that the group will be struck into a kind of awe. The person who thought he/she was bringing out a totally unacceptable part of the self is suddenly met with 'Wow – that was powerful! That was *some* Queen of the Underworld!' The repressed aspect of the Self and the power that gets repressed with it thus come together in a recognizable way: there is a sense of the person recovering power and stature that can actually be seen in the way that person stands, moves and speaks.

In these ways people become reunited with aspects of themselves that they didn't know were there. They discover themselves. Sesame can thus be said to achieve one of the central objectives of psychoanalysis, only by a different route – enabling the participant to activate, through the imagery of story and myth and the more abstract gestures of pure movement, empowering symbols of the self.

The psychoanalyst Masud Khan (1974) wrote about the 'experience of self' as an important, but elusive, concept in psychoanalytic practice. It was paradoxical because 'no one can communicate directly from his self or can be related to directly in his self'. The self, Khan observed, could only become known through symbolic forms. Hence 'The self is as much created by its symbols as expressed by them.' Khan also states that 'Self-experience is intimately related to body-ego.' Could it not be said of Sesame drama and movement that, in its most intense moments, the participant is engaged in expressing and creating the self – like the patient in analysis, only in a more embodied and physical way?

Khan reports from the consulting room that 'Clinically, the self-experience of the patient is characterized by *a very archaic and simple state of excitement, expressed often by motility*' (my italics). He contrasts the simplicity of 'self-experience' with the structural conflicts that take up much more attention in the analytic literature because they are more interesting to write about and states with engaging candour that:

> The difficulty about recounting this…type of clinical experience is that, although it may take years of very careful facilitation, when it fact it actualizes and one reports it to one's colleagues, the narrative strikes them, and oneself as well, as singularly banal and unsurprising. (1974, p.295)

So self-experience *is* a difficult area for words. It is one in which it isn't really possible to argue a logic of meanings: statements about self-experience can only be met, subjectively, with straight recognition or straight denial. But, from my own experience and that reported by colleagues and clients, I recognize in Khan's description something that rarely and wonderfully happens from time to time in a Sesame session. We even have a name for it: in the colloquial language of the work, these moments are known as 'Sesame golden moments'.[1] When they arise, they are unmistakable.

These moments represent the pinnacle of what can be achieved in the way of self experience through drama and movement. As on the couch, they are the moments people remember, the moments 'to die for' (to employ another colloquialism); and the essence of them defies description. In Khan's words, anything one can say about such moments, including our own catch phrase for them, is apt to sound 'banal and unsurprising' by comparison with the experience itself.

We are talking about experience that is outside language, that feels more real than language and cannot be translated into it. Khan looks to other writers for accounts of 'self-experience' and equates it with Balint's 'new beginning' and Winnicott's 'true self', 'a conceptual ideal that is known concretely mostly by its absence' – yet we all recognize what is meant by the 'false self'. Turning to literature, Khan likens the experience of self to what James Joyce termed 'epiphanies'.

---

1   The expression 'golden moments' originated with Peter Slade: its continuing use among Sesame therapists today is just one instance of the way his influence has been absorbed into the Sesame tradition.

Figure 1.1. 'Energy is eternal delight' – Sesame students (1993–94) running in the studio (photograph by James McCormick)

Figure 1.2. A student-led dance session on the theme 'Journey to Paradise Island' (photograph by James McCormick)

Khan presents us with a concept of self-experience associated with *psychic* movement, taking in the relative stillness of the analytic consulting room, which often turns out to be a crucial step in the direction of mental health and growth. I believe there is a correlation between such moments in analysis and those 'golden moments' in drama and movement therapy when the participant finds release and growth through touching on a symbol of the self. Such moments can arise when involuntary connection is made to an image in the session, which may come about as a consequence of a more or less unconscious choice of role and movement pattern. Most people who have taken part in Sesame sessions for any length of time carry within them memories of particular moments that correspond with experiencing profound psychic insight or change. Sometimes these are better expressed through an image from art or literature than by prosaic description. Obviously the inwardly cherished images will vary from person to person.

Since this is my chapter and my testimony, I will conclude with two images that speak for me about the inner experience of Sesame. The first is Picasso's drawing *The Flute Player* – the energy of the leaping dancer set beside the ancient, mythic image of the goat – which appears on the cover of this book. The second is to be found in William Blake's words 'Energy is eternal delight'.

References

Balint, M. (1952) *Primary Love and Psychoanalytic Technique.* London: Hogarth.

Blake, W. (1971) 'The marriage of heaven and hell.' In W.H. Stevenson (ed) *Blake: Complete Poems.* London: Longman.

Bollas, C. (1987) *The Shadow of the Object: Psychoanalysis of the Unthought Known.* London: Free Association Books.

Khan, M.R. (1974) *The Privacy of the Self.* London: Hogarth.

Winnicott, D.W. (1971) 'Playing: a theoretical statement.' In *Playing and Reality.* London: Tavistock.

CHAPTER 2

Beginning with the Body

Di Cooper

> Returning to the sources is stillness, which is the way of nature. (Lao Tzu)

To begin writing a chapter for a book about a subject that is essentially non-verbal is something of a challenge. It is my experience that sometimes words can be an intrusion and may detract from what is actually happening. It is my challenge here, in the beginning, to share some thoughts concerning ways we can begin to look at our movement awareness. I believe it is possible to be more in touch with ourselves and others if we begin with the body.

At birth we are suddenly thrown into a totally different environment with movement and rhythms and some very different sounds. If we are fortunate we will continue to be contained, supported and nourished throughout our childhood and we will have a healthy physical, mental and emotional pattern of growth and development. In this chapter I shall be referring to positive aspects of development rather than exploring the difficulties encountered if the stages of growth are interrupted in some way. I shall begin with a journey with which you, the reader, may be able to identify, or perhaps what you read here may be just the beginning of an awareness that may set up new thoughts on something which is, essentially, fundamental.

As a young, inexperienced and somewhat anxious new mother, I can recall how I often wondered whether my small son was still breathing. As he slept safely in his cot his movements were almost indiscernible. I would sit by him quietly and watch intently until I could sense, and then see, the even, peaceful rhythm of his gentle breath, the rise and fall of his tiny body, the minute movements as he slept, innocently unaware of my concern. I would study his small, curled hands and remember the delight I felt when he was awake. Our hands would meet and he would firmly clasp my extended finger as we made contact. I observed every movement, savouring each one, and feeling such awe that this tiny human being was so dependent on me.

During his waking hours he was beginning to find a variety of ways to tell me of his needs. Through each facial expression – perhaps just a grimace, a smile, a yawn or a burp – I was able to recognize the meaning of his movement activities and respond to them accordingly. Later, as his eyes focused more easily, he began to explore his environment. He absorbed new sounds, watching and listening. Along with all this, he explored a variety of body movements such as reaching out, withdrawing, pushing, pulling, bending, stretching and rolling. Kicking his small legs into the air seemed to express freedom, pleasure and independence. He discovered that one movement could lead to another and that he could communicate with me by using gesture and mime.

Crossing Boundaries: Infant Mobility Versus Adult Conditioning

We first experience ourselves through movements of the body. Our first reactions to life are in the form of movement. It's amazing to think that children will roll, crawl, stand, walk, run, skip, hop, tumble, turn, jump, race, chase, creep, hover, float, and glide, all without a book of instructions to guide them! Children invent movement games and movement sequences with repeating patterns that involve skipping, hopping and running, rhythm, space, flow and energy. Comfortable in their play, they are at home in their bodies. Their movement is free, confident and uninhibited. They have a strong sense of themselves as they go on to learn the next skill.

Language is developed alongside movement skills: the first sounds that accompany a movement, the first repetitive noises, then words, sentences, phrases. So as we grow and develop, language is an integral part of our natural progression. We use language more and more to survive. To achieve our educational goals and our career prospects, we become dependent on our ability to verbalize our thoughts, ideas and ambitions. We frequently find ourselves being judged by our ability to use words.

So what happens to our movement as we progress into adulthood? It seems that we suddenly find ourselves inhabiting a body that we no longer understand. We come to see our bodies as either fat or thin or comfortable or uncomfortable. The movement spontaneity of our childhood seems to have disappeared. We forget the sheer fun of creative physical play. Our life styles become stressful, hurried and crammed with activities which sap our energy. How can we recapture the expressive use of the body as a means of communicating?

Nowadays there is much talk and reference to something called 'body language'. What exactly do we understand by this? A simple example may be a woman who is nodding her head at the same time as saying that she doesn't want to leave her husband: her words are saying 'No' but her body is saying 'Yes'. In all walks of life, consideration is now being given to the attitude of the body while we are speaking. People are beginning to look for the tell-tale signs of what the body is saying rather than just listening to what the words are saying. This is a fascinating subject, but many of us can read almost anything we want into the body language of others. Reading body language is a highly specialized skill and can be open to abuse and misinterpretation. Nevertheless, it is true that our bodies may be conveying one meaning and our words another. There is certainly a connection and we do give out signals with our bodies that we are not always aware of.

While we use our bodies daily as a means of completing the necessary tasks in order to live, how many times do we actually stop and become aware of our own physical self? Someone else's physical condition can be, and often is, blatantly obvious. When a friend is tired, ill, happy or sad, we notice the attitude of their body, the quality of their energy. But what do we notice about our own body attitude when we are doing the laundry, rushing to work, writing letters, answering the telephone, meeting the demands and needs of others? We do know when we are tired, busy, 'rushed off our feet', hot or cold: the body tells us and we have a real sense of that physical and mental condition. We also know what it is like to be in a crowd, to sense the quickness of the heartbeat, to shiver with excitement or tremble with fear. We know these body feelings. But the fundamental question is: what do we understand about our physical self? Are we aware of how emotional changes will affect our body feelings? We become expert at managing objects as we cope, but give little thought to managing ourselves.

Most people have experienced some kind of structured physical activity – a sport, perhaps, or dance of some kind. As we learn these skills they become part of us, never forgotten. We know what we are about when involved in our physical recreation hobbies. We sense the feel of the game or the pleasure of sharing the dance. Through movement, we gain a confident sense of ourselves.

Here I am inviting you to think about, if not try out, a different kind of movement experience: a more creative experience which may recapture the playful, spontaneous nature of moving as you did when you were a child – daring to find a way of moving without editing, without following someone else's instructions or rules. This will enable you to listen to your own body and allow yourself to move into unknown movement and perhaps, eventually, into unknown emotional territory.

The minute we are challenged to move our bodies in an abstract or creative way we become confused, embarrassed, feel stupid, shy and insecure. We may feel overwhelmingly inadequate at using our bodies without language or a set of guidelines, without being given an explanation first, before we move, or being given the opportunity later to give our reasons, to justify our movements. How can we change patterns so long established, change the rhythms, begin to listen and deepen our understanding of our bodies?

There is a vast difference between intellectually understanding the rules and skills of a game or a sporting activity, or even the intricate steps of a folk dance, and the simple awareness of being able to move spontaneously and naturally without the fear and discomfort in the 'not knowing' what the next move is.

Voyage into the Unknown: Breathing

Our breathing patterns are very much affected by our emotional states. The breath will become shallow, tight or fast when we are anxious and stressed. By the same token, our breathing will become deeper and more even when we are relaxed and calm. From the moment we are born, our lives begin to be filled with things we have to cope with. We have to find the resources to use our whole bodies in order to breathe by using our senses. We can no longer draw on the comfort and protection of the womb where we breathe naturally from the belly. As we progress into childhood and adulthood, our breathing moves into the chest and we feel tension in the neck and shoulders. Even in sleeping our minds are unable to be still. We find it difficult to relax and return to the peaceful state that existed in the womb.

Our bodies will always be holding tension somewhere so we need to find ways we can release that. In order to do this we have to take time to listen to our breathing and return to the natural rhythm of our bodies. The following exercises will illustrate some of the very practical ways of experiencing stillness, as we can begin to sense the body in a different way.

Steps to the Pool of Stillness: Exercises

Begin by standing with the feet parallel and apart, to the width of your hips, with the body weight evenly distributed over both feet. The head is balanced lightly on the top of the spine – imagine the lightness of a balloon in order to get the sense of lightness. Let the facial muscles relax and the lower jaw drop. The arms hang comfortable and loosely by the sides. Think about the back being wide and open across the shoulders, and wide and open across the lower back. The knees are soft, not locked – comfortable and easy, not turned in. Stand for a few seconds and start sensing how this position is affecting you. Acknowledge those feelings, but remain standing as comfortably as possible. Become aware of your breathing: in what kind of rhythm and in what part or parts is your body moving?

After a few seconds of standing in this way, begin raising the arms very slowly as you breathe in – the arms only need to go to shoulder height. The 'in' breath is perfectly normal and gentle: do not gulp air.

As you breathe out, lower the arms and let the knees bend very slightly until the arms once again become level with the hips, hanging easily by your sides.

Repeat this simple breathing pattern until it begins to feel more natural. Allow yourself to go with the flow of the movement as the arms rise and fall, but it must be a slow and even rhythm – not rushed or hurried in any way.

This simple way of getting in touch with your breathing pattern takes only a few minutes. Another useful way of listening to the body is just to stand completely still in the way suggested above, but without actually moving the arms. This sounds easy but standing still is something quite difficult to do: the body will immediately feel strange and awkward. Our aim will be to return to the deep, natural breathing pattern we had at birth in order to restore our vitality and our sense of the body. Once the movement pattern of the breathing exercise is absorbed, the eyes can remain closed. This will help us to focus and concentrate on the feel of the movement.

Your mind will wander. You will think of a million things you would rather be doing or think that you should be doing. Your body will probably feel strange and uncomfortable. You may feel angry, frustrated, impatient – or you may feel peaceful and calm. You may find that parts of your body begin to ache, or feel strained and uncomfortable. All these feelings and sensations need to be acknowledged as being normal, as one thing becomes clearer. You are beginning to make the connections between body and mind.

This is a first step. By giving some space to yourself and to the body, you may begin to see yourself in a new light.

To explore a little further now, let's take a look at some way we can breathe more naturally. In the beginning I referred to the breathing pattern of a small child: the uninterrupted, even rhythms of natural breathing. How can we recapture this?

RETURNING TO CENTRE

Returning to the comfortable standing position described above, place your hands on your abdomen. Press in slightly as you breathe in, and on the 'out' breath you can feel the belly filling up as your hands move outwards. Quietly and slowly you can breathe in and out this way, concentrating on the 'out' breath in order to avoid tensing up on the 'in' breath.

We will often return to the habitual pattern of our breathing, which tends to be centred in the chest cavity. We can acknowledge this and, after a while, return to the deeper breathing. As we familiarize ourselves with this, we can learn to trust that there is this very simple way which enables us to re-focus, to begin again. By giving space to the body, the body will in turn give space to us.

MOVING OUT

The following suggestions are beginnings for moving in a spontaneous and uninhibited way, for discovering and sensing new body movement qualities. They will also lead to finding new tensions: through exploring and inventing different ways of moving, you will become aware of heightened feelings that will accompany the movements.

Starting with the head, with eyes closed we can experience tiny movements of the neck as if we might be saying 'Yes' or 'No', as if the head is a balloon balanced precariously on top of the spine, we can feel light, float, lift ourselves taller, moving gently – sensing, feeling the weight, power, mobility of the head.

Keeping the eyes closed, allow the head to rest lightly on the top of the spine and begin to be aware of the shoulders. Mentally moving into the shoulders, begin to explore the range of movement in the joints. Very slowly and gently lift the shoulders,lower them, push them forwards and backwards. Raising and lowering, rotating, pulling back and pushing forward slowly, will enable an awareness of the action of the movement.

Continue, with eyes closed, and begin to make simple, small movements of the hands, opening and closing the fingers slowly, quickly, gently, abruptly. Extend your hands away from the body, reaching, recoiling, sensing and feeling the endless variety of movements your hands can make.

You can move on and in the same way explore the range of movements in the hip joints, then in the knees, the ankles and feet, until you have sensed the action of the joints and limbs of your body in a new, untried and unhurried way. Constantly return to an awareness of the breath, finding your own breathing pattern,feeling secure in that constant, even, unhurried rhythm of your own breath.

This, then, is the beginning. Allowing ourselves the space to be in touch with the body, we gain confidence to move out into the space – to explore, reinvent, recapture some of the natural, spontaneous movements from our childhood. We can change the strengths of the movements: be strong, light, move slowly, quickly, take up a large space with our movements or keep them small and close to us.

We are able to open our body, close it, stop, extend an arm, reach out, focus our eyes on something we may not have noticed before. We move high and low, move forward, backwards, we change direction, change speed. Each time we move, we can sense, feel, listen to the way our bodies are responding to the movements we make and acknowledge some of the feelings that may evolve as we move.

Non-Verbal Expression

The movements evolving from your exploration will be peculiar to you only and may constantly surprise you. Eventually you will have a sense of freedom. If we can give ourselves permission to play again, we can free ourselves with the movement. We find pleasure and enjoyment in discovering again some of the movement exploration we experienced as children. As we feel more comfortable in moving spontaneously we can interact with a partner or with different groups of people. Gradually it will come to feel safe to leave the language of words behind.

As we become more confident and comfortable in using the body in this way, we are able not only to tune in to ourselves but our awareness of others' movement will be heightened. We are then able to respond to the needs of others through a simple movement action – extending an arm, or perhaps mirroring someone else's movement; changing body shape to complement another's body shape, being close or being distant; opening and closing movements. Inventing patterns, rhythms and phrases, we find out the sort of movements that give us pleasure, the kinds of movement that seem difficult. Whatever way we choose to express ourselves through moving the body, the movements belong intrinsically and uniquely to us. We are not judged on the skill or performance. There is no right or wrong way. Creative self-expression comes with body feelings first.

I was recently in a workshop where we were asked to illustrate a social situation by taking up a statue-like group position. We were asked to do this without language, so there were no words to help, no instructions as to how we might show what was happening. There was no right or wrong way to create this sculpture. It soon became very evident that, as we made our body shapes together, we communicated something extremely powerful. We became immediately aware of group members, we formed a bond in the situation and we understood the problem we were trying to solve – without language. When given the opportunity to verbalize our thoughts and feelings, we found it difficult: the power of movement, even though static, was enough. We went away from the workshop with a depth of feeling about the situation which had come about by beginning with the body action: without trying to put words first, we had an acute awareness of the feelings of each group member.

Can you picture a boardroom scene where the chairman invites the board to dispense with their papers, the table and chairs are pushed back to the edge of the room and everyone is invited to tackle the items on the agenda by exploring solutions to problems through movement first? I wonder if it would work and achieve a faster way of communicating? My own feeling is that, after the initial discomfort of allowing the body to speak, a more rapid understanding would result.

There is a lot more interest these days in approaching problem solving in more creative ways. Courses in communication and presentation skills are being set up nationwide. One of the more recent innovations is a conflict management school. Martial art techniques are deployed as a means of looking at relationship problems: before any language is spoken, participants will perform the movement sequence of a chosen martial art. The dialogue begins with the body action. Although one might immediately think of the martial arts as being aggressive and destructive, they actually have an important philosophical content which goes way beyond combat skills.

For centuries people in China have practised T'ai Chi Chuan. This is often called a soft martial art. It originates from a means of self defence but it has the philosophy of yielding before the attacker. In yielding, the defender turns his or her movements into harmony with, rather than opposition to, the direction of the attacker's force.

T'ai Chi Chuan is a sequence of movements which flow effortlessly. The movements constantly return to a circle. The T'ai Chi symbol, often known as the symbol of the Yin, shows the two great forces of the universe, the dark and the light, held in balance, not opposing, each embracing the other. The teaching of T'ai Chi Chuan has been handed down from generation to generation. I am told, and have read, that you can find hundreds of practitioners in China performing this ancient martial art early in the morning under the trees in the parks, before their working day begins. It is thought to have a profound effect on the well-being of body, mind and spirit. It is essentially an uncomplicated way of beginning with the body. From my own experience of practising T'ai Chi Chuan, it gives a deep sense of *being,* far beyond the martial image. This *being* is at the centre of each of us, harmonizing our intellectual, physical and spiritual energies. T'ai Chi Chuan is practised slowly and gently, allowing time for the energy of the body to find a central rhythm, allowing time for the practitioner to return to the body. T'ai Chi is a moving meditation and each movement is perfectly harmonized with the breath, the primeval life force of every being.

I am encouraged that more and more people are becoming aware of the value of using movement as a beginning, as a way into communication and understanding ourselves. I began by saying that words can be an intrusion.

This book contains many words written by a variety of people with rich life experiences: writers who will share their own ways of communicating. We can all work towards a common goal: to liberate the imagination, to free ourselves in order to free others who may be trapped in some way, mentally, physically or emotionally. It is vital that we are able to share the richness of words and language. It is also vital, from time to time, to be able to feel comfortable about working without language. To conclude this chapter, I would like to offer these words: Our body is our self. We cannot run or hide from it, although of course we do and wish to. We strive to be like someone else. We don't dare to look at ourselves. We wear many different masks. By becoming aware of our bodies through movement we are able to slip off the masks and affirm our individuality.

It requires courage and patience to accept our own creative expressive movements as a valid testament of ourselves and to trust that those body statements will not be judged or misinterpreted. We can go on later to discover the meanings of movement, and the analysis of it, which will help us to understand on a different level the difficulties we may encounter when working therapeutically with movement, as a later chapter in this book will show. But if we are intending to use movement as a tool for communication, we have first to understand what it means to us to be able to let go of the language and constant activities of the mind. We block our energy and prevent ourselves from responding non-verbally by seeking verbal explanations and answers to the way we feel. It is my believe that we all had the potential to express ourselves through movement when we were children without thinking about it. Somehow we seem to lose that sense of physical freedom as we move into adulthood.

In the context of working therapeutically with movement, the more we can discover about our own movements the more our capacity for understanding others will deepen. It is difficult to put this understanding into words. A great deal has been written and continues to be explored about body and self, body therapies and the body mind connection. But it is in the experience of moving creatively for ourselves that we find out exactly what it means to begin with the body. It is an experience that will free the mind and restore the spirit. Sensing and feeling a special movement which belongs uniquely to us will give us a totally new self-awareness that will never be forgotten.

References

Bertherat, T. and Bernstein, C. (1988) *The Body has its Reasons*. London: Cedar Books (Heineman).

Blackmer, J.D. (1989) *Acrobats of the Gods*. Canada: Inner City Books.

Cheney, G. and Strade, J. (1975) *Modern Dance*. Boston, MA: Allyn and Bacon.

Foster, R. (1976) *Knowing in my Bones*. London: A. and C. Black.

Geddes, G. (1991) *Looking for the Golden Needle: An Allegorical Journey*. Plymouth UK: Mannamedia.

Lao Tsu (1973) *Dao Te Ching*. Number 16. (Translated by Gia Fu-Feng and Jane English.) London: Wildwood House.

Minton, S.C. (1989) *Body and Self*. Illinois: Human Kinetic Books.

Pease, A. (1981) *Body Language*. London: Sheldon Press.

Reid, H. (1988) *A Way of Harmony: a Guide to Soft Martial Arts*. London: Unwin Paperbacks.

CHAPTER 3

Working with Myth and Story

Pat Watts

...through our dreams and through a study of myths, we can learn to know and come to terms with the greater horizon of our own deeper and wiser, inward self. (Campbell 1972, p.15)

Myth has been described as the poetic history of mankind by Peter Brook in his introduction to the Channel Four television programme *The Mahabarata*. As with poetry, its expression is through image and symbol. We can have a sense of resonance – almost grasping something just beyond our reach or of being struck, either painfully or joyfully, in the centre of our being. There is no one meaning: a myth is many-faceted.

Myth, far from meaning 'untruth', epitomises the eternal truths of human-kind – which it is so easy for contemporary man to ignore or deny. The power of these stories lies in the fact that they are both 'outside', in external reality, and 'inside' us. Antigone's struggle for her own beliefs, as opposed to those of her uncle Creon (who represents the State), is also each individual's need to comprehend and find expression for personal beliefs – even though they may be in opposition to the inner voice of learned authority.

The old, the sick, women and children are abused in war. Their painful plight is replicated in us today in Bosnia and all war-torn countries, and joins the tormented cries of the abused women of Troy. New horrors echo the old; new joys are timeless. It is important to bear in mind that myths are not concerned with morality, but simply with what *is*. They offer us access to our roots; they represent the ground plan of our being.

Myth is quite specific in content, and yet concerned with paradox. For this reason it is an invaluable vehicle for personal exploration in a contained and therapeutic setting. Freud believed that the cause of neurosis was largely

27

the result of repressed sexual traumata. Jung, although believing that this was sometimes true, held a different view: people can become neurotic when their spiritual horizons are too narrow. Life lacks meaning, because the ego has lost touch with its archetypal background. It is like a plant which has been cut off from its roots – therefore inner development and artistic expression assume the utmost importance for Jung, as opposed to the goal of social adaptation. *Archetypes* are regularly recurring patterns of behaviour,true for all mankind at all times. Primitive man personified these forces and out of this process a pantheon of 'gods' and 'goddesses' gradually evolved.

In working with the stories of myth, we are in some measure relating to the *archetypes*. We still have within us an experience of the 'mysterious', in which we are aware of being part of something much bigger than ourselves – an intuition of the sacred. Churches, cathedrals and mosques have been built so that in these places individuals can gather with others and together experience the sacred. Today, organized religion is in decline and many people have nowhere to be with others to celebrate the holy and the mystery.

Writing about Metaphor and Reality, Philip Wheelwright describes how early man '…did not split his world into a law-abiding physical universe on the one hand, and a confused flow of subjective ideas on the other – i.e. an 'outer' and an 'inner'. Nature and self, reality and fantasy, for him were radically interpenetrative and coalescent. …Probably an outstanding and frequently recurring fact about an early man's world, as he experienced it (for the world and the experience were not conceived as two), was his sense of a hovering, latent presence within, amidst or behind the familiar things that surrounded him.' (1968) Wheelwright uses the word 'presential' to convey early man's experience of the world and sees this as being close to the meaning of the word *numinous*.

Unlike early man, we fragment our world – and this can lead to a sense of sterility and lack of rootedness which Jung has described as provoking malaise and a lack of meaning. He recognized the potential for healing through artistic expression. Freud has observed that it is natural for people to personify what they want to understand: that the fundamental human need to assess, debate and comprehend, to clarify our private thoughts, leads us to enact and 'embody' as a way of finding out about ourselves and other people and coping with life.

In using myth within the context of drama we are working with powerful energies and this must be respected and taken seriously. It is one thing to hear or read a myth, but enacting is quite another. Enacting means engaging with the myth with the whole of our being – feeling, thinking and using our bodies; we are also relating to other people who are participating in role. No repetition of myth enactment will be identical: how a group works with the material depends on the chemistry of the individuals within the group and upon the particular mood at the time.

The leader and the narrative are the container. It is important that the leader remains outside the action so that she can be seen as a safe presence, not identified with the role. If it is necessary for the leader to take on a role, it needs to be a peripheral one.

Before working with a myth, the leader needs to be alert to the psychological implications of the story; even so, how individuals taking on the roles are going to 'engage' cannot be foreseen. We cannot know the sore places in each other's lives, nor how they came into being, nor the extent to which we are still vulnerable. It is important always to remember this. However, the story is a strong container and a vigilant leader can facilitate a sense of security in which it will be safe to explore. Because the stories of myth are primitive and powerful in their energy, I prefer to work without words in the enactment. Words can be potent and expressive but they can also keep us in the *thinking* part of ourselves and be a defence against *feeling*, so I encourage the use of sounds and of silence.

Other chapters in this book describe the shape of a Sesame session, which will by now be familiar: warm-up, main event and stabilizer. This structure works well for the enactment of myth. Since I work in the community with people who are able to cope with their lives most of the time, I always allow time at the end of a session for talking and sharing the experience of what has happened during the enactment.

The warm-up is an introduction, during which you get a sense of the leader and of the other participants, and it is very important. If the warm-up works, then it is most likely that the rest of the session will be creative. It is important that during the warm-up a sense of *playing* is encouraged – where there is no 'success' or 'failure'; where no judgement is being made as to worth or otherwise. This must be related to the attitudes and beliefs of the leader. As we go about the business of being adult, we forget how to play – something that the child in us knows so well. Play is an exploration for its own sake, involving spontaneity and fluidity. It is at the root of the way in which we learn. Being given permission to play in a safe space can of itself offer release and replenishment, a sense of coming alive. Playing means being able to relax *and* to concentrate. It is not imitating childishness, so the leader's perception of the meaning of play is important.

During the warm-up, people may begin by becoming aware of the space that they are in and experience moving with the others, both closely and at a distance. Working in pairs, sensitively moulding each other into a given shape and then offering and receiving feedback on how it felt, gives 'permission' to touch and increases awareness of our own and other people's feelings. After a number of activities in which the aim is to build up trust, relaxation and concentration, I offer themes which anticipate aspects of the story we are preparing to enact. For example, in the story someone might be seeking protection. In the warm-up it is possible to explore and experience different aspects of protecting and of being protected, of threatening and being threatened. (I say at the beginning of a session that it is not possible to see the point of some of what takes place in the warm-up until the end of the session).

As well as offering the opportunity to move and to touch, I introduce the possibility of experimenting with sounds – simply using vowels and consonants. Using movement and making shapes and sounds together, we create a group sculpture which can express different moods. Whenever possible, I offer *Lamentation* as a theme. I see this as a means for people to give expression of their personal grief, with others, in sound or chant. It can be a very important rite which is both moving and beautiful. It is a safe place to express sorrow which may, perhaps, never have been given voice. Many people have said how much they valued this opportunity and how they have been struck by powerful feelings experienced and expressed. Having 'played' with sound in the warm-up, it becomes much easier to use sounds in communicating the story during the enactment. As well as voice sounds, I sometimes offer simple percussion instruments. They can be used by people in role within an enactment or as a sensitive means of accompanying the enactment. Sometimes an instrument acts as a transitional object enabling people to move at their own pace into expressing feelings with greater security.

In myth enactment, the main event begins with the *telling* of the story: a story that is read loses much of its immediacy. This telling of the story needs a great deal of care on the part of the leader. First of all, selection of the story to be used: this is invariably in a book and needs to be prepared for telling – if it is too detailed, it can be difficult for the group to get hold of the bare bones of the story. All that is required is a skeletal outline, so that it can be filled out in enactment. A full story-telling experience is not what is wanted because that would be too complete in itself and is not a useful springboard for enactment. Preparing a story for use in enactment always requires more work than one imagines: to enjoy telling the story, you have to know it so well that it is not necessary to search for what comes next.

Having told the story and made sure that the group are familiar with it, roles need to be chosen. I always ensure that people choose their own role,

Akinidi, daughter of the Sun, became a human child in order to visit the Earth and, here played by two students, is shown around the island of her childhood by her adopted father, a fisherman (left of picture). In Sesame enactment, male parts are often chosen by female participants and if two people want to play the same part, they may play it together.

Figure 3.1. Enactment, on the Sesame course 1993–94, of the Siberian myth 'How Happiness Came' (Riordan 1989) (photograph by James McCormick)

so that from the beginning individuals are responsible for their choice. Sometimes more than one individual playing the same role may enable people who would like to explore a role, but cannot quite take the risk of enacting on their own. I remember one occasion when there was a tripartite Aphrodite: three people together were able to express her anger very freely, whereas each alone would have found it too difficult.

Having enacted the myth once, there may be various options if time allows. It is possible to move on, assuming different roles and enacting it a second time – or people may focus on a specific part of the story and re-enact that. This decision can only be made at the time. After the enactment, time must be allowed for reflection on the experience – first from people's own experience and moving towards offering feedback to others.

*Figure 3.2. The evil elders are jealous of Akinidi, who has taught the people to sing,
dance and make beautiful patterns. Prompted by the witch, Oadz, they approach the
tent where she lives, carrying a moss-green stone and eager to kill her (photograph by
James McCormick)*

The stabilizer entails relinquishing the role one has played symbolically:
coming to one's senses and feeling grounded in the present.

It never fails to interest me how deeply a group can relate when working
in this way. Very little need be said about one's own life story, but the
experience of playing, taking roles and sharing the process of the day,
endows relationships with richness and empathy.

In enactment of myth we are working with powerful energies and
personifying these forces. What lies within us on the threshold of consciousness can be stirred by the impact of myth content: it can effect us immediately
or it may finally fall into place a long time later. I think it of paramount

importance that an individual leading such a session should have looked inwards into the machinations of his or her own psyche. To have faced some of the darkness in oneself helps one to stand beside another's dark without wanting to take it away or withdraw.

In our own time, a great deal of emphasis has been placed on ventilation of feeling – almost, it would seem, for its own sake. The expression of feeling in role can be a safe and creative way of acknowledging feelings so that we can learn to contain and finally have some choice in the way we express them.

I would also like to stress the element of working with others. In participating in enactment, in embodying these often powerful forces, we have a sense of creating a sacred space which, as well as being the space of lively theatre, is also a celebration of something more vast, of which we are part. However, such creation, although in one way it happens of itself, in another it does not. Perhaps it relies on a quality I will call *attention*, which belongs to each individual in the group and is related to an ability to move sensitively inwards as well as outwards to others. To create the space where this is possible must be the main task of the person leading the enactment.

In myths and legends, basic psychic material is overlaid with cultural material – but fairy-tales, which I also use, are less cluttered in this respect and so mirror the patterns of the psyche very clearly. There is usually one clear theme and the resolution will have reference to the lack or weakness evident at the beginning of the story. For example, the weak and ageing king will be replaced at the end of the tale by a young and vigorous prince.

Enactment of myth and fairy-tale – here I have dramatherapists in mind – are for those who appreciate these tales and delight in their images and who have been stirred by their symbols. For those who are sensitive to the energy and power within them and are open to the endless flow of meaning these art forms generate, they offer a lively sense of 'something other' as well as increased self-knowledge.

References

Campbell, J. (1972) *Myths to Live By.* New York: Viking.
Riordan, J. (1989) 'How happiness came.' *The Sun Maiden and the Crescent Moon.* Edinburgh: Canongate.
Wheelwright, P. (1968) *Metaphor and Reality.* New York: Indiana University Press.

CHAPTER 4

Jung and the Symbol
Resolution of Conflicting Opposites

Molly Tuby

Therapy Through Drama and Movement

At first it may be difficult to see the link. In essence, Jungian therapy aims at bringing about psychic transformation through the 'transcendent function' – in other words, a Jungian approach, whether through analysis or through a life lived reflectively, consists in a slow process of growing self-awareness whereby a number of polarities (expressed unconsciously by the conflicts which tear us apart) become conscious, are painfully suffered and, by the grace of God, are reconciled by a 'third' which transcends them, that is, by the healing symbol.

In this context, a symbol is understood to be two separate entities which come together to form a whole. Words tell us a lot about the ways of the psyche. The word 'symbol' derives from the Greek word *symbolon* meaning 'that which has been thrown'. It was used to designate the two halves of an object which two parties broke between them as a pledge to prove their identity when they met at a later date. The symbol was thus originally a tally referring to the missing piece of an object. This corresponds exactly to the psychological function of a symbol. The American analyst Edward Edinger writes:

> The symbol leads us to the missing part of the whole man. It relates to our totality. It heals our split, our alienation from life. And since the whole man is a great deal more than the ego, it relates to the suprapersonal forces which are the source of our being and our meaning. (1973, p.130)

Wholeness seems to be the natural goal of life with the reconciliation of apparently irreconcilable opposites. If unimpeded by too hostile inner or outer forces, the ego shifts towards that mysterious and paradoxical totality which Jung called the Self, centre of both conscious and unconscious – a process he called individuation when undergone with awareness, and leading towards the paradox of becoming unique at the same time as being in touch with the deepest images and patterns of behaviour common to all humanity.

Many complex factors can block our way to wholeness and lead to mental imbalance. The unfolding of the personality faces a multitude of problematic areas, the most basic usually being childhood experiences intruding unconsciously into the current emotional situation; this can cause many disturbances such as the inability to cope with the natural changes, physiological and psychological, inherent to the cycle of life. Or, inborn traits of temperament can be distorted by pressure from the environment: whether, for example, we spontaneously react primarily to the inner or to the outer world (introversion versus extraversion), or whether we apprehend people, objects and situations by desirability or truth, potentialities or just what is – in other words by feeling or thinking, intuition or sensation and the reality function. Recognition of another polarity, that of the inner feminine in every man and of the inner masculine in every woman, is usually conducive to better personal relationships, to creativity and to spiritual growth. And then there is the all-important problem of projection on the personal level: that bewildering propensity to see in others what we have not made conscious in ourselves, especially the dark, shadowy elements. The problem of projection is at the core of the work. In the analytic situation it is referred to as the transference/countertransference relationship between the therapist and patient. It is a complex, ever-moving exchange involving far more than personal repressed material.

Here we enter into the world of the objective psyche, the world that we find represented in myths and fairy-tales, inhabited by powerful and dangerous forces which can swamp or even destroy consciousness if the ego is not vigilantly protected and reinforced. These suprapersonal forces, paradoxically, are also the instruments of transformation and healing because it is they which are at the root of the symbol emerging into consciousness and bridging the two worlds, the personal and the transpersonal.

Carl Gustav Jung, spurred by his own extraordinary psychic experiences and by certain puzzling images and ideas in his patients' material, had come to the conclusion that below the personal unconscious there exists a layer of human experience which is common to all, timeless and universal, expressing itself through myths, fairy-tales and religious rituals. These are the archetypal motifs of the collective unconscious described by the poets, the bards, the artists and the mystics. They are also lived out by the insane when the ego has been so damaged that it is swallowed up by the archetypal images and the ego\self bridge no longer exists. Following these observations, Jung launched into an unparalleled historical study of mythology and folklore, archaeology, ethnology and history of all religions, including the most abstruse Gnostic texts, and of Alchemy, where he found the model of his most original and therapeutically helpful concept, the individuation process. The wealth of symbols we now have at our disposal to understand the richness, as well as the dangers, we carry in our psyche has far-reaching consequences which we can only ignore at our own peril.

Stimulation of symbol is one important aspect of therapy. Cultivating the symbol involves, first and foremost, the imagination. Jung devised a method which he called active imagination. It consists in choosing a dream-image or a fantasy-image, fixing it by concentrating on it and watching its alterations which reflect the unconscious processes whilst the images them-selves are made up of conscious memory material; it is the combination of both images and alterations which constitutes the union of conscious and unconscious. Active imagination is like dreaming awake, except that for this inner theatre to have a cathartic effect it is necessary for the ego to participate, to be involved.

For many of us, listening to music, looking at works of art, going to the theatre and the ballet, reading poetry, are all ways of nourishing the imagination. At times it enables chaotic emotions to be experienced in more contained and structured forms. Great art activates the symbols, transforming personal pain into a feeling of belonging to the long chain of human suffering. It can bestow a sense of meaning. Aristotle spoke of the cathartic effect of the great tragedies, a cleansing of the emotions.

Dramatherapy is different. Imagination and symbols are activated in the same way but the participants improvise around the story and allow the body to speak. Jung was often quoted as saying that the hands know what the mind does not, and he was a pioneer in encouraging his patients to paint, sculpt or dance the images they experienced. Today it is commonplace for most schools of therapy to foster creativity. When patients are working on their own particular form of expression they are getting in touch with those same archetypal energies which are at the root of all art, whatever the level. Drama touches on a more ritualistic aspect of the archetypal and draws from that its powerful effectiveness: it is a group activity and the whole body is involved.

A few years ago I was invited to take on the teaching of Jung's psychology to a group of Sesame students. The emphasis was to be on the importance of symbols. I accepted with enthusiasm, but had one other priority: the therapists' level of consciousness. Unconscious entanglements between therapist and patient are always lurking and can destroy the good work that is being done. A difficult challenge occurs when the patient's ego sinks into the depths, and all too often Sesame workers are called upon to contend with such situations. The fact that they were not then required to undergo individual therapy (incidentally, many did so over the years I was teaching them) made me ask to run a weekly self-awareness group alongside the seminars. Some of the students thought they had joined the course to learn a skill and, at first, resented the imposition. In time, most of them came round to seeing the relevance and value of scrutinizing the 'I' and the 'Non-I' in themselves and in others. Discriminating between the personal and the archetypal is essential when protecting, and hopefully kindling, the fragile light of consciousness.

In his autobiography, *Memories, Dreams, Reflections*, Jung speaks of the early days of his discoveries, when he began to realize the enormous power of the energies he was exploring. This is what he writes:

> About this time I had a dream which both frightened and encouraged me. It was night in some unknown place and I was making slow and painful headway against a mighty wind. Dense fog was flying along everywhere. I had my hands cupped around a tiny light which threatened to go out at any moment. Everything depended on my keeping this little light alive. Suddenly I had the feeling that something was coming up behind me. I looked back, and saw a gigantic black figure following me. But at the same moment I was conscious, in spite of my terror, that I must keep my little light going through night and wind regardless of all dangers. When I awoke I realized that the figure was a 'spectre of the Brocken', my own shadow on the swirling mists, brought into being by the little light I was carrying. I knew, too, that this little light was my consciousness, the only light I have. My own understanding is the sole treasure I possess and the greatest. Though infinitely small and fragile in comparison with the powers of darkness, it is still a light, my only light. (1990, p.107)

References

Jung, C.G. (1990) *Memories, Dreams, Reflections.* London: Fontana.

Edinger, E.F. (1973) *Ego and Archetype.* Baltimore: Penguin Books.

CHAPTER 5

Why Oblique and Why Jung?

Kharis Dekker

Why does Sesame employ an oblique approach and why does it draw on the psychology of C.G.Jung to root its understanding? These two questions walk hand-in-hand as the best of companions. I shall try to show how this is so.

To put it as succinctly as possible: Sesame uses the oblique approach of movement and drama as a therapeutic art form for those who are unable or unwilling to put their problem forward verbally, and also because it is likely that the core of any problem lies in the unconscious and is not accessible for verbal discussion. Sesame roots its understanding in Jungian psychology because this recognizes that the emotional inner forces of the unconscious psyche need an imaged form or personification as a channel through which to emerge and be made conscious. Movement and drama can give channel and form. This is to put it simply. Let me now sketch in with some broader brush strokes.

The Sesame Method

Sesame uses what it calls an 'oblique approach', meaning simply that it uses an art form as the therapeutic medium. The art form of movement and drama is the means of expression, the language of communication between the therapist and individuals engaged in the session.

The aim of a Sesame session is to create a safe space in which to explore possibilities. Within the containing shape of the session structure, the individual participant can become involved and absorbed, can explore and can risk, to whatever degree he or she chooses. If the atmosphere is right, we can recapture something of the playfulness, freshness and spontaneity that we had in childhood, when we had a readiness for trying things out and did much of our growing through rehearsing.

The therapeutic purpose of Sesame's approach is in the allowing that it affords. We allow whatever is in the unconscious to come into play in a safely receiving and containing way, so that we can integrate it meaningfully into our lives when we are ready for it. The underlying intent is to work in recognition that in the psyche of each individual lies the knowledge of what is needed for growth and for healing. Recognition of the psyche and basic trust in its processes is the bedrock of this method of approach.

Sesame aims to create a link between the physical, emotional and mental aspects of ourselves and to bring these into harmony through embodied imagination; to explore undeveloped areas of ourselves and try new ways of being; to help us feel at home with symbolic forms of expression and so to establish rapport between the conscious and unconscious sides of ourselves, leading to a more integrated state.

Sesame's method is to engage the body creatively and allow the emotions spontaneous expression within the freedom and protection of role and metaphor. We do not go into personal material at a factual or literal level but rather find the symbolic equivalent or metaphor for the emotion. To approach issues through metaphor, where images stand figuratively in the imagination, allows for privacy of personal interpretation. It is possible to recognize and come to terms with inner problems through this indirect method, which is less exposing than a more confrontational approach and more likely, for this reason, to catch the hidden thing.

The method is cumulative in effect, allowing each individual to go at the pace indicated by the needs of the individual psyche. When a person is ready to make an unconscious problem conscious, the symbolic material offered in the session will act as a bridge from unconscious to conscious. Unconscious aspects of the personality will respond to the language of imagery and use it to meet inner needs. This affords a release which is safely channelled and held within the containment of the dramatic context. Recognition of and coming to terms with aspects of the unconscious, and the opportunity to develop personal strengths to cope with these in a creative and positive way, is likely to be of real and lasting help.

Well chosen working material that is metaphoric rather than literal is accessible to all and so can be shared. Symbolic imagery strong enough to carry the emotional charge can be found in story. Well chosen story offers powerful content in a containing context and is universal in application. Archetypal energies need strong images or 'characters' to hold the degree of emotional current they generate and the structural form of a role can carry strongly felt emotions. The fragile ego personality in itself cannot do this. Because of our vulnerability, the psyche naturally resists when confronted –

but when previously repressed emotions are ready to surface they can be given life within roles, as holding vessels which allow for their expression. Then we can begin to face them. Through being given manifest expression, painful emotions can in time transform into positive energies for life. The purpose of enactment is to offer to surfacing emotions roles in which to manifest without damaging the fragility of ego development.

The value of physical movement and enactment, as distinct from verbal therapy, is in the bringing through of emotions into the body, where they can flow and be 'earthed'. The oblique approach is an 'Open Sesame' to the interior world of the unconscious areas of the psyche. Cultivating an active involvement with the images of the psyche is at the heart of the therapeutic process. We move within the psyche's own language when we employ the imaginative medium. It is in respect for the psyche and in recognition of it as our best guide that Sesame offers a medium to give it scope.

So much for the outline brushwork. Not let us look at what happens in a session and what a Sesame therapist actually does.

In a Sesame Session

The human body in movement, however minimal that movement may be, 'speaks'. The person moving feels freer and less self-conscious if movement is given motive – and so a drama builds up with moods, inner states or characters being given living form. The drama may be a spontaneous improvisation or it may have a given story as a framework. Movement alone may be the language, or the spoken word may come into play. Sometimes actual text may be used, though sparingly: often it is only key words, strong verbal images with their potent emotional impact, that spring out of and help to carry the heightened moments that are being experienced bodily. Such imaginative creativity opens doors of possibility which may have been locked for years. Sesame sees itself as offering a key.

The therapist is there, ready upon the instant to initiate action, precipitate its development and then see it through to a close. The therapist participates in the creativity of the moment, sometimes in role as a character or changing into any number of different, temporary characters, and by this means interacts with the participant, ensuring a full spectrum of experience and helping to bring about a balancing of opposites. By engaging in the action, the therapist helps to maintain the integrity of the dramatic reality, so that what is happening is more genuinely experienced and fully felt by the participant. The therapist may, for instance, take on the character of a supportive companion standing alongside, or may step forward and represent a difficulty to be overcome, or may hang back as the weaker one requiring help; may precipitate clashes and conflicts in order to further dramatic tension; may refrain from action in order to allow room for the participant's invention and input, then respond to this by picking up on it and bringing it into the context in a meaningful way; and finally will make sure that somehow a solution is arrived at which will bring the action to a resolved ending within the time frame. The practised therapist makes all this appear a simple matter, easy and inviting as child's play, which is wonderfully releasing for the participant. The most beautifully unexpected things will happen in such a conducive atmosphere.

The crux of the therapy lies in the therapist's response to a participant's input. What comes from the participant can be supported, mirrored, validated and made more real by the way in which it is received and developed. The therapeutic interaction occurs within, and by means of, the art form. In the drama the therapist engages in role according to the observed need of the participant within the dramatic context. What the participant needs will not be known beforehand. Even the participant will not know the needs of his/her psyche, which will erupt without warning. The therapist must be available to respond within the immediacy of the moment.

It is the therapist's responsibility to see to it that where the participant is left at the end is resolved in the participant's own way. How is the therapist to know what a participant's own way might be? What resolution might be called for? The clue comes from *careful observation* of what the participant is actually doing and indicating. The therapist then works intuitively along with this, in tune with it, and never imposes his/her own personal material on the participant's work.

The skill of the therapist lies in being able to foster a working atmosphere in which all these aims can be realized in whatever way and to whatever degree is appropriate and possible for the individuals in the group.

Now let us look at Jung in relation to Sesame work.

Jung's Insights into Transformation and Healing

Jung recognized that the psyche can best be heard, attended to and befriended by our engaging in some form of creative and imaginative play. Play, as structured art form, acts as a vessel wherein many healing transformations can occur, as in an alchemist's alembic. Jung always recommended the practice of an art form to an analysand.

A Sesame session is just such a vessel, in which imagination is liberated. Enactment grows out of some piece of given stimulus and within this we can be any age we choose, of either gender and any type of character. By imaging these, we discover, and come into relationship with, the many aspects of ourselves and of the human condition. All that is in us in potential, but lying dormant, can be 'kissed awake', so to speak. We may be able to tap repressed areas in such a way that by giving these their chance, their stage for presentation, they can become more friendly to us: instead of our being the victims of fears and angers driven underground and made vicious, we can find the bodily and the vocal means of giving them constructive release, eventually making way for their transformation into positive energies. We need a freedom from restraint to be able to effect this change and we can give ourselves this freedom within the safe bounds of the imaginative activity.

Jung's analytical psychology sees that distinction between the elements of the unconscious psyche is necessary. One aspect or strand must be differentiated from another before any conscious synthesis or integration can be achieved. 'Only separated entities can unite' is an oft-quoted saying.

In enactment, these elements can be stepped into in a personified form – and they can be stepped away from at the end of the enactment. They can therefore be seen separately and reflected upon consciously. Thus the original state of unconsciousness, where all is felt as a confused mass, can be broken open. The now separated parts can be consciously seen and integrated. When previously denied parts are owned in consciousness, they are less likely to project themselves upon other people and events. By withdrawing projections, we become more gathered and less prejudiced.

Psychic contents may be not only in a state of potential, but in a state of woundedness. They may lie not only undifferentiated and latent, but as if 'hurt' by their banishment. Complexes, perhaps initially grown defensively around our vulnerability, may through time become virulent. They may continually weep in our system, like sores, and we may experience only their poisonous qualities. How are these to be treated?

'Cure' cannot involve removal of wounds, for one cannot change the past, the case history, in a literal sense. Only a standing in creative relationship *with* the woundedness, only acknowledgement, acceptance and befriending of pain through a genuine suffering of it, has any healing effect. There is no blueprint for how to go about this, except to say that listening to the psyche will make the way known to the individual. Within the play of a Sesame session, the psyche may find the freedom to make its needs and its intent better known.

Deeply embedded in the shadowed depths of the unconscious are those basic primordial instincts and imprints for behaviour which Jungian psychology terms the 'archetypes'. These can quite overthrow the rational mind and act in us with an autonomous imperative, making us 'act out' when we are in the grip of their compulsions. Sesame's enactment of myths, which are the stories of these protean forms, helps to give the archetypes a mirror and a mould. The fires of 'affect' – the emotionally hot issues, seething like molten metal – need their mould or cast in which to cool and be contained. Enactment is a means of helping this to happen. There will be no need to 'act out' literally, in life, if we can 'enact' in the imaginative context of an art form.

If madness could be described as a state of being so swamped by the chaos of inner drives, with their overwhelming swirl of voices and fantasies, that consciousness has no orientation and one feels drowned; and if sanity is being able to hold and contain the images that chaos spawns in a meaningful context of understanding which orientates consciousness and the ego personality, then one can say that the enactment of myth serves well.

Or it may be fairy-tale that Sesame uses. Jungians agree that fairy-tale embodies the universal experience of mankind, as does myth. Fairy-tale depicts the basic structure and dynamics of the psyche – more so than myth, which has some kind of cultural overlay and gives the simplest and purest expression of psychic processes. Fairy-tales represent the archetypes in their barest and purest form and they offer an anatomy of the healthily functioning psyche. Thus we hear them with gratitude, our illnesses specially so. Illnesses, above all, need to have the sort of pictorial maps that fairy-tales provide. Psychotherapy's developmental as well as curative aims can be met by bringing these 'maps' to life.

As psychotherapy expresses it, the cure, the 'medicine', is made out of the very 'poison', once this has been transformed. The medicine is imaginal, not literal. It is our child of the inner labour. It is an interior realization, real in its own terms and in its effects. Once our pain, our stumbling stone, our suffering – now it becomes our 'bread', our succour. Or – still speaking metaphorically – this transforming rebirth could be described as the opening of an eye, a new way of seeing, a light in the mind. We see the threads of our life weave into a meaningful story. Transformation of pain, through suffering consciously, changes us. Revelation reconciles us with our story as a meaningful destiny. The most reconciling feature of this enlightening process is that what has been achieved is more than the raising of an already existing consciousness: it is actual *creation* and evolving of consciousness. We have made a brave new world. We have made our way, hazardous though the journey may have been, from initial biological enslavement into the promised land, the kingdom of inner psychological gold. This gold, this Philosopher's Stone, which is not a common stone but a common problem turned into a jewel of understanding, a bitter aloe that has ripened, is the fruit of experience glowing in consciousness like a dawning sun. By this we lighten our darkness, as understanding begins to dawn in us.

Such a process of understanding cannot be forced, for it is not an intellectual achievement only: to accomplish it requires movement of heart – and this is a matter for the individual. When Jung said that his analysands went through a process of 'individuation', he meant that these great events become humanized within the individual. The place of the experience is not, of course, in the outer and literal life. It is the psyche that houses the experience. And standing in relationship with the psychic contents is the ego personality, differentiated from them but conscious of them.

Jung said that the most important thing is 'the art of letting things happen in the psyche'. Sesame tries to facilitate this art and also helps to ground it. Entry into metaphor, experienced as real in its own imaginal mode and differentiated from it in careful de-roling, helps to ground us in the double realities of both inner experience and outer life.

In Conclusion

I would like to end with two images:

> The first is of a sheepdog. To bring all the sheep into the fold (all parts of the psyche into consciousness) he doesn't run straight at them. This would only frighten and scatter them. Instead, he runs round behind and approaches them slantwise – gathering them, coaxing them, from oblique directions.

> The second image is given us in the saying of the alchemists that 'The Sun and its Shadow complete the Work'. The Sun, wheeling in the heavens, is orbited by the Earth. The body of the Earth, as it rotates, will find itself in shadow in different places at different times. Psychologically, in the full course of life, we have the chance of bringing different regions to light. If we remember that 'Enlightenment does not come through imagining figures of light, but by making the darkness conscious', as Jung said, then we can see that what lies in the shadow is as much a necessary part of our journey's pattern, for the dawn comes out of it.

In therapy, Sesame respects necessary shade as well as light, gestation as well as birth, with a finely sensitive feel for the ready season. The season will always be the individual's own and the Sesame therapist remains ever mindful of this fact.

CHAPTER 6

Drama as Therapy
Some Basic Principles

Graham Suter

During the period preceding the creation of the full-time Sesame training, a group of us spent some time talking with psychiatrists and others working in the field of mental health and exploring the aims and usual methods employed in their work with patients. The group involved in this research consisted of Marian Lindkvist (Founder of Sesame), Ursula Nichol (a teacher of drama and movement), John Hudson (a school drama teacher), Audrey Wethered and Chloe Gardner (two Laban movement teachers) and myself (an actor and adjudicator of drama). At the same time, we set up, among ourselves, a number of working experiments with drama and movement. The basic principles upon which the Sesame training was based were evolved from these meetings and explorations.

It swiftly became clear that the activities should aim to encourage clients (we used the term 'patients' in those days) to produce material from their unconscious. The most accessible way seemed to be by involving them in spontaneous drama improvisations. In this way they would be spared the need to derive actions and characters from a given text and enabled to select actions and roles to suit themselves. And we realized, just as swiftly, that a sense of privacy was essential. Fellow actors, even if not at that moment involved, were acceptable, but outsiders intruded and inhibited us.

We went out to many hospitals, where members of the staff would explore the methods with us. We found that we often had to begin by suggesting simple actions and familiar themes – treasure hunts, exploring jungles, fairy-tales and pieces of music are typical examples of what we used as a stimulus. We discovered that it was not easy to find music with an atmosphere and a structure to suit dramatic events. We also found we had to emphasize that it was the people in the group, not we, who were to choose what to do and what parts to play. The group nature of the action imposed certain demands on the actors, as society does, generating and controlling individual response. If something went wrong, as it sometimes does, it was for us as leaders to intervene *within the make believe* by assuming a suitable role, so that the mode could still be trusted and believed in,

Accidents taught us things. I was once sent to get lunch at what proved to be the patients' canteen, where the attitudes of the staff coping with my bewilderment made me very aware how the environment can affect anyone.

Once, a group of people we had trained over some years, who had achieved some success with using our methods, told me they were getting up a show by the patients for the rest of the staff and patients to watch. I begged them not to, but in vain. In the event, it turned out to be a fiasco: the staff in the audience had come expecting ludicrous results and the other patients had laughed inappropriately at the players, which was very upsetting for those taking part. It took many months to restore dramatherapy to a point where it was trusted again.

From these experiences and from running, for a while, a weekly Day-Release Course at Watford, we were eventually commissioned to set up a full-time course at Kingsway Princeton College, London EC, with a clearer sense of the safeguards we needed to convey to our students. That early period of research and experimentation provided us with the basics of the theory upon which the Sesame Course rests to this day.

The Sesame Theory of Dramatherapy

Drama explores how diverse personalities come into conflict – or, perhaps, how one's desires may conflict with what one's circumstances force one to do. Comedy tends to examine ways in which, for example, one's behaviour may seem surprising or odd in contrast to what it seems reasonable to expect: a highly respected person having a cosy session with a prostitute. Where there is no such conflict there is no drama, much to the sadness of some clergy who deplore the lack of plays about heaven!

Since action springs from character and circumstance, great opportunity arises for self-expression. Also, because it is 'only a play', no one need face any close inquiry into what is being done and why. The action is realized to be a metaphor and, as such, open to more than one interpretation, leaving the actor to do what he desires, although those desires may be imperfectly perceived or only half understood.

People may be able to reveal deep troubles with more comfort and ease when playing a part than by more direct and confrontational routes. The actor may be able to see and work at a personal problem *through the metaphor*, which often conveys what is being felt and expressed with far greater clarity than is possible in ordinary speech. The drama is, therefore, a way into hidden depths, particularly for people who may be linguistically inept. It is this that makes it a valuable tool in the psychiatric field.

Improvisation is a generally acceptable way into drama, particularly for people who would be inhibited by scripts. They are not asked to pore over a script and think what they are going to do with it. They don't need their reading glasses, nor are they embarrassed by not being 'good' readers; and even a 'good' reader, when reading, may not find it easy to discover a character or sense a situation in a script. They are not faced with having to become someone totally unlike themselves, or required to put up with the endless repetitions of rehearsal, robbing the action of its impact. Therefore, we opted for an improvisatory approach when working in therapeutic settings.

To get an improvisation going often requires careful planning by the group leader, as well as great alertness to cope with any untoward events that may arise. These must be dealt with unobtrusively within the framework that has been set up, with the leader making the necessary interventions *in role*. He/she will usually avoid taking on an important role in the play, staying free to take on subsidiary roles and deal with any emergencies that may arise by quickly becoming a probable character, such as a 'doctor'. People have a way of getting 'hurt' and falling by the wayside during improvisations, which may be a bid for attention or an attempt to avoid some dramatic action that they find unacceptable. The best way to deal with hazards like this, which can disrupt an improvisation and even cause it to break down altogether, is to find a means of addressing the problem within the action, becoming a doctor, applying remedies, bandages, etc. and helping the person on his way. This avoids cutting across the action with some intervention as leader or therapist, which feels authoritarian and destroys dramatic reality for the group (see Chapter 22 for an example of this).

Some improvisations need to be set in a clear and well defined manner to protect the play's believable reality and to avoid the kind of confusion that can cause the dramatic reality to break down. For example, if 'treasure' is going to be found, the leader must launch the action from a specific point in the space so that it can move within that space towards the key spot where the treasure is. Any 'journey' that is undertaken in a play must begin and end in space as well as in time because this is an important aspect of the dramatic action. If the action is going to be divided by a river, or if the space is surrounded by a forest, these must be established clearly within the space for the people taking part to believe in the need for the journey and the nature of the journey.

On the whole, 'properties' such as crowns, jewels and teapots are best imagined, rather than represented by objects, because this leads to much richer and more interesting effects. An imaginary chest filled with treasures, to give an example, grows in interest as different people 'find' different treasures – each according to his or her imagination. The treasures then acquire a symbolic value, an effect which is greatly diminished when solid, visible props are used and which some people are nervously unable to handle correctly.

Before the start, the group needs a short physical warm-up, which can incorporate some basic work on the actions in the story: walking in sticky mud, climbing rocks, pushing through forest growth, wading through water and so on. Physically-based warm-ups of this kind liberate the imagination and make the action feel more real.

Scripted drama can, in appropriate settings, produce experiences from which people can discover things about themselves. It may enlarge our experience and understanding of the way character shows itself: for example, the way duplicity lurks behind the more or less correct behaviour of 'nice' people in *The Importance of Being Earnest,* when the two young women score off each other while remaining 'correctly' behaved on the surface, each revealing surprising resources under carefully cultivated, sedate formality or apparent ingenuousness (comedy contrast). The underlying humanity in this contrived comedy comes across brilliantly.

Session work with Shakespeare can also offer a great opportunity to experience our common humanity and our emotions, often on a large scale, demanding corresponding imagination, energy and colour in speech. When he demands conscious work by the actors on creating moods and atmospheres (in *Macbeth*, for example), working with Shakespeare can be a great help to trainee dramatherapists, strengthening their ability to do the same when leading a group.

All acting has a performance element in it, even though outsiders may not be present. Whether drama is scripted or improvised, it may be said to 'seek an audience'. Usually it is a good working rule to exclude outsiders, only those involved being present; but it should be remembered that even when the only audience is the other people involved in the session, there *is* still an audience, whether conscious or not. All art is rhetorical and seeks an audience – whether it is a concert or play in front of an auditorium, or a picture on a wall. Discussion may arise as a result, but is ultimately irrelevant. What is sought at the point of performance is the individual's reaction.

In life we are left to work out why people react as they do: are they aroused by what we do, or by our manner, or could they have been aroused by something in themselves? Many times we long to know the truth of the matter, but it is naïve to expect that discussion will reveal it, since speech can as easily be used to cloak, not reveal, what is thought and felt. Some people are clearer in speech than others. Some see more deeply. An unstudied gesture may recall what is being felt much more than words – though even a gesture can be ambiguous.

A dramatherapist needs to be able to observe accurately in order to catch the things that are being said through movement and gesture. This is where the Laban training in Sesame comes into its own, enabling a specialized form of observation that makes it possible to encourage the truth that lies below the surface to emerge (see Chapters 9 and 10).

Basic Guidelines for Leading a Session

A session needs to be planned in advance with the needs of the whole group in mind, rather than a particular member of the group (especially as planning for a particular person tends, by some invisible law, to ensure that person will not be present on the day!) Having clarified the aims of the session, the leader selects appropriate material – usually a story or a poem. When using a fairy-tale, it is important not to change any of its essential details. It is also important to think in advance about the areas of action in a story and how they will fit into the given space, since the action has a physical shape that expresses its nature. Would some music or special effects help? Chairs and tables can become buses, planes, shops – or a boat, by being turned upside down – helping to create a sense of place and make it feel more real. On the other hand, the use of 'hand props' (as I said earlier) tends to hinder this. The basic rule is: places matter, props don't. Timing also needs to be thought about in advance to be sure there is enough time for de-roling at the end. Having a session plan gives the therapist a solid base from which to begin, though things may subsequently happen which cause him to change or even abandon the original plan and improvise something that feels more appropriate on the day (see Chapter 18).

After the physical warm-up, the leader introduces the Main Event by telling the story, or reading the poem, very clearly. In doing this it is important to believe in what you are presenting and to let your voice have colour and atmosphere, so that it lives. In casting, the members of the group must be allowed to choose their parts without pressure. It should be remembered that some people enjoy acting parts of the environment: I remember one occasion when a 'church' materialized, formed by people standing and leaning together, and was then used for a spontaneous wedding.

When the main action has come to an end, the group needs time and some activity to return them to everyday reality: for example, a session with a lot of action and journeying may be followed by a measured dance of the Renaissance period. At the end of the session people may have questions and comments arising out of what has been done. These must be carefully addressed, usually along the lines of 'What do *you* think?' But discussion should not be initiated by the leader, because this can be interpreted as a 'condition of taking part' and acting ceases to be an end in itself. Asking for discussion can be felt as intrusive and a breach of trust.

When the session is over, time needs to be taken to note one's observations – partly with an eye to Laban's analysis of movement. Because it takes time to learn to observe and read movement, this detail receives a lot of attention during supervised clinical work on the Sesame training with the clinical placement tutors giving detailed feedback to individual students, helping them to become skilled observers of their clients. After training, Sesame practitioners continue to record their observations as a form of de-briefing, using their records to think about the progress of clients and to work with them in supervision.

It feels important to end this practical summary with a word about mask work, which can feel very inviting to people using drama in therapy because of the way masks are able to release submerged thoughts and feelings. Faced with one's masked face in a mirror, one may be drawn to fantasize if one's feelings are touched off by the mask. A 'witch' mask, for example, may evoke aspects of one's 'shadow'. A danger arises from the fact that such fantasies may become very hard for anyone else to control or modify. In such a situation a therapist may be forced into an authoritarian role as he seeks to control or neutralize the outburst, resulting in mere suppression, with the additional pain felt by the participant at being made to take off the mask. If such a situation is not controlled, other members of the group may be attacked (even physically) and bewildered or hurt, since the masks they are wearing do not equip them to cope. Therefore a mask, which can be an effective means of release, is, at the same time, in danger of becoming a serious threat to a group, calling for great resource and confidence in the leader. A leader who has 'in depth' experience with mask will know ways of helping people to prepare for and manage its effects, but with anyone else in charge they are probably best avoided.

CHAPTER 7

Marian Lindkvist
and Movement With Touch

Jenny Pearson

'Follow the man who follows the dream…' (Finian's Rainbow)[1]

In January 1964, Marian Lindkvist had a dream. She dreamt that she was
visiting a hospital, as she often did with one of her two daughters who was
eventually diagnosed autistic. In her dream she walked into a hospital ward
and noticed that the people in it were not looking bored and unhappy, the
way she had come to expect them to look on her visits to hospital: they were
animated and communicating with one another in a lively way. Watching
them, she suddenly recognized what was going on: they were doing drama!

The dream was the product of two facets of Lindkvist's personal experience coming together in her sleeping mind. At that time she was doing a lot
of acting, as a member of a company directed by Ursula Nichol. She had
played Tituba in *The Crucible*, Polly Garter and Mrs Dai Bread Two in *Under
Milk Wood* and other parts, which absorbed her to such a degree that she
was able to get right away from her very troubled home life and find another
kind of reality in the world of imagination. The dream placed this good
experience right in the setting with which she associated her saddest
experiences – a hospital. By conflating the two, it gave her a potent image
to inspire her life's work – the creation of a new kind of therapy based on
drama. She woke up, remembered the dream, and immediately set about

---

1 From the song in the film *Finian's Rainbow* (1968), quoted by the late Gordon Moody,
   Vice-President of Sesame, at a gathering to mark the Marian Lindkvist's retirement as
   Director of the Sesame Institute in November 1993.

making it come true. From that day she never looked back, but 'followed the dream.'

Lindkvist ('Billy' to all who have worked with her over the years) has been writing a history of Sesame in a book of her own, which is why this chapter is written by me and not by her. Her book will give the detailed story of those years, telling how she immediately set about finding people from pioneering days: how she set about creating a team of professional actors who went with a director into hospitals and day centres, running drama sessions for the patients and setting up short training courses for occupational therapists and others. An important part of the experiment was the creation of the famous 'Kats' troupe of mime and movement artists, directed by Ursula Nichol, which toured hospitals and special centres with 'action plots' that drew members of the audience (who were also patients) into active participation. The Kats attracted public interest and press coverage, as well as helping to promote the cause of drama therapy with health administrators. It was from these beginnings that Lindkvist and her team developed the idea of a specialized training for therapists working with drama and movement, gradually expanding the basic training in drama to include a grounding in Laban's Art of Movement, the psychology of C.G.Jung and relevant aspects of Peter Slade's Child Drama.

The purpose of this chapter is to acknowledge Marian Lindkvist's pioneering role in the creation of dramatherapy and in the development of the quite complex training now thriving at Central and to describe her very special and original contribution to the Sesame approach, a way of working that she calls 'Movement with Touch'. This aspect of the Sesame way of working is of fundamental importance, no matter what setting we are working in. Billy taught it to Sesame therapists in training for 30 years, both in the studio and in the clinical placement in which she was the tutor: an educational centre in which she worked regularly with a group of adults with autistic tendencies. The drawing of Billy on page 70 was made by a West Indian man who was in this client group for a number of years.

Billy had no knowledge or experience of the medical world when she began her experiments with a therapy based on drama. She was, in her own words, 'just an ordinary woman who had a dream'. But her personal experience of drama and movement over eight years of training and acting in plays showed her insight and the camaraderie that could develop between people working together on a production. She also recognized how the joy she experienced when taking part in a production had helped her to survive the personal agony of trying to understand a mentally ill husband and get help for her daughter. The dream – displacing and condensing two disparate subjects within a single setting, as Freud observed dreams to do – opened up the possibility of bringing these previously unconnected experiences together in a creative way in real life. From the moment she dreamt it, she knew this was what she had to do.

Billy was not, of course, the first therapist to make a creative discovery with a dream. Freud linked his discovery of dream interpretation to the famous 'Irma dream', which left him with a fantasy that 'some day one will read on a marble tablet on this house: *Here, on July 24, 1895, the secret of the dream revealed itself to Dr. Sigmund Freud*' (Freud 1895). Freud got his marble tablet, literally. Billy's dream has been marked in a manner more characteristic of her. It is recreated every time a Sesame therapist creates a session with a client group. At the AGM marking her retirement, a lively and moving celebration of her work left some unforgettable images on the inward eye: the towering figure of Mitch Mitchelson careering across the Sesame Studio on his unicycle and Billy handing him skittles to juggle with; a beautiful improvised dance, by a group who had taken part in a Laban workshop with Susi Thornton that morning, on the theme of *The White Bird*, Laurens Van der Post's story from the Bushmen (1961); and a lyrical memoir of Billy and the pioneering days of Sesame by Gordon Moody, quoting 'follow the man who follows the dream'. It feels affirming to know that Sesame came from such a deep, archetypal source – especially as drama therapy, like psycho-analysis and like dreams, functions as a bridge between the unconscious and the conscious mind.

I doubt whether anyone who has worked with Billy would support her claim to be 'ordinary'. She is *extraordinary* in the determination and passion with which she pursued her inspiration and made it come true. She is also extraordinary in the way she has retained her simplicity – the straightforward, personal touch with which she deals with clients and students alike, even in the most challenging of settings, as I discovered at first hand when she helped me to set up a project with disturbed children shortly after I finished the training (see Chapter 22). She has a unique way of communicating straight from the centre of her being, which has clients and students responding with a matching directness. Because she is real with people, people tend to believe in her and respond with confidence both in her and in their own capacity to do what she suggests. And it works! This can feel truly miraculous in a tricky mental health setting or working with a client group where excitement is running high and verbal communication is almost non-existent.

This personal quality, which it is Billy's special skill to share and evoke in those who work with her, is at the basis of her Movement with Touch.

The central importance of this way of working within the context of Sesame as a whole emerges as you read accounts by individual therapists of their work in a variety of settings (see accounts of clinical work in Part 2, Mainly Practice). Though this 'hands on' way of working may initially seem to have a limited usefulness, being primarily intended for people who lack verbal skills, it turns out in practice to have an extremely wide application. Even those of us who work with sexually abused children have found that they respond with evident relief and an appropriate, childish sense of fun to a whole range of tactile activities that are clearly and unequivocally non-sexual. For elderly people living in residential homes, the simple experience of holding hands in a circle and 'dancing' the hands to music can produce a lively sense of being 'in touch' and connected. These are, however, relatively sophisticated uses of an approach that Billy first pioneered with people for whom verbal communication was impossible: she just had to find other ways of reaching them in order to discover what they wanted, to offer what she felt they might want and then to check out with them if that was right.

Billy began to develop her Movement with Touch on an early research project in a hospital setting with people who were mentally disabled. She developed it further in other settings where people's verbal communication was poor, including an early project with some autistic children. Movement with Touch really comes into its own when it isn't possible to work with movement unless the therapist physically holds and guides the limbs and body of the client – a simple, direct measure that goes to the heart of the client's problem and can at the same time be turned into a means of communication. If people have very poor verbal skills or none at all, and/or have difficulty in moving, there is going to be some heavy resistance to making physical movements that are suggested to them verbally. Likewise, they will be in difficulties when they are asked to imitate or respond to movements that are simply 'shown' to them. Billy's discovery, simple enough once you think about it, was that by making physical contact it became possible to communicate effectively with people in this kind of difficulty, as well as helping them to move.

Essentially, Movement with Touch is communicating and responding in a physical way, bypassing the normal channels of speech, sight and sound – though non-verbal sounds often come into the communication in a secondary capacity. When the therapist takes the trouble to 'read' the client's body language, the person begins to feel 'heard' and this can initiate a gradual movement towards reciprocity. So there is a lot more to it than simply communicating the movement you want the person to make. Billy's emphasis in this work is always on a two-way communication: picking up from the client what is going on for him/her through watching, listening, empathic touch, and being able to read some of the feelings that are expressed by the way people move. Laban principles help with this, but the process can be fine-tuned by applying Billy's very subtle, empathic way of working. Any movements that are suggested to the client in a session are communicated only after careful negotiation, first of all empathising with the client's own movements and very gradually extending, perhaps elaborating, the movement taken from the client, all the time testing the person's reactions to the point where it becomes possible to encourage him to explore other possibilities. This whole process can be brought about through the touch of hand against hand, foot against foot, or sometimes backs and shoulders. Often a good session will end with the client completely relaxed, with eyes closed, lying in the supporting arms of the therapist. A more vigorous session ending on a humorous note can, of course, be just as satisfying.

Lindkvist's Movement with Touch has features in common with the pioneering work of Veronica Sherborne (1990), the Laban movement therapist, which is not surprising as the two women did their basic research among people with roughly the same range of problems and disabilities. Lindkvist and Sherborne met and talked in the late sixties, finding that they had a lot in common: as Billy observes, there's a finite number of things you can do with people in such restricted circumstances. But though their experience overlapped, there were fundamental differences in the way the two women approached their task. While Sherborne's starting point was basically her Laban-based material, helping the client to achieve what she, the therapist, had devised for the session, Lindkvist's method has always been to begin by observing her client and join in with the client's movements, establishing a communication in the client's 'language' before going on to find some kind of 'bridge movement' to take the person by easy stages towards doing something new. Throughout this process, Lindkvist's emphasis is on 'listening' to what is coming from the client, even if this means that the session doesn't proceed very far in the direction of a new movement. In this way the client is eased by gradual stages into trying different kinds of movement which might feel alarmingly strange and frightening if introduced less subtly. With certain clients, particularly in the mental health field, Lindkvist takes care to warn her students that the sudden introduction of certain kinds of movement can actually bring about a psychotic episode.

The effect of working through movement to enable people to have these new bodily experiences seems to be a freeing-up, both physically and mentally, of the person's capacity for life and enjoyment – though Billy always reminded her students that such a statement was impossible to prove.

One can only observe how the bodies we are working with become softer and more relaxed, eyes lose their frightened watchfulness and take on a dreamy expression, and people who have been tense and suspicious may gradually begin to smile.

The Benefits of Stamping

It was Billy's way of beginning with her clients' input that led her to discover, when working with psychiatric patients in a South African hospital, a movement sequence that is now an important part of the Sesame movement vocabulary: an age-old healing ritual which involves moving anti-clockwise in a circle and stamping the heels into the ground. Having learnt the benefits of *stamping* with her South African patients, for whom it was an established part of tribal ritual, she introduced it into her work in Britain, where it turned out to be equally beneficial. She then began teaching it to the Sesame students – who found that they, too, enjoyed *stamping* for its own sake. It is an exhilarating warm-up at the beginning of a session, focusing attention and energy with a strong 'grounding' effect. To experience it is to recognize its value in clinical work, particularly with people whose energies are very unfocused.

In my student group, I remember how we began with the *stamping* ritual each week as a warm-up during our studio sessions with Billy, so we were thoroughly at home with it by the time we came to use it with her in a clinical placement. I remember vividly how we would proceed around the circle, one behind the other, anti-clockwise, our eyes slanting towards the centre of the circle, stamping our heels to the majestically slow rhythm of her magnificent, fur-covered drum. ('Does everyone fall in love with your drum, Billy?' I asked her one day. 'Yes!' she replied.)

She had already shown us what she meant by *stamping*: a step forward in which the heel leads, striking the ground with a strong, downward movement to 'send the sound down through the earth to the ancestors.' (She was careful to explain that this image was intended to inform the quality of the movement, not to have us pretending to a belief that belonged to another culture.) We circled and stamped, at first to a very slow rhythm, and then very gradually the drumming and our stamping became faster. By the end, our movements found a rhythm very like a ritual dance – but still stamping sharply with the heels. I was aware of the whole group's attention and energy becoming concentrated in the moment, in the rhythm, in the room, held by the quickening beat of the drum. By the time the drumming ceased we were all very *present*, ready for whatever might happen next.

Stamping produces a strong sense of well-being, which we all noticed. Billy has written in her own book about the scientific reasons for this, which she has researched in some depth. Having proved the benefits of *stamping,* Billy went on to find ways of giving this experience to people whose disabilities made it physically impossible for them to stamp – either because they were unable to stand up or, as often happens with people who are psychologically disturbed, because they didn't have strong a strong enough ego to make such a strong movement. She found it was possible to simulate the experience of stamping if the person lay on the floor and she took hold of a foot, keeping the leg straight and pushing the heel quite hard with a regular rhythm. If you get this movement right, the person on the floor can end up with a sense of well-being like we felt after stamping. This is just one detail of the kind of research with which Billy built up the repertoire of techniques that she calls Movement with Touch.

Working with Autism

Stamping played an important part in the clinical placement I was lucky enough to do with Billy as tutor. We worked with a small group of adults with autistic tendencies who knew Billy well. The experience was surprisingly enjoyable. To begin with it felt quite scary. There were four of us working with four clients, which meant that we were able to work one-to-one with the clients. This we did for two mini-sessions of ten minutes each on four separate mats in different parts of the room where the session took place. The mats made it comfortable to sit, lie down, even roll on the floor. They also acted as containers, establishing an area for each pair to work in. Apart from the two sessions on mats, we worked as a group. Billy stressed the importance of keeping to the overall session plan, which acts as a containing ritual for everyone: the clients have come to rely on its familiarity and can become quite upset if it changes, she warned us. But there were parts of the session where the content was expected to vary from week to week.

Among those attending the sessions was John, a big, excitable, West Indian man who had worked with Billy for several years. He was visibly delighted to see her. However, when he first arrived in a session he would often be so excited that he couldn't stay in the room. He would jump up and down in his trainers making small, excited sounds, a bit like a kettle coming to the boil. If his excitement boiled over he would run out of the room, down the corridor, into the toilets and out again, and then back to the room where the session was about to begin. Two others, a woman and a man, also tended to arrive quite 'high', darting and leaping around, while the fourth person, Ned, was so shy and withdrawn that he found it terribly hard to enter the room at all. The person working with Ned would have to make contact with him on arrival by engaging his attention through sound and gesture from just inside the door – participating in his quick, angular movements and perhaps holding his hands to establish some kind of rapport, then gradually finding a way to calm his stereotypic movements and introduce others that felt less jerky and slightly more flowing. On a good day this might enable Ned to let go of some of his tension and enter the room, though it might take half the session to achieve this: some days he didn't even make it over the threshold. The first three participants had some language, mostly monosyllabic, but I never heard Ned speak. One day it struck me that only a few months back I would have been completely at a loss in this setting, not having the first idea how to begin to make contact. Movement with Touch gave us a language in a place where words were almost without meaning.

The overall plan for our sessions here was a set plan, for the reasons I have given – but it never felt static, partly because we were physically on the move for most of the time and partly because the songs that were built into the session plan had a lot of movement in them, most of them being around the theme of journeys: 'The Runaway Train' (sung as we moved around the room in a Conga), 'She'll be Coming Round the Mountain'; 'Michael Row the Boat Ashore' and, sometimes 'Swing Low, Sweet Chariot'. Billy led the first two sessions to familiarize us with all this: after that, we took turns to run the session. There was room for small, unthreatening variations within the basic structure.

The weekly ritual with its familiar songs and movement patterns was entered into with every appearance of joy and enthusiasm by all the clients except, to begin with, the reluctant Ned. The *stamping* warm-up was a little different from the one we had done back at the studio, where we moved round the circle one behind the other with our hands free. Here we held hands in the circle, stamping on the spot, with the students encouraging and sometimes physically helping people to stamp by lifting a leg from the back of the knee area and letting it drop so that the heel struck the floor. (To the weak, autistic ego, stamping doesn't come naturally: the rationale for assisted stamping is that this grounding movement helps the person to have a sense of 'being there', in the room and in his/her own body).

For the group, this *stamping* served two purposes: to release pent up energy and to channel it into something we could share and enjoy together. One of the students would beat the drum, starting slowly and accelerating the beat as we had done in our studio sessions. Billy would work with us in the circle, encouraging the movement. She would often take John by the hand and say cheerily 'STAMP, John! STAMP!' As he stamped with her he would begin to relax and smile: you could see the tension going out of his broad, strong shoulders.

We would each lead our partner by the hand to join the stamping circle. Everyone would stamp together saying, almost chanting, 'STAMP – STAMP – STAMP', with the exception of Ned and his partner who, at this stage, would still be negotiating an entrance. In words, none of this sounds very exciting – but words can't convey the dramatic effect of the cheerful sounds, the smiles, the sheer *élan* of the stamping circle, or the sense of being part of something these people have looked forward to intensely. The stamping is a dance of greeting. In effect, John was the only one able to suit the action to the word and actually stamp. The other three, whose ungrounded movements were more in the range that Laban described as *flick, dab* and *light touch*, were inclined to trip airily from foot to foot – unless, as I have described, one of us got down on the floor to facilitate the movement.

All four participants brought a kind of eagerness to the session. The third man, Allie, had an endearing way of chanting 'Billy! Billy! Billy!' and smiling at everyone. Because he was epileptic, we had to take special care when he became over-excited, finding ways to slow down his jumping and skipping movements. He was the first person I partnered and Billy talked me through a gradual process of introducing quieter movements. Towards the end of the session, I was surprised to find myself sitting on the floor holding Allie between my arms and legs as he leant back against my chest, eyes closed and smiling blissfully as I rocked him gently, singing 'Swing low, sweet chariot'!

Even Ned, having at last been persuaded over the threshold, could usually come to a point of enjoyment by the end of the session: an image comes to mind of him holding the sides of his mat and rocking wildly back and forth with a grin on his face as we all sang 'Row, row, row your boat, gently down the stream!' It was part of the ritual that the mats became boats for each individual client during this song, after which we all stood in a circle and rocked on our feet to the final song 'Michael, row the boat ashore, Alleluyah!'

Within the overall plan for the two sessions on mats, each of us improvised in relation to the needs of the individual client we were working with. The overall aim of the first mat session was to release and channel energy and the work we did was often quite vigorous. A standard exercise was *pushing*, in which I might stand or kneel opposite my partner, raise our joined hands and lean my weight against his, hand to hand, saying 'Push!' as I did so. Usually our partners would say the action words with us as part of the exercise – something which can feel natural with the autistic, as their use of language tends to be more 'echolaic' than communicative. Another exercise is *pulling*, which changes the direction of the energy. *Pushing* has many variants: it can be done with hands against hands, with feet against feet as you sit on the ground, with shoulders against shoulders and back to back. The action is made in such a way as to elicit a response, both physical and verbal, saying the word to help focus on the action. The speeds of movements can be varied and their effort qualities can be changed – from firm to light, from quick to slow: this is where the Laban training comes into its own, enabling us to think and direct our actions with clarity about what we are doing.

The second session on mats is more gentle. If the release and focus of energy in the first mat session has worked, it now becomes possible to go for more sensitive, creative movement – even, sometimes, to release hands and do some 'mirroring', which can become quite lyrical.

Then the group gathers in a circle, sitting on the floor, for a shared experience of Movement with Touch – a meeting point in which there is a conversation of movement, gesture and physical contact. I may say, reaching across the circle, 'Jenny's hand is touching John's hand'. Billy follows: 'Billy's hand is touching Elena's hand' and so on. The movements are initiated by one of us, reaching out to one of the client group. Sometimes there is touching of foot against foot, which generates laughter. Sometimes we all reach outside the circle – and then all reach towards the centre. Reaching out can feel quite risky: in a non-verbal group, action carries a lot of meaning and 'outside' feels less safe, less contained, than 'inside'.

By this point in the session, people are often quite relaxed and playful: the surplus energy which was so explosive at the beginning has been dissipated and there is a gentle focus, a capacity for deliberate, delicate movements, which Laban calls 'fine touch'. It feels as if we are really encountering one another. It's fun and it can also feel quite moving. Time to end and part. Time to go back to the mats and turn them into boats, rocking together and singing the grounding song 'Michael row the boat ashore'. End of the session. See you next week. Good-bye! Good-bye!

At the end of the penultimate session in the series, we announce 'Next week will be the last week'. Everyone says 'Aaaaaah!' – a sad sound, so that sad feelings are voiced and not left floating around in people's minds as they leave but have a chance to be acknowledged and expressed. 'Never mind. Billy will be back again with some more people some time.' I notice John's face: after hearing that it's all going to end, he looks so sad. This is a big, gentle man who lives in a small house with a devoted mother and quite a young baby: all the time he has to be careful and restrained in his movements. This is a man who is severely autistic, who will never know the tenderness and release of a sexual partnership, though he is sensitive and musical with a gift for drawing. He has come to rely on the physical and emotional release he finds with Sesame. He is going to miss us.

This placement was exceptionally rewarding because of the feeling that came back to us from the client group. If what I have described sounds like a childish, 'inappropriate' way to work with adults, I can only say that the playful aspect of people which gets released in drama and movement often *does* have a child-like quality, however grown-up we may all seem on the surface. This could be because the adults in today's world get so little chance to play that a session like this taps into a neglected side of us all. In the long term, the rationale for working with people in this physical way with movement and song can be experienced psychologically as changing the way people feel about themselves. If, in Laban terminology, you can influence tightly restricted, *bound* movements in the direction of *free flow*, even a little bit, there's a good chance that the closed, tight, withdrawn feeling inside may be able to relax and open up a little, giving the person some relief. The movement may be minuscule, but the relief can feel quite important and if it is repeated there may be progress in the direction of a happier relationship with life.

Working in this placement with Billy, though scary at first, quickly became familiar and even comforting – to us as well as to the client group. I think we were all sorry when it ended. No wonder the 'autistic placement', as it has been called for years, is such an important point of reference in the work so many people trained on the Sesame course,[2] informing what they do for the rest of their working lives.

In the Beginning…

Billy chose to talk rather than write for this chapter because she was concurrently working on her own history of Sesame. What she has to say follows naturally on what I have just written by way of an introduction. Interviewing her felt quite nostalgic, recalling how some of us would invariably stay behind at the end of her studio sessions, plumbing the depths of her experience for insights into the Sesame techniques we were all struggling to learn. I noticed how often she would look for answers to our questions within herself, within her own body and the way she, personally, felt in relation to the subject in hand, as well as her long experience as a therapist. She taught us to look to ourselves for answers in the same practical

---

2   Note many references to this placement in Part 2: Mainly Practice.

way, so that we would be able to find them for ourselves after we left the Sesame training.

Billy first used Movement with Touch in some work with multi-disabled people, going on to apply what she had learnt in a research project with some autistic children in 1973–74, when autism had only recently been recognized as a category of mental illness and very little was known about it. I asked how the project came about:

MARIAN: I hadn't consciously met children like these before, but there was a kind of vague familiarity about them, because of my daughter. I found myself very drawn to them. They were quite different from the disturbed children I had worked with before. They didn't seem to be able to participate in anything. I found myself, once or twice, relating to an individual child when the music was playing: the child seemed to be responding because the music was there as something that was attractive to both of us. I was intrigued and asked the consultant psychiatrist if he would be willing for us to do some research with these children. He replied that he would.

The central focus of our work was on interacting with the children through movement. Audrey Wethered, the Laban specialist, was a member of the team. What we were doing was trying to change the children's stereotypic movements. Stereotypic movement is part of the autistic illness: it's a compulsive habit movement. Stereotypic movements are often very rapid: for example, the rapid movement of the fingers in front of the eyes, which is said to make the people feel more cut off from the world. I suppose one could say that all autistic behaviour is a form of withdrawal from reality and communication and that stereotypic movements are part of this general pattern. I remember Audrey commenting that a stereotypic movement had nothing to do with the natural movement patterns of a child.

JENNY: Stereotypic movements cut across natural movement, don't they?

MARIAN: Yes, they are jerky: all sorts of different movements. They are usually done with the hands or the head, but they may be done with the foot.

JENNY: Would you say that if you work with autistic people and get them making more natural movements, this has its reverberations inside them?

MARIAN: If we're looking at human beings holistically, everything you do affects every part of you – so, from that point of view, movements that are open and warm and healthy and outgoing, if they can be tolerated, are likely to give people a good feeling. But one has to be very careful to remember that if someone is so into themselves, escaping from reality, then one has to go very slowly towards these opposite movements – even if they are natural, healthy movements that the rest of us do.

JENNY: In what ways were the autistic children so different from others you had worked with?

MARIAN: We could never get them to do anything together. We had to work with them one-to-one. I can remember following my own instinct (which was what we were all doing) and trying to pick up the rhythm of a child who, for instance, would make a rhythm on a rocking horse. I would try to work from that rhythm because it wasn't a stereotypic movement – it was a rhythm. It was my first experience of finding it absolutely necessary to forget about the group and work with the individual. One had to be very much aware that there was a group, but nevertheless this was individual work taking place within the group.

One thing I insisted on from the start was that none of the children wore shoes in the session. That was because I had begun to recognize that the stereotypic movements were most often made with the child's hands or the arms or the head: it seemed to me that these children were not aware of their feet at all. So I started working with their feet, not bothering about relating to the child. I felt they must have a chance of looking at and experiencing their feet. I started to push at their feet, at the whole foot, mostly with my feet, getting the whole focus on the feet and legs. I also got them pushing each other's hands. That was my base and it worked out very well, particularly as autistic children seem to feel very threatened when you concentrate on their faces: they will often react with something near terror if you look in their eyes.

I'm grateful to have found that way of working so early on, although later I moved away from that base. I often realized I was doing what looked like the same things for different reasons, depending on the person I was working with. For example, when I push, hands against hands, with autistic people, it is to get a feeling of balance – not to see who is stronger. There might be a context when it might be very good to see who is stronger, but not in this setting.

JENNY: With the children at Beech Lodge, where some of us work now, pushing is often about who is stronger – at least at the beginning. The children seem to need this feeling of a contest as a focus for their aggressive feelings, though once they have used up some of their surplus energy and aggression we sometimes get around to *balancing* (see Chapter 22).

MARIAN: Yes, but there you are dealing with totally different children: your children *need* to feel their strength against yours. The people I mostly worked with at the time I am talking about, which includes autistic children, could never be as strong and vigorous as I could. A lot of them spent their time lying on beanbags and couldn't move much without help (see Chapter 24). So I'm not going to pit my strength against these people. I'm going to try to get them feeling that they have *some* strength by offering *some* resistance when I get them to push. The feeling that the Beech Lodge children need – that they are strong and ready to contest with your strength – is a stage that the people I work with are most unlikely to reach.

JENNY: It sounds as if in these settings you are moving people towards having a feeling that they have got *some* physical strength – perhaps, even, towards a feeling that they have a *self* – that they *exist*.

MARIAN: Yes, I am. That's right. I can do this.

JENNY: Because if you are just kind of floating on a beanbag, it must get to feel as if you haven't got much of a body.

Without some kind of resistance to the movements you make it must be difficult, in a sense, to feel that you have a self. But if you can *push*, even just a little bit, and come up against the physical reality of the other person, that would give you a feeling of 'I exist. I can make my presence felt.'

MARIAN: Yes. Your *will* is doing something. You are coming up against resistance and pushing against it. When they push, I would never just disappear so that they are left simply making a movement. That has no value. They have to come up against resistance – but the resistance must never feel stronger than they are.

JENNY: So by your physical resistance you are enabling them to assert themselves?

MARIAN: Yes, it *is* a form of assertion – though it can be difficult to think of such a gentle thing in those terms.

JENNY: I have noticed that when you push with people in the kind of setting you describe, you very often make a sound, a kind of grunt, that seems to be descriptive of effort in a non-verbal way. When the person you are working with pushes and makes a sound with you, even if it is a quite little sound, even that can feel as if they are saying 'I AM.'

MARIAN: Yes. Also, if I'm making a sound which is *big* and my partner makes a noise which isn't very big, he is joining in with the bigger noise and this can feel, to him, as if he is making a much bigger noise than he actually is. The experience this gives is a bit like the experience you get singing in a choir. In my experience, if you sing in a choir your own voice becomes divine because you are mixing in with all the other divine voices, even if yours isn't very good. What I've been describing works in this way. It's a kind of choral speaking.

JENNY: You seem to use your voice a lot in this work, as well as your body.

MARIAN: Yes – the voice being part of the body, as Laban observed.

JENNY: It takes a particular kind of person to be able to lend their voice and their body to other people, doesn't it ? Is this why the training has to be so intensive, giving the students time to change and become the sort of people who are able to do this?

MARIAN: Students find this Movement with Touch work very difficult, initially. I don't really like teaching it on the course because very often people can't see the point of it in the studio. I prefer to teach it in the field. It becomes easy to teach in the field because the person you are working with is there, their need is there. You respond to their need. You get their reaction. People come to see the sense of the studio work with hindsight. I notice this with the students every year: when they come to write about their fieldwork, they will describe how they have used Movement with Touch because that's the only thing they *can* use in certain settings. I think it should go on being taught on the course after I retire because it is unique in work with movement and drama. Of course the students gain tremendously from reading Veronica's books (Sherborne 1990) and learning about her work with the same kind of people, but what she did is very different from this thing of mine, which is so hard to teach – except in the field.

JENNY: This is part of the difficulty we are all having in trying to write for this book. It's hard to get across, in words, the kind of things we have all learnt experientially – both in the studio and in the supervised fieldwork. This need for experiential learning, particularly in Movement with Touch, means, doesn't it, that we have to have fieldwork placements with supervision on the spot from people who actually do the work? To me that is the most important single feature of the training.

MARIAN: You have to have it in order to learn Movement with Touch, because it can't really be learnt unless you see the person who has the need. It's only when that need calls up the theory you have learnt that the whole thing comes together and you begin to understand.

JENNY: This is why we have given quite a lot of space in this book to stories – examples with real people which show Sesame in action. Have you got some stories of your own

that we could use to show Movement with Touch in
action?

MARIAN: There are two stories from a hospital in Hertfordshire
where I did some work. Two children were born there
that day with twisted limbs. One child had both legs
going sideways in the same direction: the official term for
this is 'windswept'. I was able to do something using
Movement with Touch because I've known people who
find it very difficult to move, but who can sometimes
move if you just touch them in a particular place in
relation to the part of them that isn't moving. You can just
indicate a direction, push them very, very lightly, and they
will gradually be persuaded to move outwards.

This little boy was going to be put in some splints so that
his legs would straighten. I just touched him with my
fingers, very lightly, on the bend by his knee, and his legs
straightened out. Everybody became very excited about
this, though in fact I wasn't: I thought it would probably
happen because the bones were so unset. I am sure he
would have needed the splints subsequently. What I did
was no miracle cure, but as an indication of the way
Movement with Touch can work it was quite dramatic. A
similar thing happened with another child with a *lordosis*,
a twisted rib and arm. I just touched him lightly, inside
his thumb, and the arm straightened out. A
physiotherapist could probably have manipulated and
moved it, but I'm not a physiotherapist and what I do isn't
manipulation: often it's just a light touch that gets people
to move themselves. I honour the physiotherapists, in fact
I would never work with people who were physically
disabled without consulting a physiotherapist first to
make sure I do nothing that could harm them. For
example, I like to be able to take the person away from
the beanbag or wheelchair and get the whole body
extended, so that I can work with the whole body – but I
always check with the physiotherapist first that this will
be all right for them.

The point I'm making is that what I do is totally different
from physiotherapy. Those two cases I've described were

Figure 7.1. Jo James, Sesame Course Tutor (right) with a member of the group she describes in Chapter 24 'Poetry in Motion' (photograph by Rebecca Mothersole)

examples of the way a very gentle touch in the right part of the body can start the movement that's needed to straighten out a limb.

JENNY: From your description, it sounds as though you did those two things by a kind of identification with the children's bodies – working out of an innate knowledge of movement that you get from your own body.

MARIAN: Yes. That is how I work it out. I know perfectly well that if my hand is twisted round like this, and I touch here, my hand will move away from the touch like this. You have to get into the body of the person – otherwise you can't imagine what it's feeling like. So I'm in that body, I'm like that, and I say to myself 'How am I going to get my hand from that position?' I keep a little bit of myself in my body, but a lot of myself leaps into the other person's body at the same time. And then I begin to feel what I need to do.

JENNY: So it's working partly from your own body and your knowledge of the way it moves?

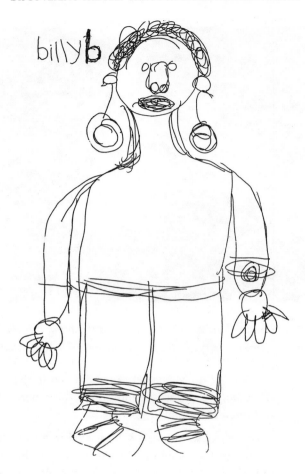

Figure 7.2. Drawing of 'Billy', by a member of the small group of adults with autistic tendencies: he noticed every detail, even the ear-rings and watch

MARIAN: I think it is – yes. It's what Audrey Wethered called
            'informed instinct'. I think that's a very good description
            because it says that you must have information. It's
            automatic for me to work in this way. I still don't think in
            Laban terms when I'm actually working with people,
            though I sometimes use Laban's language to explain what
            I mean. Like when I say to the students 'It's no good
            when somebody is pushing somebody unless the pushing
            is *sustained*'. 'Sustained' is a perfectly good English word,

but it's also a Laban word. The point I am making in this example is that only against *sustained* movement do you feel your own strength. If somebody gives a short, jerky push, the person at the receiving end doesn't feel as if they have any strength at all. So I have learnt Laban terminology to use when I teach.

JENNY: Did you do any Laban training yourself, Billy?

MARIAN: No, never. I read Audrey's book at the time I was working with her (Wethered 1973). I've talked to Audrey and other Laban people about the work I'm doing. But I've always worked in my own way.

JENNY: So in Movement with Touch you work entirely from yourself and then use the Laban language to communicate about what you do?

MARIAN: Yes, I think that's right. I suppose there have been times when I've thought 'My God, I've got to teach now! How am I going to explain the theory to people who are supposed to be able to write down a theory?' These were the times when I began to see how the Laban terminology could help me to convey what I was doing.

Note: Laban was originally taught on the Sesame Course by Audrey Wethered and Chloe Gardener. It will be clear from my account of Billy's clinical placement that by the time students on the Sesame Course go out to apply Movement with Touch in a clinical placement, they are already familiar with the Laban. This means they have a language in which to discuss the finer points of the work.

References

Freud, S. (1895) *The Complete Letters of Sigmund Freud to Wilhelm Fleiss 1887–1904* (Edited by G. Masson 1985). Cambridge, MA: Harvard University Press.

Van der Post, L. (1961) *The Heart of the Hunter*. London: Hogarth.

Sherborne, V. (1990) *Development Movement with Children*. Cambridge: Cambridge University Press.

Wethered, A. (1973) *Movement and Drama in Therapy*. London: Macdonald and Evans. Second edition (1993), London: Jessica Kingsley Publishers.

CHAPTER 8

The Unique Voice That Lives Inside Us All[1]

Frankie Armstrong

The Bird was found by a young boy who heard such a Beautiful Song that he had to go and see who was singing. When he found the Bird he brought it back to the camp to feed it. His father was annoyed at having to give food to the Bird, but the son pleaded and the Bird was fed.

The next day the Bird sang again, it sang the Most Beautiful Song in the Forest, and again the boy went to it and brought it back to feed it. This time the father was even more angered, but once again he gave in and fed the Bird. The third day...the same thing happened. But this time the father took the Bird from his son and told his son to go away. When his son had gone the father killed the Bird, the Bird with the Most Beautiful Song in the Forest, and with the Bird he killed the Song, and with the Song he killed himself and dropped dead, completely dead, dead for ever. (Pygmy legend from *The Forest People* by Colin Turnbull 1984, p.79)

I have found myself preoccupied with many questions about the nature of the voice, vocal expression and its relationship to our sense of self since 1975, when I began developing my particular approach through Voice Workshops. How and why is it that something as apparently simple as encouraging and giving people permission to make loud and powerful sounds, and to enjoy using these to chant and sing with others, often has such profound and

---

1 Line from Leon Rosselson's song '*Voices*'.

startling effects on participants? I have no ultimate conclusions or answers to these questions, but let me put forward a few ideas born of my years of experience and reflection.

From time immemorial, it is probably true to say that the voice has been central to the human expression of emotions and feelings. In tribal and pre-industrial rural cultures, the voice was used as part of ritual, rites of passage, celebration, grieving, to accompany work and dance – in fact encompassing every aspect of life from the cradle to the grave. We wept, wailed and keened at grave sides, sang celebrations for birth and marriage, placated wrathful gods; we chanted prayers, sang paeans of praise to seen heroes and unseen hosts. We sang lullabies to soothe crying babies and accompanied the myriad of tasks that tribal and agricultural communities undertake for survival with sound and song. Animals were sung to when being herded and milked and the soil was tilled and ploughed to the accompaniment of chants and songs, as was the gathering, threshing and pounding of grain and the spinning and weaving of yarn.

I do not believe that we did this simply to pass the time. Raising our voices individually and/or collectively in song is a way of releasing and giving form and shape to a state of heightened emotion. So what happens to us if, either individually and/or collectively, we feel ourselves to be robbed of the power and expression of our voices? I believe that in our present culture we are being denied part of our birthright. To move/dance, to voice/sing, are part of what it means to be fully human. To my knowledge, no pre-industrial community has ever been 'discovered' where people do not, or did not, *all* sing and dance. I believe the need for this expression is as alive in us today in the 'Industrial West' as it was for our ancestors.

It is both through social evolution and individual development that we can be, and, alas, frequently are, robbed of this central tool of expression. A small baby begins exploring the world through movement and touch, smell and sight – and also by making an extraordinary range of sounds. Some of these sounds undoubtedly are functional – cries of hunger or distress – but many seem to be born of what we might call primal curiosity. We must all have experienced and shared in the sheer delight that babies find in their gurgles, squeals, trills, growls and croaks – displaying a remarkably wide range of sounds, both in pitch and timbre. Most children, as toddlers, spontaneously 'play with their voices' until, sadly, they are educated into thinking this is not 'proper' singing – or else, simply in the process of growing up, they come to feel that such play is embarrassing or foolish, as it isn't something that adults usually appear to do.

For some children, I believe a more profound form of inhibition can take place. It is through the voice that we experience our first ability to affect the world: we have our first sense of our potency, or our impotence, as a direct result, or non-result, of an adult responding when we vocalize our needs. The baby is able to bring comfort to herself in the form of her parents or carers by giving voice, by crying or screaming, if she is in distress. This is the first time she can affect the world 'at a distance'. If the people who feed, clean and console her are out of sight and she is able to summon them with her cries, this must have, however pre-consciously, a profound effect upon our sense of ourselves as separate beings and of our power. My guess is that for most of us our carers come most of the time and that this can give us, in Winnicott's words, a 'good enough' experience to enable us to grow up with a realistic sense of how we can call upon others when we are in need and how, realistically, they may not always be at our beck and call in the instant. For those babies, however, whose cries go unheeded too often, a sense of impotence and powerlessness must cathect around the use of the voice and remain associated with it.

If we feel we are not being heard, we may feel we have no right to be heard – even that we are not worth hearing. This may sound like a simplistic hypothesis, but it is my experience that many people, on being given permission, encouragement and skills to make strong, open sounds from deep inside their bodies, find themselves very moved and may cry or laugh and say such things as 'Was that really me? – I've never made as big a sound as that in my life – I've never felt the right to take up so much space with my voice – I never thought anyone wanted to hear me before!'

Some of these expressions may arise out of childhood deprivation; others could be the result of the accumulated inhibitions of social conditioning. Either way, the response seems to be the same – a sense of release, relief and empowerment which can very easily be guided and coaxed into melodic and musical expression, adding enjoyment and a sense of achievement to the previous list.

As all the Sesame tutors do, I put great emphasis on movement. The idea that singing is done while standing still is of very recent origin (a few hundred years at the most in a history that goes back tens of thousands). Giving voice, after all, is movement – the movement of breath, the vocal folds, bone and muscle. Letting the body find the natural impulses that lie behind giving voice can be a very important part of finding that organic relationship between body, voice and psyche which allows us to feel that our singing is the expression of our true selves.

The theatre director John Wright said 'Behind every moving voice is a dancing body'. He doesn't necessarily mean this literally – though people often find themselves with a much greater range of vocal expression, both imaginatively and melodically, when they are moving or dancing. The necessary movement can also be an inner dance, an inner awareness of movement and flow, though to the observer the person giving voice may appear to be quite still. It is not stillness but stiffness that is the enemy of the expressive voice. Stiffness comes with anxiety and inhibition. Anxiety and inhibition all too often come from an unhelpful and critical adult who told us when we were a child 'You can't sing' or 'You've got a horrible voice' or 'You're tone deaf' or 'You're a growler. Would you please go to the back of the class and mouthe soundlessly during the concert!' I have had adults of ages ranging from 20 to 80 years and older remembering clearly the exact moment and the precise words that stamped them with the identity of 'non-singer' when they were impressionable youngsters.

Encouraging simple, collective rhythmic movements such as simulating work actions – hoeing, pounding, scything – or giving people space to follow spontaneous impulses can free people from the fear and anxiety that holds their bodies stiff and their capacity for self-expression in chains. The body knows about these things. We have many expressions in the idiom of everyday language that graphically describe the relationship between psyche, body and voice. To give a few examples: 'I felt choked up – I choked on it – It really stuck in my throat/gullet/craw – I just couldn't swallow it – I felt a lump in my throat.' These all relate to the throat area. There are equally telling expressions that relate to the mouth and jaw: 'Biting back my words – I could have bitten my tongue – It left a bad taste in my mouth – Grit your teeth and bear it – Hanging in by the skin of my teeth – stiff upper lip – Taking it on the chin – Biting the bullet.' So many of these expressions refer to holding things in, holding things back, and generally repressing our feelings. It's little wonder that our throats so easily become the sticking point when we find ourselves in conflict about what we want or need to say, when we feel unheard or unlistened to, and when we feel we don't have the right to be heard. So helping to free up the area of the throat and jaw and deepening the breathing can in itself be powerfully therapeutic, aside from any beneficial effects on the voice itself.

I believe that all art has therapeutic effects and for me it is the chance to work with these in the process of creating sounds and songs collectively that is the joy, challenge and magic of the Workshops. Of course there is a role and function for voice therapy and I always seek to make it clear that I am not a voice therapist, a term which implies a very specific, technical and complex training that I have not done. What I feel drawn to do is to help people rediscover the joy and power of singing, while being aware that the therapeutic aspects will inevitably happen, if they need to, in the course of our explorations. As someone with nearly 40 years' experience of singing in public and 24 years' involvement in professional and group work, it feels to me quite natural and appropriate to have these two processes happening side by side in my Workshops.

Finally, I would like to say something about the non-verbal way of working with drama that I found such a delight when I first took part in Pat Watts' Myth Enactments, which I then found to be one of the great liberating factors in the work done by Sesame people. While I love and value words passionately, finding them as important as melody when I am selecting songs for my personal repertoire, in workshop settings I often work with made up languages or vowel sounds and I teach chants and songs from other cultures, often in languages that the people I am working with do not know. I realize there are several reasons for doing this. Getting outside the structure and content of our daily language and returning to something like a pre-verbal state can help us to get away from fears of the old patterns of self-criticism and negative judgement that so many of us carry. On a purely technical level, it is also true that exploring an open vowel allows us to sense the source and vibrations deep in our bodies in a way in which the speed of conversation, and of many songs, does not allow time and space for. To chant or sing in *gobbledegook* or a in foreign language, especially those languages which encourage a tribal quality, invites us to stay with a voice that comes from the earth through the soles of our feet and gathers its power and expression in the centre of our body, the abdominal muscles, the diaphragm, and the solar plexus – the seat of emotions – and releases sound through open lungs and open throat, feeling ourselves to be a bridge between the earth and the sky. The voice I want to help people to find is that which comes from deep inside us, literally comes out of the darkness into the light, forming a bridge between the below and the above.

In my work with Pat, going on from my initial enjoyment of a series of Myth Enactments she led one autumn at the Westminster Pastoral Foundation in Kensington, we created workshops together in which my voice work was incorporated as permission and encouragement for people to chant, sing and improvise with their voices in the course of exploring and enacting a chosen myth. It was a revelation to discover how the 'extra-ordinary' use of the voice can invigorate the enactment of a myth, fairy-story or ballad. Some of the most moving, dramatic moments I have ever experienced have been in these myth-based workshops, when my spine has tingled to an outpouring of jubilation or chilled to an outburst of anguish and I have been moved to laugh or cry in a way that is too rare in our modern, commercially dominated theatre.

Whether I am running workshops in an overtly therapeutic setting such as the training for Sesame students or running a workshop in a day centre or psychiatric hospital, whether I'm working with a community group or doing voice work with a theatre company or rehearsing with a choir, whether my emphasis is on releasing sound and truly embodying the voice or whether it is on our innate musicality, ability to improvise, harmonise and to sing in communion, I always hope for the possibility of simple but profound changes. In the process of finding, and feeling more confident about, the use of their voice – by feeling that they can make themselves heard and that they have the right to be heard and that they and others can actually enjoy the sound and feel of their voice – people are so often able to feel an increased sense of well-being, aliveness and self acceptance. This in turn fosters a belief in one's self, a greater sense of one's own worth. The exhilaration that goes with 'finding one's voice' in the literal sense has not a little to do with finding one's voice in the metaphoric sense. The reason that I love to sing Leon Rosselson's song *Voices*, always with the full audience supporting me in the chorus, is that I believe the words: that we all have a 'unique voice inside us' (Rosselson 1992, p.300) with which to contribute – in words, sound and song – to the collective of our shared human experience and its expression.

References

Turnbull, C. (1984) *The Forest People.* London: Triad Paladin.

Rosselson, L. (1992) 'Voices.' *Bringing the News from Nowhere.* London: Fuse Records.

CHAPTER 9

Laban and the Language of Movement

Sam Thornton

The astonishing structure of the body and the amazing actions it can perform are some of the greatest miracles of existence. Each phase of a movement, every small transference of weight, every single gesture of any part of the body reveals some feature of our inner life. (Rudolf Laban 1980, p.19)

'The aim of a Sesame session is to create a safe place in which to explore possibilities,' wrote Kharis Dekker in November 1990.

Since the Sesame course leads to a professional qualification in the use of movement and drama in a therapeutic situation, it is worth considering why the founders of the course settled for Laban's concepts as the movement foundation of this unique training.

Few people, today, would challenge the statement that 'What you eat is what you are', but the claim that 'What you do is what you are' is not so immediately acceptable. However, working with movement suggests that the second statement is equally true. The term 'body language' has been in vogue for some considerable time and an increasingly large number of people now profess to be able to read it with great accuracy and fluency. The ability to read 'body language' is not the prerogative of the few but an ability that everyone possesses to a greater or lesser degree. The only limiting factor is the reluctance to believe in what is actually happening in front of your eyes.

When you 'read' another's body language, you respond to the rhythms, patterns and results of their movement actions – not only what they do, but how they do it and to whom they do it, is the message that carries the meaning. These patterns and rhythms have become known as 'body language'. So it becomes evident that every person speaks two languages: one with the mouth and another with the body.

It is not unusual for these two languages to be at variance. Herein lies the human dilemma: to which language does the responder give credence? In an extreme example, one person tells another that he holds him in high regard and at the same time kicks him heavily in the shin. The same words and action are repeated for a second and third time. I think the receiver of these kind words and hard blows would very soon come to the conclusion that 'actions speak louder than words' and respond, either by ending the relationship or by learning to keep out of kicking distance when such honeyed words are spoken.

This example illustrates how movement behaviour, or body language, can change a relationship: the action is a clear and accurate communication about what is going on, in spite of the words. But the languages of speech and movement are seldom as concise and 'dictionary-accurate' as my example. It isn't always possible to say exactly what needs to be said: a frame of reference, either wide or narrow, is often all that is possible – indeed, all that is needed. Verbal communication can be helped by the use of a dictionary, a thesaurus, an encyclopedia, but there are no books to help us interpret or understand our own or other people's movement language to a comparable degree. Academicians would say that evidence for the accuracy of movement communication is largely anecdotal and, by this argument, lightly dismiss the evidence in their own lives and experience. Yet the proliferation of many kinds of courses which involve movement – recreational programmes involving dance and every kind of sporting activity – suggests that movement is recognized by many millions of people as a significant factor in their lives and their well-being.

Whether people undertake movement in order to keep fit, to relax from the tensions of the day, or to involve themselves in purposeful, shared endeavour towards a competitive goal, all movement has certain fundamentals in common. These fundamentals are most clearly understood when Laban's concepts of movement are studied – whether in education, therapy, industry or recreation.

Certain fundamentals are central to Laban's thinking:

- that each and every person is unique, has worth and is therefore of value
- that the inner life of every person is as inimitable as their fingerprints
- that this inner life is expressed through movement, whether consciously or unconsciously
- that movement is the bridge between a person's inner life and the external world

○ that this bridge very often resembles a loop, for what happens in the outside world affects us internally and significant internal movement will affect how we present ourselves in the external world

○ that internal change will be made visibly manifest.

Viewed from this standpoint, movement is not simply an accidental, irrational and uncontrolled response to an event to be ignored or dismissed. Laban's view invests cohesive movement experience with the power to initiate change and growth and the ability to develop new skills. These are the reasons for the continued popularity of Laban-based work and its capacity for application in various situations.

It has long been recognized that what happens to an individual in the course of his/her working life can set up internal vibrations which can be extremely damaging. This damage can be repaired or minimalised by a realization and acceptance that movement experience, learning more about 'body language', is a form of self-protection. While it is not always possible to change one's place of work, movement training based on Laban's principles can mitigate the effects of continued emotional mistreatment.

Movement can also be a tool for positive growth and change, as well as for personal therapy. Through movement we can learn about the world and actualize or change our place in the world. It can enable us to allow our inner, creative/expressive voice to speak. We all have a creative, expressive voice. The ability to express and create is not the sole prerogative of 'the artist': it is everyone's birthright.

It follows that genuine creative expression through dance – the artistic manifestation of 'body language' – is not owned by professional dance companies or choreographers. Dance is of the layman; if it belongs to anyone, it belongs to the layman. Long before professional dance companies were thought of, man danced. He danced to propitiate his gods, to celebrate his triumphs, to share his times of despair and loss or, simply, to express his sense of community and well-being. We no longer dance for most of these reasons, but discos are still popular and dance classes continue to attract large numbers of people.

This universal interest in dance stems from the fact that dance is the most immediate and totally involving of the arts. Dance is of the body and the body is used to bridge the internal and external worlds. Before words and language, man experienced despair, joy, fear, wonderment, isolation and all the other emotions. The pre-language infant is not debarred from feeling simply because he cannot speak. Infants may not be able to name what they feel, but they do feel it and they express it through their movements. Their dance of hunger, of feeling lonely, of feeling uncomfortable – like their sense of joy at the sight of a well-loved person or object – is very clear and explicit. It is up to the observer to interpret these 'dances' and make an appropriate response.

The body has its own language – a language that we all speak. Essentially, the language of the body and the language of dance are one and the same. Laban's approach to movement enables us to refine this language, to increase our movement vocabulary, and then to use this new-found vocabulary to express states of being in a more explicit and artistic way. He provided maps for us to follow, while giving us the confidence and ability to colour the map according to our own needs and personality. His work stems from an attempt – the most comprehensive attempt to date – to grapple with and elucidate the language of movement. Dance forms, which stem from a need for technical mastery as the first pre-requisite of progress, can be regarded as a dialect and not a language. While dialects have their own energy and colour and are valuable for what they are, they cannot be regarded as the language itself, but only a regional variation of the language.

Laban furthered our awareness of movement to a quite remarkable degree. Through him, it became possible to distinguish between the varying factors that he called *Effort, Spatial Form and Space Harmony* and, most significantly, *Body Awareness*.

Body Awareness means much more than simply training the body so that it becomes stronger, more supple and able to master ever more complicated patterns of movement in a shorter time. These things will happen in any situation where constant repetition and practice are undertaken. A dance class which is based on violent patterns of movement, aggressive and harsh use of space and an implicit expectation from the teacher that there will be one person in the class who is recognized as 'the best' will produce a particular environment, both within the room and within the individual members of the class. Laban recognized that what you do to the body will affect how you feel and so his approach to body awareness is to ensure that there is always a balance between angular movements and gentle, flowing actions and that, by the end of the class, the body is at peace with itself and the members of the class are in harmony. There is a profound difference between a body that is physically exhausted due to the rigours of the session and a body that is equally quiescent, but has a sense of cohesion and unity. The body is both the medium and the message and it is unwise to maltreat it in pursuit of technical excellence.

It should not be assumed that in Laban work there is no element of training aimed at mastery of the body. There most definitely is this sort of experience, but it is not undertaken for its own sake. It is undertaken in order to help the participants to express themselves more fluently and accurately through dance. A person's mastery of his/her spoken language is a constant process and the only way that movement language can become more specific is also through a regular opportunity to listen to and use this language. New movement words are learnt and new expressive forms are discovered through exposure to *Effort* and Laban's *Space Harmony*.

At its simplest, *Effort* is survival. We all want to survive and so we make the necessary *Effort* to survive and we do this in a way which is particular and specific to us. How we do things is the clue to our inner, or *Effort*, life. In everyday life we perform actions that are appropriate to the thing we are doing or using. Washing-up, ironing, sewing, hoovering, digging in the garden, all have their own patterns of movement which, in *Effort* terms, are aimed at efficiency and speed of execution. Inappropriate effort either takes too long, is too tiring or is expensive because of cups that are broken and clothes that are scorched. Even in 'objective' situations like this, the way in which each person uses his body is distinctive and characteristic. It is not that we are being consciously expressive but that we are taking up a covert, or inner, attitude to the four factors which govern all movement: *Weight, Space, Time* and *Flow*.

Our use of three of these *Motion Factors* can be measured and is often very easily visible. *Weight* is the way we use our muscular energy to control the weight of the body in all the various things we have to do (some call this *Force* but, in my opinion, this is not accurate). The body has only one system to deal with its own weight in relation to gravity. When gravity is suddenly felt, the body, as if by magic, has weight. When the effect of gravity diminishes, the weight of the body is also magically reduced. How we use our muscular energy to control body weight and gravity establishes our *Weight* attitude.

Space, in *Effort* terms, is not the visible display of spatial form and pattern but rather how much or how little of the available space we use. Our first perceptions of space come from an appreciation of the shape and size of our own body. Objects are either reachable or they are not. We either think 'laterally' – that is, spatially – or we do not. We are either flexible in our approach to life or we are not. In these three instances we display an inherent, underlying attitude to space and this attitude has little to do with formalized spatial structures but everything to do with an inner driving force which has, over the years, taught us that to respond in a particular way is the most effective way for us to survive.

Time, in *Effort* terms, relates to the passage of information. The body system which is concerned with the passage of information is the central nervous system. It is not unusual for the result of the Olympic Hundred Metres Final to depend upon a 'good start'. Information from the ear to the muscles to 'get up and go' is a key factor and this transfer of the instruction to move comes from the central nervous system. All top-class sprinters have fast reaction times: they all have an innate capacity for 'suddenness'. Without it, they would always be left in their starting blocks. We all have a capacity for suddenness, but this might only manifest itself in the most extreme survival situations. We all also have the ability to indulge in *Time* – to ignore the clock and the information it is supplying and sustain our activities regardless. Whether we naturally tend towards suddenness or sustainment is neither good nor bad: it is the way we are and, provided our natural inclination is in keeping with the situation we are in, we will experience success. If it is inappropriate, we will know frustration and, possibly, failure.

This sort of activity is usually aimed at our physical survival and so the flow of the inner life rarely manifests itself. But there is more to survival than the external, physical world. The internal world needs to have a vehicle in order to express itself. The reason why so many people are in deep trouble is because the flow of their inner life is denied expression. They have lost the ability or the opportunity to express themselves through dance, through their body.

Reference

Laban, R. (1980) *The Mastery of Movement*. Fourth Edition, revised by Lisa Ullman. London: Macdonald and Evans.

CHAPTER 10

Dance as You've Never Danced Before!

Susi Thornton

...releasing the body into spontaneous movement or play constellates the unconscious in precisely the same way as does a dream. (Marion Woodman 1982, p.78)

A circle is formed. One by one, individuals move into the centre, sharing themselves by giving a name and a movement. They are acknowledged by the group, who mirror the body patterns and the quality of each person's sequence. The new term has begun on the one-year, full-time Sesame Course. We see boldness, hesitancy, caution and humour, those who love the act of moving and those who have not yet arrived at that place. Some leap, some crawl: there are flowing and abrupt rhythms, economic and abandoned use of space. Some share previous dance training, terrifying their new colleagues whose only experience of moving has been the disco floor. What a lot we have learnt each other and about communication through movement in that first exercise in the circle.

It has been found that, under pressure, the individual needs to work from his or her personality and this is manifested in particular constellations of movement happenings. So in this first exercise, certainly stressful, it is highly likely that we will be given important movement data about a person's true strengths, preferences and attitudes. At this stage, all that we, the observers, can hope to gain is a first impression. We will need to check out these impressions throughout the year. How fascinating it would be to be able to play back a video at the end of the course, comparing these impressions with a video record of each student's personal dance piece, the final assignment of the academic year. We would see an enormous increase in confidence and movement vocabulary, a sense of enjoying personal creativity and the act of moving, but we would also see common patterns from the very first movement event.

> It seemed that my fellow students moved with ease and grace – they could turn and twist and leap, they could follow each other's movements. They could make creative responses to what was being asked. My horror was so great I could not hear what was being asked. It was all devastating… Week by week self hate began to become self acceptance – 'if you want a thing to change, it can' I heard. I *wanted* to dance. I longed more and more for freedom in the body I had been given. And it happened. (Sesame student essay)

It is the study of these patterns that constitutes the Laban movement aspect of the Sesame Course – a study of the fundamental principles of human movement, observed and codified by Rudolf Laban (Laban 1980).

The first term is spent searching how to be creative through movement and how it serves as a means of personal expression and communication. Students have the opportunity to improvise moving without thinking, getting in touch with a body 'knowing' which guides them into favourite, comforting rhythms. Sometimes the challenge is inspired by words of Gabrielle Roth, a dance shaman: students are exhorted to find their feet, give themselves up to the beat of the music and dance as they've never danced before.[1]

> Rocking, quietly, on the floor, Body heard the Mind say,
> > '*You* can't dance!
> > I have told you all your life
> > Your movement's lumpy – full of strife.
> > Sit this one out! Don't show yourself!
> > You can't dance!'
>
> Rocking, quietly on the floor, Body heard the Beat say,
> > 'Why *not* dance?
> > Let your hesitation go.
> > Feel my rhythms build and grow.
> > Answer now the music's flow, for
> > You *can* dance!'
>
> Legs and feet were not enough
> to get me through this dancing stuff!
> It called for arms and chest and head

---

1   From the sleeve of the dance music cassette *Dancing Towards the One* by Gabrielle Roth and the Mirrors. Produced by Otto Richter, The Moving Center, New Jersey.

and made me do strange things I dread!
But I could feel new peace inside,
And Mind had lost its voice to chide.

Oh what a joy of choice I found.
Controls were off, so I could bound
and freely leap and whirl or march.
Such happiness at being in touch
with what my Body felt was right.
(By now my Mind was out of sight.)
I danced and danced, I gave it all.
I sang my Body, danced my Soul.

(Poem by Mary Smail as a Sesame student)

Repetitive constellations of movement will eventually be recognized at a conscious level by the individual or observed by others and lead to a deeper understanding: for instance, one student is liberated, once he understands his need to leap and twirl and be 'off the ground'. Should he subsequently find himself in constricted circumstances, held down for too long, he will understand why he becomes frustrated and will know that his gift to himself must be to utilize these flying motivations.

Laban always talked and wrote about harmony and balance, action and reaction, so the 'flyer' needs grounding and the 'controller' needs to experience 'chaos'. The recognition of a person's strengths and preferences and the acquisition of harmony and balance come about through the study of the four fundamentals – *Body, Space, Effort* and *Relationship* – understanding of movement through the physical function, through spatial awareness, through experiencing the variety of dynamic changes and through moving with others. By the end of the first term, each student should be on the way to having a rudimentary understanding of these fundamentals, enabling them to move more eloquently and to observe the movement of others.

Many students have never had the opportunity to take space to study their physical self. This can be a joyful, but also a painful, experience as they draw life-size body maps and with crayons and pastels colour in the positive, free parts of themselves. At the same time they may discover blocked, dark areas which exclude the conscious mind and bring back long forgotten memories. Often this is the first time individuals have encountered movement as a process of healing. One student recalls how this experience enabled her to realize, for the first time, her own, personal power. This was her body and she had the right to move as she wanted. Another student recalls that she was suffering from kidney pain during the first few weeks of the course:

We danced our whole body and coloured our energy on to our body maps and I was stunned to see how much energy I had in my body and how small the area of pain then was. I think this was something of a healing dance – and empowering experience.

The early sessions enable students to find their feet, not collapse at the knee and elbow their way through. They work to connect one body part with another, to move as a whole – spreading, twisting, bending into the space around them and on the floor: '…how strong and powerful it was to follow my direct elbow round the room, to allow my little finger to float me over the room.'

Here students can relive the fun of crawling, rolling, sliding, creeping and, with much hilarity, go over, under and around each other. One student writes:

Before working with Laban I had very little body awareness and was somewhat identified with the thought processes going on in my head. To begin to experience life through my body was a profound awakening and gave me a sense of wholeness and presence which had previously been unavailable in the fragmented, dispersed sense of myself before. It was a 'coming home' to my body as the ground of my being: a connection to the physical world.

Movement is a major part of the inner, creative child and enables people of all ages to get back in touch with that part of themselves. In experiencing this for themselves, students understand why Sesame work is made up of movement and drama.

The concept of space as a living entity which can be shaped and moved, and move you, is a revelation to many. Students discover in themselves a preference for moving at high level, medium level and deep level and, as always, these actions can lead to joy of discovery or tears arising from an inability, at first, to master the body in an alien space: 'I rise, I fall, I open, I close, I advance, I retreat – and so I did, feeling a connection with my own centre as I moved the difference through the body.'

I share with the students how Laban used people's natural way of moving in his movement choirs – using high dancers, medium dancers and deep dancers, in the same way as people group themselves for a vocal choir. It then becomes quite understandable that certain ballet sequences will not be easy for someone who is adept at falling, rolling and kneeling, and vice versa. This has implications for a therapist working in the field to be open to observing clients to see what their natural preferences could be and helping clients to recognize these and feel secure.

One of the great gifts that Rudolf Laban gave us is the facility to name and record aspects of movement. Learning about this helps to introduce the symbolic nature of movement and, thus, its link with the psychological concepts of Carl Gustav Jung, which are such an important part of the Sesame work and training. This analysis shows how movement underpins the flow of facial expression and communication in drama, myth and voice work. It also enables us to look at movement objectively. A short movement phrase is invented and written down, stating which body parts are making gestures or postures and in which direction, or where in the space, they are being made. A partner has then to interpret this written phrase in movement and, finally, the two people dance this phrase simultaneously while another pair watches. Are the two dances the same? Are they different? The observers will see a difference because no instructions have been given about the timing of the phrase or its general expression. And so we move, as a group, into learning about *Effort*.

Effort is an aspect of movement that at one level we all know about but, in trying to understand and observe dynamic changes, students often have the same kind of sensation the centipede might have if told he had a hundred legs with which to walk. For a while, disorder reigns. Then, gradually, members of the group discover the rhythms with which they are most familiar. They begin to model and imitate one another's movements, discovering new rhythms and widening their movement vocabulary. They play with different combinations of elements, experiencing subtle changes and great contrasts where just one element is changed and two stay constant (Press-Glide) or where one element is held and two elements change (Press-Float).

Laban described *Effort* as man's need to express and communicate something of his 'inner being':

> He has the faculty of becoming aware of the patterns which his effort impulses create and of learning to develop, re-shape and use them. The actor, the dancer, the mime (*and the Sesame student!*) has not only to master these patterns but also to understand their significance. In this way imagination is enriched and expression developed. (1984, p.68)

These patterns are the individual's inner attitudes to what Laban called *Motion Factors: Weight* (= gravity), *Space* (= environment), *Time* (= measurable degree) and *Flow* (= energy). A student bears this out when she writes:

> I was stuck in a *dabbing,* fine touch/sudden/direct relationship with myself, others and the world. Observed first through my movement,

I could see this pattern also in my behaviour, in my relationships, in every corner of my experience. I had momentary contact and then would withdraw again. My thoughts darted from one idea to the next and then off again in some tangential direction. When I could apply the principles and began exploring through the body what it felt like to move in a sustained way, to flow, to follow one path for some time, it was an immense sense of relief and joy. I discovered the emotional/psychological equivalent within… I could feel a grace and harmony I had not ever known before.

She continues to describe how experience of the motion factor element of *firmness* helped her to 'come down to earth, to be more present and accept what was going on inside her instead of trying to escape'.

Working with *Effort* offers choices and again this is necessary for field work. Clients are observed and, following the rule 'go where *they* are', they can be met and then guided to increase their capacity for choice. A student wrote in a movement essay of a client who moved very repetitively, using fast, light but 'all over the place' movements. In working with her, the student chose to incorporate focused movement and slower movement. Eventually the student was delighted because the client chose to incorporate a slower pace into her 'all over the place' pattern – a new experience for the client, who was still able to hold on to her favourite attitudes in other respects, that is, her attitude towards gravity remained *light*, and towards space, *flexible*.

Laban was interested in qualities of movement which are latent: that is, they are not directly expressed by the mover but the mover has an innate capacity to use such qualities. One student found she was very happy being strong and powerful in her movement: she liked movement which focused downwards and she constantly moved in heroic and dramatic fashion. Her crisis occurred when she tried to experience an opposite quality, to work with delicacy. The fact that she could work in one pole meant that the opposite quality must be latent. Eventually the moment came when she could rise on to her toes, draw up her energy into her upper chest and move like gossamer across the floor. This revelatory experience was taken to therapy and started a breakthrough for her. It was also the beginning of a rhythm where new movement experiences manifested themselves in deeper personal growth and inner awareness.

The fourth *Fundamental*, in Laban's analysis of movement, is *Relationship*. Although working with myself, with another, with a small group, are challenges from the very start of the course, we also look in some detail at the development of this *Fundamental* in relation to the work of Veronica Sherborne. After her Laban training, Veronica went on to work with people of all ages with learning disabilities and she found a model of three categories – *Equal, Against* and *Supportive/Dependent* – to be a very useful one for her students and client groups. Once again, it empowers people, giving them choices.

Students have explored the myth of *Ceres and Persephone* through dance. The relationship between the mother and daughter gives insight into the *supportive/dependency* mode, the fine line between mothering and smothering, enjoying and rebelling. This pattern is further explored when the house guardians try to keep Persephone happy whilst her mother is away. Persephone escapes from their arms and finds herself alone in the forbidden territory where the ground suddenly opens and she is caught and kidnapped by the henchmen of the underworld god Hades, and brought before him. At first there is anger and fear, but in most pairs of dancers in the parts of Persephone and Hades there is some change towards respecting and enjoying, borne out by the difficulty that Persephone has in making a decision when Ceres arrives demanding the return of her daughter. As one student wrote: 'I remember being given the chance to choose (who does Persephone choose?) and finding it too difficult to give up either Demeter or the Underworld and I felt this reflected a truth within myself – an avoidance of the pain of loss.' Another student recalled this moment: the enormous feeling of power and responsibility. I saw her 'grow' as she became in touch with these feelings within her and the knowledge that she could make this decision.

The students' experience on the Sesame Course demonstrates the value of working with an oblique approach, using story and myth to make connections if the time is right for the individual. Using the myth of *Ceres and Persephone* and the *supportive/dependent* relationship demonstrated the principle of being able to ask for what you want. The Guardians would support Persephone in ways of her choosing. Another student wrote:

> I wanted to be stroked. I then changed this to patted on my stomach and this felt good: there was something grungy in there waiting to come out. I asked my partner to carry on and imagine that she was untying a knot which was in my stomach. She then pulled this imaginary string out of my stomach and it really felt that something inside me was coming out... I felt strange, but fine... I remember I was starting to move downwards and energy and pain were coming out of me. It was as if I had this real pain in my stomach. I heard Susi's voice telling me to keep moving and I remember thinking yes, keep moving. As I continued, the energy seemed to flow through me and become released. It was like I was being cleansed of a lot of grungy

stuff. I had a memory of a feeling about forgiveness. I wanted to forgive myself. The pain was like something locked inside me, something that had been locked away for years. As the energy passed through me I had the sensation of clouds parting. (Student essay)

The Movement course also offers the opportunity for creative leadership. The students each take responsibility for facilitating a session, using movement as the material. To be able to do this task, students have by this time explored and experienced different ways of preparing the body for movement. Gradual awakening of body parts and feeling the flow between them is known as *body alphabet* (a term first heard from Hilary Mathews[2]). Watching and picking up on individual movement in the group, keeping the flow going, starting small and leading to large, mobile happenings, is called *intuitive limber*, a term coined by Audrey Wethered.[3] During the year we look at 'safe exercise' – adapting movement phrases from Yoga, T'ai Chi, Contemporary Dance and Ballet, which do not strain or over-use the untrained body. We experiment with phrases of movement which limber the body in a dance-like manner.

The choice of starting material will be made according to the needs of the *main event* and will develop into a preparation stage which awakens and challenges the body and encourages awareness of the space around and the different changes of energy which will be needed in the creative work to follow.

The *main event* may be a dance drama, a story, a poem, a picture or a response to a piece of music. One group had great fun with a large swathe of scratchy red fabric; someone else brought along shiny silver survival bags. We have danced to a student's song, drawn with a partner and danced the picture and been offered, for inspiration, the shapes and form of natural objects. There doesn't have to be an external stimulus: one session comes to mind in which the challenge was to touch, be touched, move around and bounce off one another.

Much energy is expended, much excitement is engendered and bubbling creative forces have to be allowed to subside in the *grounding*. This is the time when the session leader checks that the movers are 'back' into the reality of everyday life in the room in which we are working. Dreamy, hypnotic moods

---

2 Hilary Mathews was a dancer who taught at the Laban Art of Movement Studio. She now works in the healing arts.

3 Audrey Wethered became a movement therapist after studying individually with Rudolf Laban. For a brief account of her involvement in the early days of Sesame, see Chapter 7.

have to be dispersed gently and gradually by making body action important with more abrupt rhythms: wild leaps and jumps and twirls will be slowed down; the rhythm of breathing long and deep will be encouraged; characters from the story will be peeled off prior to making contact with the self through slapping and rubbing and saying our own names. Contact with each other, acknowledging the sharing of the session, is symbolized by passing a *hand squeeze* round the circle, clockwise and anticlockwise (often at the same time!)

Mention has already been made of the final assignment of the year: the solo piece. Although this causes considerable anxiety beforehand, all the students agree that it is one of the high spots of the year. It is the culmination of all our work together, where the student's individual creativity is made manifest through an understanding and experience of the fundamentals of movement. Students choose their own accompaniment – mostly taped music, but some students have sung and danced, some have worked without vocal sound, some have moved to percussion accompaniment. Optional costumes and props complete the picture.

Each piece is a personal gift and often these dances chart the student's personal journey through the stimulating academic year. It is a time of creativity and many times shows a process of healing, acceptance and moving forward. We laugh, cry and applaud the courage and bravery of expression of the students, few of whom would call themselves dancers – but at this moment they are living proof of Rudolf Laban's belief that dance is the primary form of expression and available to all. The Sesame Course has added the rider to this belief: available to all, however limited mentally, emotionally and creatively they may be.

Dance is one way of awakening the soul. A student writes: 'Laban's work was an empowering influence on my life: a process of integration, of making whole, not only within my personality but also within the larger natural world.'

Laban himself wrote:

> There exists a writing of God. It is the happening in Nature. Everything that is awakened to transient existence, that which becomes, grows and vanishes, is word and letter of this writing. Becoming, growing, withering, vanishing, these metamorphoses of existence speak about the deeper sense of God's writing in Nature. We can get nearer this deeper sense only through movement, which is embedded in her utterances (1984, p.95)

Thanks to Dan Burningham, Jo James, Pam Marshall, Jenny Pearson and Mary Smail for quotations included in this account of the Laban work on the Sesame Course.

References

Laban, R. (1980) *The Mastery of Movement.* Fourth edition. (Revised by Lisa Ullman.) London: MacDonald and Evans.

Laban, R. (1984) *Vision of Dynamic Space.* Compiled by Lisa Ullman from the writings and drawings of Laban. Sussex and Philadelphia, PA: Falmer Press.

Woodman, M. (1982) *Addiction to Perfection: The Still Unravished Bride.* Toronto: Inner City Books.

CHAPTER 11

Child Drama
The Peter Slade Connection

Jenny Pearson

Peter Slade, drama teacher and researcher whose theories about the art form he called 'Child Drama', had a revolutionary effect on drama education in schools, was a strong influence in the early days of Sesame and was taught for a while on the Sesame Course when it was at Kingsway Princeton College. Although Child Drama is not taught as a subject in the training today, Slade's classic book Child Drama (1954)[1] (and a shorter, introductory version from the same publisher) remain on the reading list and his influence remains enshrined within the art forms of Sesame session work.

Slade, during the time he was drama advisor for schools in Somerset and, later, in Birmingham, observed thousands of children both at play and taking part in a range of drama and movement projects. He kept careful records of what he saw and these observations add up to a body of research which could be said to relate to dramatherapy in ways comparable to the relevance of infant observation to psychotherapy.

His central contribution was to draw, from his very wide and detailed observations, a consistent account of the way children, left to themselves, move and communicate as they play – particularly at those times when they spontaneously enact scenes from their imaginations. He saw this kind of *dramatic play* as a basic and primitive form of theatre. Most people who have had children, or remember anything of their own childhood, can recall instances in which they have found themselves taking part in, or observing,

---

1 All quotations in this chapter are taken from this book. For an overview of his ideas on the theory and practice of play, see Slade, P. (1995) *Child Play: Its Importance for Human Development*. London: Jessica Kingsley Publishers.

dramatic play. As I write, I remember a boarding school in the country for children aged eight to thirteen whose parents mostly lived and worked overseas. In its large, wooded garden, we enacted dramas in which we rode 'horses' made from small branches of trees and which we stabled and fed and owned individually over a long period. There were also dramas of pure imagination, without props: I remember a 'deer hunt' in which one person would be the deer and the others formed the hunt, riders and hounds. I remember the fierce excitement of these hunts and the terror of being the 'deer', having evaded the 'hounds', lying breathless and hidden in the laurel bushes while they searched for me, hoping desperately and that they would go away and then I would be safe and free.

The value of Slade's carefully recorded observations is that they give us details of the way children imagine and play which are archetypal and which can therefore be drawn upon when we initiate the shapes and movement patterns of group work with drama. The reason for doing this is that the patterns which are basic to the child become basic patterns within the unconscious memory, so that by connecting with them we connect with an aspect of the client that is deeply rooted and real. Whatever the age group or client group we are working with, all were children once – and if the clients are themselves disturbed children then we may be able to open up the possibility for them to find more healthy ways of playing within the dramatic form, which might not otherwise be accessible to them.[2]

In the long term, working within the basic shapes and rituals of Child Drama can seem to reach people at a very deep level, where it may help to establish and build within the psyche a sense of the shape of things which is both universal and timeless but without which it may be difficult to feel a sense of belonging as a member of the human race. It's to do with being in touch with one's archetypal roots – something which happens at a non-verbal level – and to be quite closely related to some of the things children do when they play. More superficially, in the short term, working within the recognized shapes and energies of Child Drama tends to give session work a more comfortable feel, which is especially useful in the early stages of introducing drama and movement therapy to a new group.

Examples are the shapes that Slade observed when children were coming together to play or engaged in 'running play' – the way they form circles and run in spirals – and his observation that when children run in a circle, they invariably go anti-clockwise. We can speculate about reasons for this:

---

2   See references to work with disturbed children in Chapters 22 and 29.

Slade thought in terms of the heart being on the left and therefore towards the centre when people run anti-clockwise. Whatever the reasons, the observed fact is that anti-clockwise running predominates over clockwise running. The rationale for preserving this pattern in our session work would be to preserve the pattern that comes naturally to healthy children, since this is most likely to resonate with the healthy aspect of any client group. In psychoanalytic terminology, shapes and movement patterns that fit in with Slade's observations are more likely to feel *ego syntonic*, while shapes and movement patterns that go counter to what he observed may feel uncomfortable and *ego dystonic*.

When working with people who are feeling fragile and disturbed in their minds, this kind of feel for unconscious connections in a drama session can make quite a difference in the way individual clients respond as they work with us and how they feel after a session is over.

Another observation of Slade's that becomes important when enacting stories is that in dramatic play, children are often very particular about the shape and structure of the space within which the drama unfolds: certain areas are designated to represent areas within the story or scene that is being played out. In the same way, a drama set up in the classroom or studio needs to respect this rule of place – for example, if the drama is about an expedition that ends in a picnic and a swim in the river, you need to have a clear ground plan specifying where the river is and where on the grass, or in the wood, the picnic is to take place. If this isn't clear, the group may find itself swimming on the spot where it was picnicking a few moments before and this seriously diminishes the power of the dramatic experience.

Slade trained and worked as an actor and ran his own theatre companies and training studio, becoming actively involved in experimental theatre during the early 1930s when he worked with both adults and children. Subsequently, as a drama advisor for schools, he travelled around Britain and worked with thousands of children, keeping notes on his observations over a period of 25 years.

One of observation of his that I have seen reflected in both child and adult groups in dramatherapy is a contained in a concept that he named 'The Land' – his term for a place of imagination that children can enter when fully absorbed in the kind of play that goes go beyond self-conscious 'pretending', reaching a level of total absorption in which they visibly 'become' the kings, queens, monsters or Batmen of the story they have created. Another order of 'reality' seems to take over. This is the spontaneous theatre of the playground. Slade's work with drama in the classroom sought to create conditions in which the same degree of absorption could be attained. The role of the adult was to establish conditions under which this could happen and then keep out of the way – a fair description of what a Sesame dramatherapist seeks to do in session work, as people have demonstrated in their different ways throughout this book.

The magic of Slade's phrase 'The Land' works particularly well for me because it seems to convey, through associations and overtones, something of the magical, mythic quality of the place people get to in a good session – the place in the story which is not of this world: the country where, as P.L. Travers puts it, 'the wolf and the hare say goodnight to each other' (1991).

Slade describes how children who were allowed to approach drama in a free way would sometimes create a presentation without any help, among themselves, doing everything in secret up to the moment they surprised the teacher by asking if they could present what they have been doing:

> These are improvisations and the flow of dialogue is often amazing for its wit, charm, and mixture of naivety and deep philosophical content.

> At the best moments of playing they are...unconcerned with audience; they are far away in 'the Land'. But sometimes a petering out gives an indication of the 'near finish' and we can feel them slowly coming back to earth. Nevertheless, if they are not entirely convinced that any adults present understand that Play is temporarily finished...they will often turn and say 'that's all' just to make sure. Sometimes the end is so abrupt that it is very difficult to be sure of its arrival, particularly as under these conditions the Players often stay absorbed in 'the Land' and remain coma-acting for a minute or two... (Slade 1954, p.55)

He describes how the inventive flow of language and imagery that children produce while they are in 'The Land' can become self-conscious and stuttering during the transitional 'near finish' phase when 'things are becoming more conscious.'

Facilitating a comparable entry into an inner space where it is possible to make a living connection with the worlds of myth and story has obvious parallels with Slade's beautiful description of children entering into 'The Land'. Self-consciousness recedes and people suddenly discover a freedom to improvise with movement and voice, 'becoming' the figures in the story so that their experience in role is for the moment indistinguishable from their experience of themselves. The outer world is left behind and the drama takes over, with the same kind of present reality as in a dream.

Setting this experience of the inner world becoming almost tangibly real in a Sesame session beside Slade's observations of 'The Land', it would appear that what happens may be a kind of creative regression to a way of experiencing which, though it may feel new, could also be connecting unconsciously with a long lost mode of play. Where the patient in psychotherapy may regress to infancy, perhaps the client in dramatherapy is regressing to a slightly later, but still archaic, experience of the playground. If this is the case, it could account for the surprising ease with which so many people take to the Sesame art form – even those who declare themselves to be 'bad at drama' and find the prospect of 'acting' an alarming one.

If this parallel to childhood experience holds good, then what Slade said about its contribution to the well-being of children could logically be extended to include people of all ages and conditions for whom the Sesame key has opened a door to the boundless treasure house of the imagination:

> Play opportunity…means development and gain. Lack of play may mean a permanent lost part of ourselves. It is this unknown, uncreated part of ourselves, this missing link, which may be a cause of difficulty and uncertainty in later years. Backward children often respond to further opportunities for play, for this and other reasons. They build or rebuild a Self by Play, doing when they can what should have been done before. (Slade 1954, p.35)

Thus Slade's descriptions of children at play, and in the more specialized setting of drama, provide dramatherapists with valuable insights into what feels comfortable and right in a session and what is more likely to be felt as disturbing, though for quite unconscious reasons. He observed two main shapes, or symbols, that frequently appear both in the art of children and in the way they move around and group themselves in a room: the circle and the spiral. When entering a room where music or drumming could be heard, children would run and dance in a spiral, which Slade described as 'the shape of happy entry'. The spiral would turn into a 'filled in' circle, the children being more or less equidistant over the floor space. As the sounds stopped, the ring shape would appear – including just about everyone. Among very young children the ring was generally a large one, including just about everyone, breaking into smaller group rings from time to time. (Sesame sessions traditionally begin with the group large circle and frequently break up into smaller groups for the initial warm-up.)

These patterns and symbols that Slade observed in drama sessions were not imposed by adults: they were natural forms that arose from the children when they entered the studio, as well as out-of-doors in the street. Outside, because of the child's intense absorption in these forms of play, they can be a serious threat to safety. Slade noted a fascination with time and beat in the 'running play' of the street: how a younger child would often run with one foot in the gutter and the other on the kerb and then turn, so that the other foot took the higher level. Occasionally, this was combined with trying out rhythms. Older children would extend these forms of running play into the road, where it became intensely dangerous because of the exclusion of traffic consciousness due to their absorption. He noticed the circle appearing just as dangerously in this street play, usually near right-angled junctions. These forms of play were solitary and personal, rather than social and Slade observed that they were closely bound to 'Self-experience' (see Chapter 1). The age at which it appeared was around five, attaining its full beauty from about seven years upwards – the point when the runner was nearly as much a master of running as of walking:[3]

> The running play of the street, which also includes mixed walking and rhythmic skips or hops, so delicate and lovely to behold, is quite different from the careless running out after a ball or away from a companion... Running play of the street has recognizable Music and Drama qualities, and in itself can be a first-class theatrical experience. It is clearly a tremendous personal experience, too. (Slade 1954, p.47)

The transformation that Slade noticed in children when they were absorbed in forms of play which engaged their whole selves, physically and emotionally, has its counterpart in Sesame work with people of all ages and abilities. When the imagination is highly engaged, a kind of beauty takes over the face and movements of the person for whom this is happening (see Chapter 24).

This link between Sesame experience and Slade's research reinforces the impression that what we are partly doing through our drama and movement is to enable people to recapture in our sessions some earlier state of being in which such enjoyment was possible. In some extreme cases it feels as if we may even be making such experiences available for the first time (see Chapter 7).

More generally, and perhaps especially for the Sesame students in their studio work, being put in touch with the kind of exhilarating 'Self-experience' that Slade describes re-awakens the energy and vitality that most of us can remember dimly from childhood, but may have thought we could never

---

3   See Chapter 23 for description of a child who had never gone running until he encountered Sesame.

experience again. I recall an occasion shortly after I finished training when I was preparing to run a drama session with a colleague in the big space we use as the Sesame Studio. We got there half an hour early and put on some music – part of the soundtrack of *Dances with Wolves* – and we ran. The space was wide and toughly carpeted, like an indoor field. We just ran round and round for the joy of it in a kind of trance, our feet flying, running in a huge circle and laughing across the space between. Reading Slade, I can now recognize that we had returned to the enjoyment and absorption of running play.

Observing so many children across a wide social spectrum, Slade noted that the general pattern of development was roughly the same for every child. He saw this as evidence supporting Jung's theories on archetypal experience:

> The constant repetitions and use of symbols in the realm of Child behaviour, also the acting out of situations sometimes before they have been experienced, is entirely in line with the Jungian conception of the collective unconscious. We find story themes concerned with birth, marriage, parenthood, death and resurrection. People...are killed but often get up again (resurrection). We also hear references to the hereafter...and at five years there is already apparent a certain recognition of good and evil, or at least of opposing forces...

> Dramatic play is constantly fluid, and is quite unlike our conception of theatre. Indeed, where our theatre is introduced too early...the child does not at first even connect the joys of its own form of drama with what it attempts to do to please us. To begin with, the child is still greatly concerned with Self, and has been from babyhood. But because of the expanding recognition of things and persons around it (the 'me' and 'not me'...), gradual domination over ever-widening circles of attention begins to take place. It is not surprising that this attitude of the child is continued in dramatic play. Given a flat floor space and a happy atmosphere, there is, with each child, the tendency to *absorption* which marks genuine creation; and, whilst absorbed, they are not conscious of being watched. They act outwards from the Self around the body...

> When a child is absorbed, it neither needs nor wants an audience, and, because it needs no audience, it faces in any direction and moves where it will. It is during this movement-at-will that the child begins to cover the actual floor space in so interesting and beautiful a manner, filling the space as if it were a picture... The joy of dramatic play is that it is the creation of the moment. The energy and imagination *can* be

interrupted, and then the 'moment' is gone for ever. Audience is often the enemy of the 'moment'. (Slade 1954, p.48)

Sesame drama also shares this feature of child drama: it is an end in itself and doesn't need or want an audience, other than the group itself. I have been in sessions, both as session leader and as a participant, when the most exquisitely beautiful scenes and performances have arisen spontaneously out of the moment. Participants are eased into the central enactment by means of a series of body-centred warm-ups, usually related in some way to a central story or theme. The group gathers in a circle to hear the story. This gathering creates a pause, a time of quiet transition from the warm-up to the living heart of the session. Then parts are chosen and they rise slowly to take their places around the room, ready for the opening scene. The action is set in the round. Different areas may be designated as different places in the story: for example, if the Myth of Persephone is to be enacted, her mother's home will tend to be placed at some distance from Hades with the woods and fields in between, observing the rules of spatial awareness. It is up to the session leader to see that this rule is observed, thus protecting the imaginative experience of the group.

The group itself is audience to the action. People not currently involved in the acting area may stand around the side of the room or accompany the action with simple percussion instruments or voice. Some may choose to take inanimate parts, together forming a palace or a cave, a flock of sheep, a forest or a ship. In this way everyone becomes involved, even the most reticent person who may not feel like playing a name part.

I have vivid memories of enactments during the magical year of training, which live like real events in my imagination: Orpheus being taken across the river to Hades; the goddess Inanna being challenged by the gatekeeper to the underworld in front of a series of different gates, each made up of people; 'Hans my Hedgehog' in the Grimms' fairy tale, lovingly tended by his princess after his spines had been burnt in the fire.

Slade likened child drama to jazz, also created by improvisation and with spontaneity as its main quality. Sesame work depends on these qualities. The enactments cannot be repeated, any more than a group of jazz players can repeat a jamming session. A myth or a story may be enacted many times, but each enactment will have its own shape and flavour. You can remember it, but you can't repeat it.

Slade also observed how drama seems to satisfy the appetite for adventure: 'With the child, we find adventure by drama satisfies, and improves behaviour if conducted in school'. As with dreams, so drama at its most intense seems to pass beyond the 'as if' level of 'pretending' and take the participant into

Figure 11.1 The circle, symbol of containment. At the end of a drama and movement session with Jo James, Sesame Course Leader (bottom, centre) on the 1993–93 Sesame Course (photograph by James McCormick)

Figure 11.2 'Rituals...before going to sleep' (see Chapter 12). Thomas was not yet two when he began to make circles in his bed-time play to contain himself and his toys (photograph by Peter Aylward)

an area of experience that is implied in the seemingly paradoxical phrase 'the reality of the imagination'. It is *experienced* and this can be extremely satisfying, comparable to 'the real thing'. Thus the prisoner writing about drama in Wormwood Scrubs is able to write 'The drama gave me inner freedom' (see Chapter 15).

References

Slade, P. (1954) *Child Drama*. London: University of London Press.

Travers, P.L. (1991) *The Bird and the Word*. New York: Parabola.

CHAPTER 12

Ritual
Journeys of the Heart

James Roose-Evans

Ritual takes many forms. At its simplest level there are those recurring personal rituals which we all use for waking up, going to work, settling down to work, coming home, going to sleep. All such personal rituals enable us to come to terms with the reality of each day, imposing some order on what otherwise might be total chaos. More complex rituals have evolved for whole communities – whether that of the immediate family or clan, or a tribe or nation. The classic rituals all place the individual in a larger context so that birth, puberty, marriage and death are seen as timeless experiences which have occurred to generations of individuals. Such rituals validate, providing the image of forces controlling life, and serve to reinforce our ability to cope with an unpredictable world. They heighten the intensity of shared experience, enabling us to realize that we are not alone but part of an indivisible whole.

The greatest of all rituals are, of course, religious. Religion, being a search for meaning in the universe, offers a series of rituals to mark the seasons or events in the life of an individual or a nation. Thus the stage funeral of the assassinated President Kennedy deeply affected the psyche of the nation as a whole. As Joseph Campbell observed of this event: 'The nation was unstrung. The archetypal event of his funeral allowed us to meditate upon death and the mystery of death as epitomised in the highest presence in our national life. Out of it came a sense of resolution for the country' (Cavander 1985). All true ritual marks a transition from one mode of being to another. Ritual at such a level works a transformation within the individual or community, resulting in an altered state of consciousness. Such major rituals are known as *rites of passage*. In the words of Anthony Stevens, the Jungian analyst: 'Now I am a boy leaving my mother and submitting myself to the ritual that the gods have decreed. Now I die as a boy and am ritually dismembered. Now I am born as a man amongst men.' (1982, p.169)

Yet, in our society today, we so often lack such rituals which can mark and celebrate such rites of passage. As Harvey Cox wrote: 'We are dragooned into rituals that mean little or nothing to us, yet when we need the symbolic deepening of an important experience we somehow lack the necessary gestures and images. No wonder we undergo identity crises until we die' (Cox 1973). In a similar vein, Mircea Eliade, in conversation with Claude-Henri Rocquet (1982), responding to the question 'How are we to tell children that they are sexual and mortal beings?' replies:

> Today not only has sexuality been desacralised, demystified, but death has too; it is ignored. The sight of it is repressed. In a profane society it is very difficult to initiate children into these two great mysteries. I have no answer. Is it actually possible for a child to understand death or sexuality? I don't know what one ought to say.

It will be seen in the two examples given later on that our society does indeed need to find a way of coming to terms with sexuality through ritual.

It is not only sex and death that lack rituals, but many other transitions. In her novel *Open the Door* (1983), the novelist Rosemary Manning has one character observe: 'Oh, God, why is there no satisfactory ritual for parting? The pain is raw at the edges: no healing balm of sherry.' Today we have no rituals for a broken marriage, a broken relationship, or a broken home. Churches which celebrate marriages do not want to know when the marriage falls apart and have no rituals with which to handle such failures. Today we have no ritual for a woman who has been beaten or battered or raped; no rituals for men who have been raped; no rituals for pregnancy or for puberty in the male. What rituals do we have for a child moving to a new home or to a new school? What rituals for a young woman's first menstruation? What rituals exist for the elders of our society? Why wait until someone is dead before we express appreciation of them? And while each of the major faiths has precise rituals for the dying and for the dead, what rituals do we have to offer those who have no specific faith or tradition to support them?

Even among the existing religious traditions which have their own ancient liturgy there is often felt the need for alternative forms of liturgy. A nun, having read my book *Inner Journey, Outer Journey* (Roose-Evans 1987), wrote: 'I'm especially interested in and inspired by your exploration of drama spilling over into liturgy, creating our own liturgies that are relevant to us today – and *all this rooted and fed from our deepest centre.*'

A ritual is a journey of the heart which should lead us into an inner realm of the psyche – the 'ground of our being' – and if we perform such rituals with passion and devotion they will enhance our desire and strengthen our capacity to live. The Jungian analyst Bani Shorter sums it up thus in her book on women's initiations, *An Image Darkly Forming* (1990): 'Ritual is a collective or individual attempt to conjure up or re-awaken those deeper layers of the psyche which the light of reason and the power of the will can never reach, and to bring them back to life.'

Psychotherapy alone cannot achieve this, for most therapies work on a cerebral level. A woman psychotherapist, who had received seven years of intensive in-depth training, once wrote to me:

> Like most psychotherapies my training has been mainly a conscious, verbal process; and a very effective one. It has given me invaluable help in my own journey, and has been a very humanizing influence on my Catholic spirituality. However, I am at the limit of what I can do consciously and verbally, and my personal process is no longer about personality work. I have been aware for quite a while that in spite of the very good therapy I have had, there is still something very deep inside me that is still wounded and controls most of my responses to the world; that in spite of the depth and breadth of my spiritual understanding and love of God, somewhere inside me I am still a prisoner. Somewhere I don't *know* myself. There are doors inside me that are shut and I want to open them, or, at least have the opportunity of opening them or not, as is appropriate. I stand baffled and bewildered at my own boundaries, not knowing how or where to cross, and everything, every good thing I have learned and believed up to now being no longer sufficient to see me through, I need a new knowing.[1]

In my own ritual work there are many exercises which I use to help an individual make that 'rite of passage'. The first example is of an English student at the Middlesex Polytechnic in London who was one of a group of students with whom I was working over a five-week period. The following extract from his journey shows how a simple exercise became for him a living ritual:

> Monday the 10th was one of those days that sticks out most for me in the five week period of working with James. It was the day that I

---

1   For a similar example see Chapter 21.

worked with the bamboo poles. I was told to use them as though they were part of me, as though I had lived with them always, and that I was to go on a journey with them. At first no image came to mind, and so I waited patiently, as I had been taught to do by James. Then, all of a sudden, a picture of my mother flashed into my mind. She has suffered from Parkinson's Disease for twenty years and as a child I had grown up submerged in my mother's illness. Now in this room, with these crutches made out of bamboo, I was transformed into a cripple. For the first time I knew exactly what she felt like. Trapped and yet not trapped. Unable to walk as others did and yet with the power to move. Like being caught in a slow moving nightmare which you cannot wake up from because you are already awake. Yet each day it becomes that little bit harder to walk. A little more effort is needed to do certain things until the power to do these specific things goes and recedes into the blackness of memory. I think if I have one fear in life it is to end my days as my mother is doing still, locked in a mobility vacuum, a slow motion film that is slowly, almost imperceptibly, running down. A life that is no life, a death that is no death. This I fear and yet it has taken me all this time to come to terms with my own emotions. Until that day in New Hall when I faced them finally.

As I mentioned earlier, the young in our society have no rituals which will enable them to come to terms with their own sexuality. The churches cannot help them because Christian teaching has yet to come to terms with the central drive of the sexual libido, and to evolve a theology of sexuality. It was while working in Colorado with students in their mid-twenties, that the most moving and powerful examples of such a rite of passage took place. The exercise involves a journey to the frontier. The first example is from the journal of Monica:

As I was meditating at the start, gazing at the frontier, the impulse that hit me all of a sudden was my sexuality, my virginity. At first I was happy to advance towards the frontier because it was far away. I saw myself falling for a guy and this expressed itself in the form of a somersault. Then curiosity and crawling along the ground took me a little closer, but I was still comfortably far enough away from the big decision. I was learning and growing in my knowledge, which was a good thing. This feeling slowly changed as I started to feel a pressure pushing me towards the frontier, as if this guy were pressurising me more and more. When I realized that I was really in love with him I expressed this feeling by a head over heels cartwheel. However this also brought me closer to the frontier. I began to feel alarmed at being so close to this barrier and now I began to look backwards, not wanting to face what lay ahead. I was still curious about the dangerous frontier and so, in order to get closer, I lay on my back with my head facing towards the frontier, and I stretched out my arms until my finger tips touched the frontier itself. At this moment I experienced an instant revulsion and my whole body shrank away. I felt torn between staying where I was and exploring further. So I lay on my stomach for a long while, contemplating the frontier. Then finally I advanced towards it. Being this close to it and actually *seeing* it kinda shook me up, and so I curled up into a ball in order to protect myself from the intense pressure I was feeling and the responsibility of making a decision. I knew I couldn't stay in this position for ever, so I stretched out my body lengthwise, so I lay alongside the frontier, and I waited for the big decision to occur. After nearly rolling over the frontier, tensed and wavering, I finally rolled right back to where I had started. And so remained a virgin.

This whole experience was very intense for me and I think it represents a major conflict I have with College. The guys here seem only interested in one-night stands which I have no desire to get caught up in. Yet the only alternative is to be ignored, to be left out – which results in my very strong anti-male feelings, and my being uncomfortable around guys. There is a lot of pressure to go with the crowd and as I am a virgin I am in a very small minority for students these days. Sometimes I question myself but this exercise has really helped me to realize that I'm not ready for sex and that I am strong enough to stand up for my own convictions. It means being lonely now but I know I feel better about myself for it. I hold the controlling hand.

Monica's ability to resist the pressure to go with the crowd, or to compete with her peers and, instead, to go with her own individuality, recalls a poem by Emily Dickinson who similarly stood her ground: 'I'm ceded – I've stopped being Theirs.'

The second illustration on this theme comes from another Colorado student, Dickson. He was a philosophy student, very well read, articulate, but who had never done anything like this before and his journal records how he was 'pissed off' with the exercises. But he persevered. At one point he wrote:

In two days I have had very strong images that depicted my loneliness. The effect of ritual helps men in general to circumvent this loneliness. However, James seems to push us to a better sense of self-identity. He constantly pushes students to work with imagery that emphasizes individuality.

He tried the Frontier exercise more than once but got nowhere with it:

The motions felt contrived, and the images were forced. Nothing really flowed.

Then, suddenly, he changed his strategy:

Concentrating from the beginning, I developed a central image before I even made the first movement. In my mind I pictured a girl, a Colorado College student, whom I have observed from a distance but with whom I have never actually talked. She is quite beautiful and her beauty often captivates my imagination. I picture her, as I know her, from a distance. As I moved forward, crawling first on my belly, then on my hands and knees, and finally walking upright, so gradually I draw nearer to her. My images change from a distant picture of her alone to close-ups of her and me together. The images luckily weren't limited to sexual pictures. I often found myself moving in an active daydream of a long life with this girl, of love, of true love, and the full range of activities that love consists of. I learned of the benefits and the commitments needed. I learned of the need and the desires of both her and me. The images of the two of us were closest and clearest after I first stood up, about halfway through the exercise. Then they grew distant and dull. In the end I found myself lying on the frontier without crossing over.

The frontier was the passage from life into death. The journey began, as it should, from my present state of mind. The journey focused on a love affair that lasted the rest of my life. It was a love that enabled me to beat the loneliness of death. With love I lost the existential hunger that constantly spears me at this stage of my life. I found a fuller sense of life that filled in the black hole of expectation of death that plagues the hungry human. I don't think that I could have lived this love had it not been for the exercise. I merely would have remained contented with the sexual fantasies of my daydream. I don't know if the feeling and understanding spanned by the ritual will persist, but I know that today I experienced love and can enjoy it, at least for a day.

Later on in his journal Dickson expresses what is far more prevalent on the campuses of America than authorities care to acknowledge:

> Sometimes I think that fifty per cent of my education is a lie, yup, about half of the time. I stay in school for grades and parental appeasement. What a chicken shit. That certainly is a lie and the one I'm lying to is myself. Learning should spring from curiosity. If I don't *want* to learn something then I'm obviously not curious...it's not just school or the fact that I'm lonely angers me. I think it has to do with life in general. Sitting around, I see that I'm not the only one who's unhappy. Hell, most of this campus is unhappy. And those that aren't unhappy are either too stupid or don't give a shit. But maybe that's the answer. Actually, I think I've tried that before and look where I am. Oh, well, this has got to end before my anger surfaces again: *Vanitas vanitatis.*

The majority of people today possess, no matter how unused, real creative and imaginative faculties and the individual needs to rediscover how to give form to her or his most urgent feelings, fears and aspirations, so that they may the better understand themselves and others. We have to learn how to respond directly and truly to our deepest impulses and to give them form and rhythm, above all in our worship – creating, according to our needs, our own rituals. We have to be like the youth Tito who, at the close of Herman Hesse's novel *The Glass Bead Game* (1969), quite unselfconsciously begins to dance on the mountaintop as the sun rises: 'Without knowing what he was doing, asking no questions, he obeyed the command of the ecstatic moment, danced his worship, prayed to the sun, professed with devout movements and gestures his joy, his faith in life.'

This description is matched by a real-life example of a spontaneous ritual taken from the fourth and final volume of Kathleen Raine's autobiography *India Seen Afar* (1990):

> I have on more than one occasion watched Santosh when she dances Radha. She goes every morning to Triveni before she starts her day's work, and says she could not live her life or do her work without these hours on the dance floor with her guru, who teaches her more than dance, teaches her the deep realities of the soul's life.

I once asked a therapist who had attended one of my ritual workshops how he would define ritual. There was a long silence and then came the reply: 'That which connects me, or transports me, to the Beyond'.

Our society has urgent need to rediscover ritual, to experience such journeys of the heart. 'Our real journey is interior,' wrote Thomas Merton to a friend when he was setting off on his last journey to the East. 'It is a matter of growth, deepening, and of an ever greater surrender to the creative action of love and grace in our hearts. Never was it more necessary for us to respond to that action.'

References

Cavander, K. (1985) 'Heroes when we need them' (Interview with Joseph Campbell). *American Theatre Journal,* February.

Cox, H. (1973) *The Seduction of Spirit: The Use and Misuse of People's Religions.* New York: Simon and Schuster.

Hesse, H. (1969) *The Glass Bead Game.* London: Holt, Rinehart and Winston.

Manning, R. (1983) *Open the Door.* London: Jonathan Cape.

Raine, K. (1990) *India Seen Afar.* Totnes: Green Books.

Rocquet, C.H. (1982) 'Ordeal by labyrinth.' In K.D. Coltman (ed) *Conversations with Mircea Eliade and Claude-Henri Rocquet.* Chicago: University of Chicago Press.

Roose-Evans, J. (1987) *Inner Journey, Outer Journey.* London: Rider.

Shorter, B. (1990) *An Image Darkly Forming.* London: Routledge.

Stevens, A. (1982) *Archetype: A Natural History of the Self.* London: Routledge and Kegan Paul.

CHAPTER 13

Ritual in Sesame

Morag Deane

A Sesame session is akin to a living rite. I base this conclusion on personal experience, both in training and during the ensuing years of using the Sesame Method in a variety of settings. I would like, first, to consider the structure of a Sesame session in relation to ritual, and then to move on and recount some experiences of it in relation to particular enactments.

Ritual is a complex umbrella term: a variety of definitions have been offered for it as a phenomenon. The difficulty over definition has been compared, by a number of anthropologists, to a similar difficulty in defining 'the arts'. I am aware that in considering ritual and the Sesame method I am not exactly comparing like with like and that there is a danger of foisting a twentieth-century model inappropriately. But, regardless of the differing backgrounds in which they occur, the Sesame Method and ritual are both agents of growth, development and change. There are common landmarks. Both fulfil a need variously described in terms of 'hunger' or 'a need to signify'.

Ritual is often referred to in terms of habitual repetitious forms. Some repetition and routine may be involved, but, unless an interchange is also present, rite can degenerate into rote – which is of limited value.

A parallel can be drawn between the experience of a 'living rite' and a Sesame session, since within the structure of both there is the possibility of a new and fresh dimension emerging. The structure serves as a container, facilitating the compulsion to explore the unknown in order to grow. Ritual processes and Sesame work do not guarantee transformation, but they do provide a significant *temenos* in which a transformational experience becomes possible.

The most immediately obvious similarity between a Sesame session and a rite is structural. Both are segmented into stages or phases and into sub-units with particular actions and gestures. Both adhere to a tri-partite model with a distinct beginning, middle and end. The anthropologist A. Van Gennep (1908) distinguishes three phases in a rite consisting of separation, transition and incorporation. The first phase of ritual – that of separation – approximates to the Sesame Warm-up, or limber, in as much as it clearly marks the change from one situation to another. Van Gennep described the 'limber' as differentiating between sacred space time and profane space time. In this way, ritual changes the quality of time. It may be understood as placing the process beyond or outside the time which measures secular processes and routine. So it can be said to take place 'out of time'.

In a similar vein, the Warm-up, which occupies the first phase of a Sesame session, takes participants from the 'here and now environment' of the ward, studio, etc. and prepares them, both physically and psychologically, to participate in the Main Event which follows, occupying the central part of the session.

The Warm-up sets the scene for the Main Event by focusing informally on movement-based activity, often taking place – or at least beginning – in a circle. The process can be compared to an orchestra tuning up before a performance. In observing the participants, one can certainly detect an increase in body awareness and group awareness during the Warm-up. This heightened awareness in the group can develop further over a number of sessions.

The use of movement-based activities can also mark the beginning of ritual. Richard Katz (1984) studied community healing among the Kung of the Kalahari over a ten-year period. He described the beginning of a rite in the following way:

> As the sun goes down a central fire is lit and the women who will sing and clap come together. They sit down intertwined, forming a tight circle around a central fire. The dancers, both men and women, begin to circle around the singers. Others who are not singing or dancing sit in small peripheral groups, conversing around the 'talking fires'. Initially there is a lot of warm up activity. The mood is casual and jovial. Many of the dancers are trying out and showing off new dance steps.

It is not possible to draw absolute parallels between the transition section of a rite and the Main Event section of a normal Sesame session. The nature and content of both are determined by the perceived needs of the participants. However, there are common features.

Van Gennep refers to the second phase of a rite as the transition margin or limber through which the ritual subjects pass. It is a phase of ambiguity, a sort of limbo, which has few of the characteristics of either the preceding or subsequent social cultural states. In relation to ritual, the significance of the liminal or Warm-up period (as with the other two phases) varies according to the rite of passage in which it occurs. Liminal periods are important in pregnancy, betrothal and initiation where Turner (1982) states that the emphasis of the rite tends to be laid on the transition itself rather than the particular states between which it is taking place. He states that, since we tend to think of society as a structure of positions, the liminal period may be viewed as an inter-structural situation.

According to Turner, ritual symbols of the liminal period fall into two categories: those of effacement and those of ambiguity or paradox. The former serve to remove identity by loss of name, personal clothes or use of mud and paint smeared on the body to make one ritual subject indistinguishable from another and from animals. Other indications of liminality include eating or abstaining from certain foods and complete disregard for personal appearance. Among the Tiwi, undergoing initiation rites is compared with, and referred to as, being 'sent away to college'. While 'at college' each youth is referred to only by his grade name, for example Marakumarni for year one and Mikingula for the last four years. This emphasises gender identity, as opposed to personal identity based on kinship ties. The loss of identity during the liminal period brings about a state of limbo which contains little or nothing of the past or of the future. This can have a levelling effect before elevation to a new status. The ritual subjects cannot obtain this state without renouncing all knowledge. This process may be compared to stages in the individuation process in Jungian analytic psychology, in as much as both involve a voluntary surrender of the conscious ego to transformation in order that development may take place. This surrender may be seen as a disintegration into *prima materia* which is necessary in order to be re-shaped/formed to encounter new experiences. So the essence of the person is extracted and related to the next period. This may be further illustrated by Eliade's studies of the Shaman's journey (1988) in which the ritual subject is broken into pieces and then put together as a being bridging visible and invisible worlds.

The second category of symbolism evident during the liminal period is that of ambiguity and paradox. The ritual subjects are associated with the opposites: life and death, male and female, food and excrement, simultaneously. This expresses their dying away from a former life and being born and growing into another. Turner (1982) referred to this characteristic state of liminality as 'betwixt and between' since it confounded the normal classificatory structures of society. Mary Douglas (1991) would regard this state as one of ritual uncleanliness, due to its ambiguity. This may be seen as weakening since the ritual subject has no power. However, there is a sort of compensation as a result of liberation from structural obligation. The ritual subjects may be accredited with a sacred power: hence their frequent comparison with ghosts, gods and ancestors. Just as they are considered to be in close connection with the asocial world, conversely they were also associated with the non-social world of animals and birds. The symbolism surrounding liminality may be seen through twentieth-century Western eyes as an attempt to externalize and make known to the outer world what is essentially an inner process. Anthropologists would argue that initiation rituals are just as essentially public processes as they are inner processes.

It can be a function of the transition or liminal period to prepare the ritual subject for the requirements of the new role to be assumed. The determinants of this role may reflect the social structure of the society concerned.

Although the liminal period is less conspicuous, even less dramatic, than the ordeals of separation and ceremonies of incorporation, it may be considered more important as it can involve introduction and instruction in the tribal mysteries and traditions. This, Turner suggests, may correspond to the 'sacra' of Greek and Orphic mysteries – through exhibition in the form of sacred objects, instruments, relics, for example Aboriginal Chirungas – or action – through undergoing experience ordeals – which can occur in various combinations. For example, among Wogeo men ear-piercing, tongue-scarification, circumcision and instruction, sometimes related to the cultural perception of the sacred – takes place. Myths are often an important vehicle for imparting this knowledge. The 'sacra' may then be seen as an idea common to initiation rites throughout the world and serving to educate the ritual subject in the underlying principals of his culture. There is a tendency in the twentieth-century Western world to treat the 'sacra', or spiritual knowledge, as 'secret' and for only a select few to know it. This is probably a result of socialization within a hierarchical and evaluative culture. In smaller, simpler societies where people are egalitarian, such disparities are absent. For example, among the Kalahari Kung spiritual knowledge is available to all.

Malinowski (1957) informs us that in small-scale societies tradition was held to be of supreme value and any laxity weakened the cohesion of the group. Under such circumstances, tradition became sacred and, being thus endowed with religious underpinning, it served on an individual level not only to mark external change of status but also a spiritual metamorphosis transcending the former in significance. On a collective level, socializing tradition during liminality functioned to reinforce the social structure. Giving tradition a seal of 'supernatural approval' placed it beyond question.

As traditional ways of living, relating and believing have disintegrated in the West, self-responsibility and personal choice have increased. One is primarily held responsible for what one does or does not achieve. Participants in a Sesame session can be compared to ritual participants in the sense that they can be seen as being in a liminal state. They are often physically outside the normal structures of society, as a result of hospitalization or being cared for in some way. Many experience loss of identity under such circumstances. Disregard for personal appearance, possessions and responsibilities can combine to produce a levelling effect.

The Main Event in a Sesame session corresponds roughly to the transition or liminal phase of a rite. Just as initiation rites involve 'growing a person', so do Sesame sessions. Use is made of symbolic material in a variety of story forms. Since a Sesame group may span several cultures, material tends to be drawn from a wide variety of sources. Myths, legends and fairy-tales provide a vehicle for enactment and, in using what seems relevant to elaborate the story, we make it our own. The value of the material emerges through group co-operation. Generally the participants will work together to create a symbol: for example, one person may collect the wood which another fashions into an image, others may bless or consecrate it, others bow down before it, hold it up in triumph, or enact a sacrifice before it. The power and meaning of the symbol is bound up with all the interactions of the participants in the enactment; it would have no meaningful existence without this collaboration. The experience may then be registered at group level, while retaining its personal relevance for each individual taking part.

Liminality may include a complex sequence of events taking place outside clock time but in the realm of sacred space time, which may be felt as subversive and playful. This sacred space time allows for cultural elements — images, paintings, dances — to be explored and interpreted in many ways. They may be played with and re-combined in unfamiliar ways, even in a grotesque way, since they are manifestations of fantasy as opposed to experience. Such disorder through play can take the form of costume and masks constructed to emphasise certain features — for example, body characteristics. Within these situations of reversal of norms, ritual subjects, according to Van Gennep, make raids and swoops on villages and gardens, seize women, abuse older men, steal and pillage at will or feed and adorn themselves at the expense of the community. Such play and reversal are not seen as a matter of individual choice but as 'deep seriousness', causing the ritual subject to reflect on cultural norms previously taken for granted. Reversal, while affording a short period of fun, release of energy and entertainment through chaotic behaviour as Saturnalian revelry, demonstrates to the individual, group and community that chaos is the antithesis of order and that there is a need for order. The movement from disorder to order experienced through play in the liminal period may have its equivalent in the different forms of play occurring at different stages in our own society: children moving into adulthood find their play and games curtailed and controlled according to socially accepted norms.

Embodied in the Sesame Method is recognition of the value and importance of play at all ages. A child rehearses for life through play. In both ritual and Sesame sessions, participants can do the same – just as in liminality people 'play' with the elements of the familiar and defamiliarize them. Novelty emerges from unprecedented combinations of familiar elements.

Sutton-Smith (1972) examined children's games in terms of an order-disorder continuum. He concludes that 'we may be disorderly in games either because we have an overtone of order and want to let off steam or because we have something to learn through being disorderly'. He sees liminal situations as seedbeds of cultural creativity producing new models, symbols and paradigms.

Through the art forms of drama and movement in a Sesame session, it is possible to make a reconnection with the ability to play. This can in turn serve the function of recreating the way reality is perceived, which over time can lead to the recovery of that spontaneity we think of as childlike (without the derogatory overtones of childishness).

The final stage of a ritual, that of Aggregation, corresponds to the Grounding of a Sesame session. As with other phases, the content is determined by the situation. A person can emerge from a rite, or from a Sesame session, with a sense of being altered, so it is important to mark the end of the experience and prepare to re-enter the 'here and now'. In ritual this phase may include a procession or ceremony to acknowledge new status, or eating a communal meal. In this way the ritual subject becomes established again within the community.

In Sesame terms, the Grounding is aimed at making sure that participants are returned to themselves before they go out of the session. An opportunity to share experiences by talking about them can be helpful in this. The session may then conclude with a dance or a song which contrasts with the main session content and which may be repeated in subsequent sessions, helping to create a sense of continuity being carried over a number of sessions.

Participants will then return to their classes, wards or workshops, or back into the world outside.

Ritual processes like a Sesame session can function therapeutically by bringing about a sense of interrelatedness with numinous or suprapersonal powers, which can facilitate new experience and bridge different modes of being. Through their structure the sessions create an atmosphere of sanctuary, which is conducive to, and strong enough to, contain the psychic tension that emerges during growth, development and transformation.

There are two particular experiences I would like to record to demonstrate how, through the Sesame way of working, growth can occur and significant ceremonies akin to ritual can evolve.

After four years' work in a Social Services Day Centre for adults with varying degrees of learning disabilities, the time came for me to leave. Before doing so it seemed important to find a significant way of bringing our work together to an end. Over a period of several months, four small groups began to join together until a single group of 27 participants was formed. Our aim was to focus on a theme and explore it through improvisation. It was then possible to formulate something that could be shared with family, friends, staff and others attending the Day Centre. The chosen theme was *People*. The improvisation highlighted differences and similarities. Enthusiasm for the project was boundless. Ideas flowed and took shape quickly. A larger hall was found and the request for make-up and costumes was met. The sharing of our session with others was a very moving occasion for all of us. Even at the time of sharing, fresh ideas emerged. The sense of co-operation and communication between participants was extraordinary and their perform-ance amazed the audience.

Our work at the Centre in the early days was in the small groups, allowing people to start where they were and then encouraging an increased response, allowing them to build their up confidence. Gradually this led to participants taking responsibility for parts of the session. They had absorbed the structure of the Sesame session and it served to contain.

I remember one young woman in her late teens whose level of participa-tion was initially low. The first time she really participated she chose the symbol of a rosebud to represent herself and held it in her hand, drawn in close to the centre of her body. As time passed it was a delight to see how, like a flower, she grew and blossomed. A similar process could be seen in other participants. It was rewarding to discover that changes initiated in our Sesame sessions were paralleled in the group's participation in workshops as well as in personal relationships. At the end of those four years I left with a sense of sadness, but also with deep satisfaction that the work I had done using the Sesame method had brought about a significant degree of growth, development and change.

The second event I would like to describe took place in the chapel of a psychiatric hospital. I worked there with patients attending the day hospital. It had been suggested that we do something for Christmas. Initially the suggestion was met with great reluctance, so for a few sessions we just explored our attitudes towards Christmas, using the Sesame structure. Songs and poems emerged in response to this and then it became possible to formulate some ideas and share them.

The event opened with two songs. The first was light-hearted and explored anxieties about coping financially with Christmas and giving presents. The second dealt with childhood memories. A poem followed depicting the more mundane side of Christmas and the absence of Christ. We then moved on to an enactment around a poem written and read by a patient. The chapel was lit by candles and our actions followed the sentiments of the poem. It dealt with the existence of misery, poverty and loneliness, which Christmas can exacerbate. We processed around the chapel singing and humming softly and blowing out the candles until only one remained alight. This coincided with the resolution of the poem in terms of focusing on the child within. This brought the main event to an end. It was followed by a carol, sung quietly, during which the chapel lights were switched on again. Everyone present then joined in the singing of a selection of carols chosen spontaneously. One patient, who had not participated in the enactment, offered to accompany the carol singing. This was followed by a time for everyone present to eat mince pies.

This sharing around the theme of Christmas felt real and significant. Participants said, in different ways, how it had helped them to move towards Christmas – having acknowledged and shared their true feelings about it. The session had provided a space in which this could happen and the structure had helped to contain and support the process in which all could take part.

References

Douglas, M. (1991) *Purity and Danger*. London: Routledge.

Eliade, M. (1988) *Shamanism, Techniques of Archaic Ecstasy*. London: Routledge.

Katz, R. (1984) *Boiling Energy*. Cambridge, MA: Harvard University Press.

Malinowski, B. (1957) *Argonauts of the Western Pacific*. London: Routledge.

Sutton-Smith, B. (1972) 'Games of Order and Disorder.' Paper presented to the American Anthropological Society, Toronto.
Turner, V. (1982) *From Ritual to Theatre*. New York: PAJ Publications.
Van Gennep, A. (1960) *Rites of Passage*. London: Routledge.

CHAPTER 14

Circus Skills and Commedia

Mitch Mitchelson

There is another kind of art, which speaks to the power of connectedness and establishes bonds, art that calls us into relationships. (Gablik 1991)

I attended a poetry recital by the Panrun Collective to launch the poetry anthology *Tiano-Covering Columbus* (Malik 1992), a response by Carribean writers to the destructive effects on their culture wrought by the voyage of Columbus in 1492. One of the poems by Faustin Charles entitled *Aborigine* opens with the words 'History is a madman dreaming he is sane'. In the same book John Agard writes:

Hold that seashell to your ear, you who dare the breath of history,
Now offer a flower to the sea,
Become a lover, risen from the ruins.

It was a beautiful paradox of the evening that the cataclysm of an historical effect could be meditated on through a gathering of poets, artists, story-tellers and musicians, transmuting the baseness of human behaviour into the gold of poetic and artistic creation.

As we ponder on the life-negating events that scream at us from newspapers and broadcasts, it is salutary and healing to remind ourselves that humankind is capable of the most wonderful and moving moments of creation as well as destruction. It is in our innate urge to create that lies our optimism in positive change and development, both personally and socially. This impulse towards creativity can be seen in the palaeolithic cave paintings in Lascaux, Southern France, revealing the artistic instincts of our prehistoric ancestors. In their depiction of a half human, half animal, shamanistic hunter, we see the emergence of that creative spark that moves us to dramatize our experience, to disguise ourselves, to imitate the natural forces affecting our world.

In the creation myths that permeate all cultures we see a spontaneous need to confront the mysteries of existence, the mythopoetic origins of our world and its inhabitants. The creation myth in Maori cosmology, for example, was ritually enacted, dramatized, sung and danced to cure sterility and lift the spirits. As an antidote to current ills, this journey back to the roots of creativity through a drama of creation myth has healing implications for individuals and for the tribe. Drama is a primary form within the stream of creative expression. In it we can make and re-make our world. We can re-mythologize our lives and impart meaning to our existence. As children, we feel the stirrings of dramatic play as we rehearse and re-play our developmental needs and life situations.

I have always felt intuitively that art has a therapeutic function – a conviction that was given form and shape when I trained on the Sesame Course. My introduction to Sesame came about through a chance encounter: I have always trusted coincidence as a meaningful omen. After training, I practised drama and movement therapy with a variety of client groups, taught on the Sesame Course and, as I continued to develop my interest in myth and story, began to focus on a specific area of dramatic art: the comedic world. This is the main subject of my chapter. By the comedic world I mean the world of Circus, Carnival, the Clown, *Commedia Dell'Arte* and Mask. I have explored this world from many perspectives as performer, director, drama lecturer and as therapist.

> The circus is a tiny closed off area of forgetfulness. For a space it enables us to lose ourselves, to dissolve in wonder and bliss, to be transported by mystery. (Miller 1948)

The circus exercises a fascinating hold on the public imagination. Chagall, Leger, Picasso and many others have painted it. Novelists, including Angela Carter, have been inspired by it. The Italian director Fellini found echoes of his lost childhood beneath its canvas. Tr. Lustig, in his novel *Doubling Up*, describes circus as 'a poem in the prose of our lives' (1990). Rogan P. Taylor (1985) draws parallels between the world of the circus and the initiatory mysteries of the shaman.

I do not wish to romanticize the circus: the touring schedules of the traditional circus are hard and being backstage deflates all preconceptions of glamour. Yet the imagery is compelling and there has been an explosion of circus arts in recent years. Circus Space in London and Fool Time in Bristol pioneered training programmes in circus arts. Circus theatre and circus pantomimes are regularly toured by professional companies. There has also been a proliferation of community circuses, democratizing and accessing circus skills.

The dissemination of circus skills in community contexts was an important part of the work of Original Mixture, the theatre company I founded with my partner. Inspired by the work of Reg Bolton, a pioneer of community theatre, we ran circus workshops and produced shows for schools, tenant groups, theatre workshop programmes and festivals in the UK (frequently inner city areas), the USA and Hong Kong. The ethos of the community arts movement, of which community circus is one manifestation, is the empowerment of individuals and their communities through the art form. A therapeutic dimension is apparent in this, whether through socialization and the creation of group dynamics, as in the Jacksons Lane Community Circus Show that I was privileged to direct, or with the self-affirmation that is attained through learning a circus skill. Important therapeutic principles are involved here. A sense of belonging, community and group interaction confirms and sustains our sense of individuality. The challenge inherent in tackling a circus skill means that any achievement in the medium contributes towards a sense of self-esteem and worth.

We understand this more thoroughly when we consider the poetics of physicality and imagery in more detail. In Issue 26 of the European juggling magazine *Kaskade* (Gabi and Keast 1992) there is an article on the healing power of juggling by Professor Dr. E.J.Kiphard. Beginning with a quotation from Aurelanius in the fifth century (which recommends ball games as beneficial to epileptic children), the professor lists a variety of contexts in which juggling has beneficial effects including learning difficulties, physical handicap, alcoholism and other addictions, arthritis, hemiplegia (one-sided paralysis after stroke) and rehabilitation after accidental brain damage. Reference is made to the work of Ron Lynn, who used juggling in occupational therapy with hemiplegic patients in the USA. The main emphasis is on utilizing the criss-cross pattern of juggling with people suffering from brain damage, stimulating the right and left hemispheres of the brain.

Elsewhere I have read about the value of bringing about 'free rhythmical movements of the hands' and the potential juggling has for producing fluid movements. Evoking the work of Rudolf Laban and his analysis of efforts through which imbalance in personal movement vocabulary can be observed, it seems that juggling can help to compensate for very 'bound' effort patterns by introducing flow and fluidity. It also offers experiences of rhythmic movement. So the therapeutic implications of juggling are considerable, allowing opportunities to develop concentration, hand/eye co-ordination, peripheral vision, spatial and bodily awareness, and even meditation. When I have used juggling in workshops with inner city communities and people with learning disabilities, I have seen all these benefits come into play. A workshop scaled to move from basic plate spinning on to scarf juggling, through grasping and throwing bean bags to basic cascade patterns with balls, is a realizable programme.

Other circus skills such as unicycling, stilt walking, small tightrope and trapeze can be tackled but, since these carry greater physical risks, care must be taken as to whether and how they are used. These skills can be most easily transmitted through one-to-one tuition with physical support, harnesses and soft mats. They offer new perspectives on co-ordination and balance and can also have great symbolic value.

I remember the pleasure I felt myself when I rode the first few yards on a unicycle. Achieving skills associated with the sharing of fun, excitement, exhilaration and entertainment can have positive benefits for the personality as a whole, strengthening a person's sense of self. As Clarissa Pinkola Estes (1992) says, everyone is entitled to the *Alleluia Chorus*. Working with tumbling has many movement possibilities: on soft mats, participants can be curled and uncurled, or rolled. Returning to a movement motif that is evocative of the foetal position, followed by an uncurling and emergence to a standing position, offers a safe and satisfying regressive experience followed by a progressive one. Borrowing from the Beijing Opera, where actors assume their character after tumbling on to the stage, I sometimes use an exercise in which clients are encouraged to assume heroic postures after uncurling from a forward roll.

I remember an occasion during a community education programme when a stilt walking demonstration on hand-held stilts by one of the people in the workshop resonated movingly and poignantly. The woman on the stilts recited a childhood memory involving a friend with whom she had an emotional bond as a child – a friend she used to play with on stilts. She experienced a sudden, Proustian remembrance of things past, evoked by trying the stilts after all those years. A different sort of symbolism came into play in a session I ran with young offenders on probation. In archaic societies, initiation into adulthood was traditionally defined and enacted ceremonially. We have no such rituals to counteract the role confusion to which adolescents are prone. This particular group of kids reacted with gusto to the challenge of unicycling and stilt walking. One moment sticks in mind when a member of the group was on stilts, visibly enjoying the moment of elevation which placed him not merely on a par, but slightly taller than the adults running the session. It was a sudden moment of 'Welcome to the adult world!' At the same time, he held on to me for safety's sake, trusting he would not be let down.

In other places I have chosen to evoke the circus without recourse to props and equipment by focusing on mime, movement and dramatic atmosphere. Michael Tucker (1992) describes the Shaman as 'the archetype of all artists. Image maker, dancer, drummer; actor and singer, healer and holy one', epitomizing the human need to fly beyond the mundane world 'to conjure worlds of visionary presence and power'. The circus can be re-created as a magical and fantastic ritual place where miracles can take place, echoing the world of the Shaman. James Hillman (1979) reflects on the extraordinary domain of circus. For him it is an image of the underworld of the imagination transposed to our overworld, where the vulnerability of the hero (e.g. Achilles and his heel) becomes the strength of the circus performer (the trapeze artist hanging from her heel.) New, hitherto hidden, strengths and energies can be released through dramatic enactment: a healing of the hero can take place.

Working with people with learning disabilities and children with physical handicaps, I have focused on creating this special fantastic atmosphere. The circle becomes a transformative ritualistic space, yet it also contains and secures the group. Music and drums evoke the show. Walking tall simulates the stilt walker and extends the line of the body. Animal mime engages the instincts, the primordial energies, through contained imagery. Slapstick routines ritualize aggression. The procession creates spatial orientation and rhythm. Wheelchairs are no obstacle to the miming of a flying trapeze as the chairs 'fly through the air – wheee!' Participants are stretched, but not threatened. The imagination is engaged, confidence ensues, movement and vocal vocabulary are extended, social interaction is encouraged to complement self assertion. The circus is in town! 'thank god for the circus...' (e.e. cummings)

Now it is time for the clowns to enter the ring.

> The clown shows us the bumbler, the vulnerable fool, the feeling centred man, pinned in a web of relatedness to the animate and inanimate life around him. (Ulanov and Ulanov 1987)

The Big Apple Circus in New York engages its clowns on outreach therapy programmes in the community. I devised a clowning sketch for adolescents with emotional problems entitled *The Ghost of a Clown.* I decided to take part in the sketch myself with three other members of the group and a small audience. The sketch is for three Clowns and a Ringperson and I was the Ringperson for the first run. As there were 'behavioural problems' within the group, this enabled me to keep some control over the proceedings while staying within the art form: the other three participants were Clowns. The routines involved one of them being knocked over during the introductory part of the act, being taken out of the ring as a lost cause and then returning as a Ghost to disrupt the show. The audience were then able to play parts themselves in reprises to the show. There was a very popular moment when one of the Clowns jumped into my arms on being surprised by the Ghost. For a well built fifteen-year-old to jump into the arms of another person, sanctioned by the story, is expressive and eloquent of a deep need for that nurture – a need which is normally hidden behind anti-social behaviour patterns. The Educational Psychologist assigned to the school was particularly interested in this motif. Another popular bit was the Clown experiencing a kind of ritual death and rebirth.

In our preparations for the sketch I taught the group 'clown falls' that can be executed safely by going down on one leg. To mimic the Clown fallen to the floor, I encouraged members of the group to 'glue' every part of the body to the floor, resisting attempts by adults to unstick them. This was a valuable grounding and focusing exercise for a group that had problems around concentration and centring themselves. A comic skit followed in which the fallen Clown raises a limb and then, every time the limb is pushed back to the floor, another arm or leg is simultaneously raised. If a kick up the bum climaxes the routine, so much the better. This exercise encourages co-ordination and connectedness within the body, radiating from a firm centre. As well as learning and playing with these physical routines, work on different 'clown walks' adds authenticity to the drama. A transformation of the basic movement of walking can be brought about by leading with different body parts, which also offers the participant novel experiences of body and movement. I once ran a workshop with Graeae Theatre Company, a professional company of actors with 'physical disabilities' which I had the pleasure of directing. Working in tandem with a dancer who introduced movement themes to the group, I introduced a clowning version of the movement motifs. This led to a rich and varied session. 'To remain whole, be twisted. To become straight, let yourself be bent' (Lao Tsu 1963).

Clowns have a capacity for wonder and connectedness. Adapting clowning exercises that were originally designed for trained actors, I use the theme of the clown's discovery of space, audience and clown colleagues. The clown walks into a room which is the most fantastic, magical space, a *temenos* or sacred domain. The discovery of the audience is a moment of delight: they become friends, lovers, new-born infants. I also borrow from an ecological clown show I once devised and directed with Rose Bruford Drama College. Using the theme of a Wild Life television show, a naturalist discovers a group of clown-like primates who wake from their group shape in the undergrowth, discover the 'television' audience, take great joy in each other's company, tease and make mischief with one another, and eventually return to their group shape to doze. We experience vulnerability, humour, a sense of wonder and an expanded sense of connection within the group and to the natural world around us.

It is essential to access the mischief of the clown in order to avoid sentimentality and preciousness. I sometimes teach clown fights as a way of channelling and ritualizing aggression – after all, as in cartoons, nobody gets hurt in a clown fight. In the 'Trickster' issue of the journal *Gnosis* (1988), Fred Fuller makes an analogy between slapstick and old European folk rituals in which 'people smacked each other with newly budded tree branches to impart health and fertility' – creative renewal through comedy.

Federico Fellini spoke in an interview of the shadow nature of the clown, the clown embodying the rejected part of ourselves. Jung describes the shadow as 'the sum of all those unpleasant qualities we like to hide' and integration of the shadow was the primary aim of analysis. As well as appealing to our sense of the marvellous, the clown is also 'a kaleidoscopic emblem of human imperfection', as Ron Jenkins (1988) writes: 'That is why the clown is a source of humour for us. We are laughing at ourselves.' Wes Nisker (1990) writes: 'The clown shows us our awkward human condition.' Sometimes in life we hide behind the mask of the clown, but by being conscious of the symbolism of the clown and through the opportunity to enter into a created dialogue with this neglected part of the self, healing energies can be released. The clown, with his vulnerability, naivety, ill-fitting clothes, strange gait and accident proneness, is very different from the socially adjusted persona we habitually wear. If we can only realize that 'we are all clowns, always getting fouled up, mixed up, thwarted by circumstance' (Wes Nisker), then we can take ourselves less seriously. In certain therapy contexts, without wishing to devalue the importance of age appropriateness or social skill training, the sharing of our collective human folly can be healing. I remember supervising a clinical placement on the Sesame Course in a psycho-geriatric ward, where we ran a kind of Music Hall with song and dance. The occupational therapists said our visits catalysed the elderly people into singing and dancing all week! This reminds me of a quote from the Jungian Guggenbuhl-Craig: 'Old fools may laugh and cry as they wish... The image of the fool takes the horror away from the deficit model of aging' (1991).

The clown, for all his tumbles, always picks himself up. Optimism and hope spring eternal. Positive thinking is good for our immune system, laughter for our respiratory system and stomach muscles, clown logic for our understanding of the world.

> Joy is like a river: it flows ceaselessly. It seems to me that this is the message which the clown is trying to convey to us, that we should participate through ceaseless flow and movement. (Miller 1948)

The clown offers us an opportunity to re-enchant our world.

> The terrain of comedy is, in fine, an image of the world as organic rather than mechanic. (Cowan 1981)

Commedia Dell' Arte is another form I have mined for imaginative therapeutic material. The name refers to a form of theatre that flourished in Italy in the late sixteenth century and early seventeenth century. In its most rudimentary form it was performed and toured by travelling troupes of actors. The players consisted of several stock characters, some of whom wore masks, who improvised comedy around well-known plot lines and scenarios. Highly stylized in movement form, irreverent, magical, pulsating and restorative, this theatrical genre with its ancient roots still exercises a hold on our psyches. 'We are at the fount of Pan and our blood courses with primeval energy'. For the participant who faces 'the long forgotten denizens of the forest in himself there spreads out an immensely valuable store of archetypes' writes Anthony Rooley (1990), describing the power of Commedia.

Who are these 'denizens of the inner forest?' They are the Magnifico, a prowling caricature of the Rennaissance lord; Pantalone, a miserly, lascivious but ridiculous old man; his rival, the pedantic Dottore, or Doctor; and their offspring, the thwarted young lovers Lelio and Isabella. The Capitano, a military type, is a cowardly braggart. At the bottom of the social hierarchy are the servants: Zanni, a naïve, simple character with an appetite; Columbina, an intelligent, good-hearted female servant; Brighella, an amoral, cynical liar who brings a sinister element to the proceedings; Arlecchino, the mercurial, impulsive, ribald and engaging popular figure of the troupe; the Strega, the wise woman/witch who dispenses love potions and wisdom; and some minor characters.

The first approach I want to explore is movement vocabulary. Joan Chodorow (1991), shares with us her experience of a body split: 'that even though I moved forward, I maintained a subtle attitude of avoidance and defeat.' She describes how, by exaggerating her walk and consciously working on an awareness of the emotive colourings determining her gait, 'in a way that felt natural, my walk changed.' Her walk, as she describes, resembles a characteristic of the Capitano, who demonstrates in his movement the tension between desire and cowardice with a sloping walk in which his feet go forward while his upper body and head are held back. My thesis is that different, perhaps compensatory, movement experiences can be explored through the gamut of *Commedia* characters. For instance, the impulsive physicality of Arlecchino could offer a contrast to the tentative movement vocabulary of the Capitano. The zoomorphic nature of some of the masks offers clues to the movement possibilities with which to animate them. Pantalone has the characteristics of a turkey, the Doctor of a pig. The Magnifico is somewhere between a bird of prey and an alley cat. Brighella is a dog and a panther, Zanni a sparrow, Arclecchino a cat with the strut of a cock, the Captain a blood hound. Animal mime is fun, particularly when blended into a character and a dialogue in which the instincts are engaged. Kenneth Meadows (1991) writes about the value of relationship with power animals where a power animal can serve 'as a guardian, looking after one's interests and security.' Embodying the animal instinct in this way gives our non-human selves an instinct and a voice: 'Animals can teach mankind to become wholly holy again'. In fairy-tales we encounter the motif of animal helpers. Some of the more extravagant *Commedia* plots have the magical dimension of the fairy-tale: 'Finally, after many adventures, with the help of another nymph, believed dead, and with the art of the magician, all ended happily' (Flamina Scala 1989).

Commedia plots are full of miraculous events. Arlecchino hatches out of an egg and discovers the joy of movement for the first time, finding his own, unique limbs. Long lost relatives are reunited, amazing coincidence resolves into stories, everybody is duped by disguises and feigned deaths and magic waters revive them. Plots end with pageantry and celebration of the collective life. Adversity turns to prosperity. These are all healing motifs and valuable to explore through drama and movement. The containing image of a community restored to harmony and balance allows an exhilarating exploration of some of the negative and selfish shadow characters such as the Magnifico and Brighella, offering modes of 'forbidden' expressive behaviour and self-assertion. Everything starts badly and ends well. As Louise Cowan (1981) says, comedy strengthens and confirms the inner life.

Commedia workshops are extremely animating and socializing events. The characters are in an established communal relationship with each other and, if that atmosphere can be evoked in the session, a dynamic social inter-action can be created. A sense of belonging is a basic human instinct. The rhythm of *Commedia* is passionate. It has to do with survival and is therefore urgent in tone. Our pulse beats more recognizably. I have seen participants' bodies become visibly more energized and vitalized through their absorption in these characters. I have observed a pleasure in the bringing to life of the sixteenth-century Callot engravings, with their extraordinary physicality opening up new experiences of body and movement dynamics. Lovers' breasts rise and fall as they run across the room to Vivaldi's Mandolin Concerto. The antics of the Zanni keep us firmly grounded with their slapstick and ribaldry. Even Pantalone, despite his apparent age and infirmity (usually brought on by impending loss of his money) has an exceptional vigour. As Eugenio Barba (1991) says: Pantalone 'does not imitate a bent old man's gait, but reconstructs it by means of a contrast which transmits the idea of the old man without reproducing his weakness. The back is bent, but so bent that it becomes as powerful as a compressed spring.' This is similar to the way Zeami (1991), the Japanese Noh master, describes the playing of old character: it 'should resemble that of an old tree putting forth flowers.' This is a vitalising image of elderly people. *Commedia Dell'Arte* empowers and produces new, green shoots of life. It also evokes the world of masks.

> Masks and…the use of disguise date from the very dawn of human history. (Fo 1991)

The use of mask work in therapeutic settings is both exciting and problematic. There is a Marcel Marceau sketch in which the actor is trapped by his mask. Dario Fo talks of the magical quality inherent in mask work allowing us 'to see more clearly and to act with greater liberty than with the face completely uncovered.' He also mentions the fact that the mask could induce anxiety deriving from the restriction of vision and vocal range for some people. Because of the magico-religio-ritualistic origins of mask work, immense respect and care must be exercised. The relationship of trust between therapist and client and the appropriateness of the material are of paramount concern. Also, as in other contexts, we must apply the artistic criteria of the medium. There is an etiquette applicable to mask work, which places importance on the sensitive handling of the mask and the rituals of role and de-role. The risk of someone being caught or trapped by the mask, like the protagonist of Alexander Dumas, can be counteracted by studying the dynamics of the mask. There is a movement rhythm contingent on the type of mask used, whether it be naïve, neutral, expressive or a spirit mask. An understanding of these different mask genres is crucial. There are also transitional exercises that help to graduate the exploration of mask work. For instance, the facial mimicry of a mask one is holding is a traditional Balinese technique for understanding the mask and allows an oblique approach to the medium. Similarly, masks can be manipulated by the hands like puppets. Peter Brook uses this as a theatrical device in *The Conference of the Birds*. I have used other masks in therapy contexts to interesting and relevant effect, though in this chapter I refer specifically to Comedic, naïve, neutral and spirit masks.

Masks are intrinsic to the *Commedia Dell'Arte* and represent a rich source of material as they can be naïve, expressive, instinctual or archetypal. There are some built-in safety clauses in their use: they derive from theatrical tradition, they are designed to be played and they are used to exposure. Also we do not entirely lose sight of the human face, as the lovers and Columbina are not masked. I sometimes use an exercise that plays on these facts. The actors arrive in procession in the market square. Those who have masks put these in place while turning their backs to the audience, who, for the purpose of the improvisation, are the people in the market square. The actors then turn to face the spectators and assume their characters – the masked characters interacting with the non-masked characters in short comic interludes. The actors' subsequent removal of their masks and the stylized company bow completes the enactment.

One value of the mask lies in its transformative qualities. I was first struck by this when working in a special school with a young man from a traveller family. We were working with theatre make-up and he made himself up with a white clown face. Emphasising his bone structure and changing his self-image, he was then fascinated with how he looked – magical and possibly romantic. I felt that this positive image of himself was of value to his self-confidence. I have seen the use of *Commedia* masks transform people's body imagery, bringing a degree of definition and vigour that were not there before the mask was used. I have seen women working with the Strega mask draw upon an incredible power, strength and presence in their exploration of this archetypal mask. The *Commedia* masks, because of their original use to amplify character in sixteenth-century squares or candle-lit rooms, exaggerate the movement attitudes of the wearer. I observed one client whose habitual movement attitude was to look at the floor. This attitude became more noticeable when the mask was put on. It did not work dramatically as the mask was being used outside its range, but when I introduced an improvisation, in which this Pantalone character was asked to interact with someone on an imaginary balcony, this man was able to modify his normal movement pattern and experience medium- and high-level perception with the accompanying physicality. Relatively small changes such as this can then be built on and developed. The masks are half masks, leaving the mouth free. A kind of vocal acrobatics – urgent, voluminous, primal, yet colloquial in tone – can be explored to animate the mask further. The exploration of mask and voice has great potential. A language of gesture can be used to complement the spoken word. I have taught clowning and *Commedia Dell'Arte* in Italy (taking coals to Newcastle with great humility) and the Italian actors used gesture in their commedic improvisations almost as a second language. Participants wearing masks have used Macaton to great effect. *Commedia Dell'Arte* masks move and they are moving, which means that they have a therapeutic dimension as they take on different expressions according to the dramatic situation and the rhythms of the body.

This leads on to neutral mask. Neutral mask was devised by Jacques Coupeau, the twentieth-century French theatre director, to discourage actors from relying on habit-formed reactions, particularly as these manifest in facial expression. Developed by the French theatre school of Jacques Lecoq, emphasis was placed on entering 'a different realm of emotional conscious-ness through a precious mastery of the body as a means of expression' (Marcia 1980). Neutral mask offers an opportunity to engage in body consciousness. I like to use it in an almost Zen-like way to perform simple actions – sitting, walking – alternated with immobility and tranquillity. This returns us to a sense of what Lecoq refers to as the gravity of things, an appreciation of basic human actions re-experienced. Copeau's actors 're-ported a new sense of confidence and authority, a power and unknown security – a sort of balance and consciousness of each gesture and oneself.' (Rudlin 1986). Neutral mask can also focus on the ability to tell a story with different emotional effects conveyed through the body. It can be subtle and graceful work, intimately connecting us to our sense of being in the world.

Spirit masks convey another dimension of mask experience. By Spirit Mask I refer to masks that have ritualistic and mythological resonances from different world cultures. My instinct is that feet have to be firmly on the ground for this sort of work. Shamanistic masks that symbolized the spirit and ancestral worlds were often designed to represent half-human, half-spirit figures. Sometimes the spirit totem mask opened to reveal a human face mask behind: the human must be the container and the vehicle for the mythic and archetypal. I am interested in the cultural evocation and linkage that masks from different parts of the world can create, since we live in a multicultural society where assimilation is counterbalanced with cultural diversity. In psychiatric settings I have sometimes noticed clients needing to express their own cultural identity – for instance, a Bengali man evoking his home village through mime. People sometimes experience a kind of bereavement when they feel cut off from ancestral roots. Masks can re-connect people with their cultural history through the imagination. For example, a Chinese man with hearing impairment who attended a centre for people with learning disabilities responded with expressive and vigorous movements to a Beijing Opera mask. These archetypal masks can release a thrusting, grounding, stamping movement (a movement in Japanese and African dances that contacts the ancestors). The expression of such a vigorous physicality can bring about emotional release. In Noh theatre a ghost would perform a dance to expiate emotion, perhaps of betrayal, from the ghost's mortal past. I have seen someone able to express anger through a mask-inspired dance, perhaps finding himself less self-conscious with the disguise of the mask.

> The occasion of singers, musicians, storytellers, mask makers, and dancers joining together is the flower of daily life. (Snyder 1990)

A procession of carnival characters has danced across these pages. In Medieval Europe, a Festival of Fools would take place annually, reversing the hierarchic order, demoting bishops and promoting choir boys in their place, parodying in the Mass and the fixed order of things. I once ran a session with young offenders and a probation officer, casting along these lines: the probation officer played a master criminal and the kids were detectives. I think the probation officer enjoyed his role as much as the rest of the cast did theirs.

The carnival tradition is not, of course, limited to Europe. There is a carnival, or Maas, in the Carribean. The African ritualistic tradition predates the appearance of the circus in Europe. Some masks from India and Bali resemble those from the *Commdedia Dell'Arte*. There are clowns in the sacred ceremonies of the native people of North America. There is a universality about this kind of imagery: it is an expression of the imagination, as described by Blake, arousing us from Newton's sleep. Gillian Clarke (1994), compares the beginning of the therapeutic process to 'the slow movement of spring water or the first bird of the year in the breaking darkness.' Joan Chodorow writes of the imagination as taking us to 'the emotional core of a complex' and, also, leading us through it. I have tried to indicate some routes for that journey – sinuous, twisted, muddy, but with the stage of the imagination as its goal and a trunk full of dramatic effects at its disposal. Clarissa Pinkola Estes has written 'To create one must be willing to be stone stupid, to sit upon a throne on top of a jackass and spill rubies from one's mouth. Then the river will flow, then we can stand in the stream.' (1992) Perhaps there is a green antlered and horned fool seated at the foot of the Tree of Life, beating his drum for us, summoning us to the festival and feast.

References

Barba, E. (1991) *The Secret Art of the Performer.* London: Routledge.

Chodorow, J. (1991) *Dance Therapy and Depth Psychology.* London: Routledge.

Clarke, G. (1994) *Selected Poems.* London: Carcanac.

Cowan, L. (1981) *The Terrain of Comedy.* Dallas: Pegasus.

Estes, C.P. (1992) *Women who Run with the Wolves.* London: Rider.

Fo, D. (1991) *Tricks of the Trade.* London: Methuen Drama.

Fuller, F. (1988) *Gnosis.* San Francisco: Lumen Foundation.

Gabi, E. and Keast, P. (1992) *The Healing Power of Juggling Kaskade,* Issue 26. Weisbaden: Babi and Paul Keast.

Gablik, S. (1991) *The Re-enchantment of Art.* London: Thames and Hudson.

Guggenbuhl-Craig, A. (1991) *The Old Fool and the Corruption of Myth.* Dallas: Spring Publications.

Hillman, J. (1979) *The Dream and the Underworld.* New York: Harper and Row.

Jenkins, R. (1988) *Acrobats of the Soul.* New York: Theatre Communications Group.

Lao Tsu (1963) *Tao te Ching.* (Edited by D.C. Lau). London: Penguin.

Lustig, T. (1990) *Doubled Up.* London: Penguin.

Malik, A. (ed) (1992) *Tiano-Covering Columbus.* London: Panrun Collective.

Marcia, A. (1980) *The Commedia Dell'Arte and the Masks of Amleto and Donato Sartori.* Florence: Usher.

Meadows, K. (1991) *Shamanic Experience.* Shaftesbury: Element.

Miller, H. (1948) *The Smile at the Foot of the Ladder.* New York: New Directions.

Nisker, W. (1990) *Crazy Wisdom.* Berkeley: Ten Speed Press.

Rooley, A. (1990) *Performance: Revealing the Orpheus Within.* Shaftesbury: Element.

Rudlin, J. (1986) *Jacques Coupeau.* Cambridge: Cambridge University Press.

Scala, F. (1989) *Scenarios of the Commedia dell'Arte.* New York: Limelight.

Snyder, G. (1990) *The Practice of the Wild.* San Francisco: North Point Press.

Taylor, P. (1985) *The Death and Resurrection Show.* London: Blond.

Tucker, M. (1992) *Dreaming with Open Eyes.* London: Harper.

Ulanov, A. and Ulanov, B. (1987) *The Witch and the Clown: Two Archetypes of Human Sexuality.* Chicago, IL: Chiron.

Zeami, F. (1991) In E. Barba *The Secret Art of the Performer.* London: Routledge.

Part 2

Mainly Practice

CHAPTER 15

The Drama Gave Me Inner Freedom
In Wormwood Scrubs

Colin[1]

When I first arrived here on the Annexe, a couple of the lads persuaded me to go along to Sesame. I'd never experienced anything like it – well, I suppose it did strike a faint memory of something in junior school when I was a child. For the first couple of weeks with Bernie I laughed so much I had tears rolling down my cheeks. It was hilarious! I tried to be serious until Bernie said I had permission to laugh. Then I just enjoyed it for the humour.

A lot of people are very timid and vulnerable when they arrive here. I arrived with a long sentence and a gigantic image problem. People used to go on about my aggressive nature, but deep down I think a lot of it was shyness. Before I came here I'd been moved around a lot and I was reacting very violently. Each move got worse. They expected me to be violent and I was. I think they moved me here in desperation, as a last resort.

I was very suspicious at first. A prison officer called me by my first name and I told him not to. I got into trouble and in a few weeks I was in segregation, but then they brought me back up here and asked me why I was angry and why I wanted to break the place up. For about six months I was going one step forward and one step back, but gradually I got myself out of it.

I encountered Bernie and Sesame very early in this process. I went to my first session with her in the first week I was on the Annexe. Bernie used to make me giggle with some of the stories she told. And the expressions on her face! Everybody thought she was crazy. She'd let you do anything. I'd been locked up for four years and meeting Bernie was quite a culture shock!

---

1 Serving a ten year sentence in the Annexe, Wormwood Scrubs.

There was one fellow used to burst into song – pop songs like *I don't like Mondays* and Pink Floyd sort of music. He couldn't really sing but he'd suddenly start and Bernie would sing with him and everybody would burst out laughing. He really was funny. He was quite a regular member of the group when I was in it.

She would tell us a lot of old stories – fables and that. Greek myths. I used to like that. Prison libraries tend to have crime and fiction, biographies tend to be about famous criminals and there's daily papers like the *Sun* – no *Times* or *Guardian*. I used to go and look for Greek mythology – the stories that Bernie told us – but they didn't have them in the library.

Those stories made sense. You could think 'It could never have happened', but then you'd have to look for the story in the story. A big spider doesn't eat people, but you can look at it in another way and say it's the right punishment for the person that got eaten. It's symbolic, like fairy-tales at bed time. I think a lot of my problem was that people use to tell me 'Act your age!' These stories are a form of release you can be allowed without being told you're doing wrong. I enjoyed the freedom of expression. In the early days I used to think 'If anyone walks in here we're all going to be locked up.' Then I'd think 'Well, we *are* locked up!'

Sesame was a break from being in prison. There was a time when I looked forward to it, week by week. If Bernie was ill and couldn't come I felt disappointed. After I'd done it, I would be physically tired. Sometimes I used to go into a session and get rid of a lot of anger. I remember one story – something about a King in a far-off country. I was the King and my boat sank and I was swimming, releasing all this pent-up anger by swimming. It was like throwing punches. I can't remember what the story was.

We used to act out long stories, sometimes making them up as we went along. The first person would tell the first five minutes, the second one the next five minutes, and so on, acting it as we went. I went through a stage when I was almost everything in the story – a rainbow, a bit of sun, a deer. Then you'd go back through the story afterwards and wonder why you did it. There was no set plan, so whatever you did was right. It couldn't be wrong! That improved your confidence. At first you might think 'I don't want to be the one to mess it up'. Then you'd find you couldn't. That helped your confidence.

I enjoyed Bernie's music, too. She brought in relaxation tapes, music, sounds of the sea, flutes, bird songs, and she made copies so that I could listen to them in my cell. When I got wound up and angry, she could bring me down and help me to take time off. I did Anger Management sessions as well as doing Sesame – that helped, too, but the drama gave me a lot of inner freedom and a capacity to look at things coolly. Just lately I've begun to do meditation: I can sit in my cell now and just switch off.

I still get tense in the day, but I've got that switch-off point at night now. It's like I used to do with drugs, with cannabis, but now I can go in and just bring myself down. I'm not an expert yet, I'm still learning, but I *can* do it. When there are disputes now, I can sit back a bit and then politely tell them that they're out of order.

I've seen Sesame help different people in different ways. Some people who are really 'Jack the Lad' go to dramatherapy and it can bring them down. Others are timid and it can give them confidence. Some people just go in for the break, for a giggle, and it does them good too. Often people go on Sesame for eight to twelve weeks as their initial therapy up here. It's purely voluntary. I experienced it before I had time to think about whether I wanted to go. Some people think about it but don't go in.

I rarely go to Sesame now because, though it sounds incredible, I don't have a lot of time to spare. I'm in my second term of office as Chairman of the Community, which means a lot of hard work – liaising between staff and inmates, sitting on committees and settling the little disputes that arise all the time. And I edit the Annexe inmates' magazine, collecting bits that people write and trying to reflect what goes on in here, aiming to knock the walls down a bit and show people outside what goes on in here. It feels really important to do that. I'm also involved in raising money for cystic fibrosis: we have raised over £3000 with four concerts here and two at Holloway.

I'm hoping to move on to a community programme for the last bit of my sentence. I've still got two years to go, maybe a bit less. I've never worked for my living before, so I need to get used to working…

CHAPTER 16

The Minotaur in Three Settings
Prison, Acute Psychiatry and with Elderly People in Hospital

Bernie Spivack

The purpose of this chapter is to show how a story can be moved around from one clinical setting to another, even used in settings where it may not seem to be a very safe or suitable choice, so long as this is done with real understanding of the setting. The myth of *Theseus and the Minotaur* is a powerful story containing elements which can stir up strong feelings. It wouldn't necessarily be the first story you would think of for a prison setting or the volatile atmosphere of an acute psychiatric ward.

If you really know the place where you are working, which means understanding the issues present for the people there, knowing the people themselves and them knowing you, then what might otherwise feel too risky to attempt becomes possible. There is a feeling of confidence within the group from which many things can flow. Choice of the material that you are going to use flows from your knowledge of the people and theirs of you.

In the same way, how you present your material, how you tell a story, will vary from place to place. When I worked with a group of Jewish patients in a centre in North London, my style was more ethnic than in other places. Because I am Jewish, my Jewishness came out in a natural way and helped to promote a feeling of comfortableness for us all. When I was worked with prisoners at Wormwood Scrubs, I was more overtly *animus* than *anima*, keeping my more masculine qualities well to the fore, taking care not to let the emphasis fall on the fact of my being a woman. This was my way of adjusting to the feel of the place so as to get a comfortable working space in which the chaps would not be constantly reminded of the absence of women in their lives. I realized it was working at the point when I was directing my first play with the lifers and the actresses were going to come in for their first rehearsal with the cast. The week before this happened, one of the chaps said 'Oh, isn't it great, Bern? The girls are coming in. That's going to make a real difference!' I laughed and said 'Oh, gee, thanks, that's very nice!' The poor man was covered in confusion and said 'Oh, no, Bern, I didn't mean to be offensive!' In fact I was really pleased because his remark meant that my way of presenting myself alongside the chaps was being received the way I hoped it would be. I was being seen as Bernie the Director and not necessarily as Bernie the Girlie and this made things easier for us all. I think it's important to be able to make a conscious choice about the way you present yourself.

When you choose a story to work with it's important to choose something people will be able to identify with and make their own. Ways of doing a story can vary tremendously and this also helps when you move a story around from one situation to another. The first time I worked with *Theseus and the Minotaur* I didn't bring it in myself: it was brought in by a group of students I was supervising. We were working at a hospital day centre for the elderly. The people taking part were in the hospital for some kind of rehabilitation before returning home – a straightforward client group of bright, elderly people, some of them in wheelchairs and none of them very mobile. The overall theme that the students had devised was about 'weaving threads', with a warm-up about weaving leading towards participation in the myth. The symbol of weaving was used to give shape to the session and to encourage individual responses. The students brought in actual thread, the real thing, something that on my own I don't often do. We were in a circle with students dotted amongst the client group for the warm-up and the telling of the story. When the parts were put on offer an elderly lady who was relatively mobile chose to be Ariadne. She held one end of the thread strongly in her hand while Theseus, played by a student, made the journey through the labyrinth. Where was the labyrinth? We the circle, seated in chairs, became the labyrinth. The student, as Theseus, made her way round and about and through the chairs, all the time with this real thread, travelling towards the Minotaur. No one took the part of the Minotaur at the heart of the labyrinth: it was imagined. I watched Theseus creating an impassable barrier out of all this thread and wondered 'What is she going to do? How is she going to get to the Minotaur?' Acting on the spur of the moment, she ended up going out through a door and slaying the Minotaur out of sight in the toilet. As Theseus disappeared round the corner, some of us in the circle made dying monster noises (only a few, as the killing was happening out of sight) and then, having made the journey in imagination, Theseus returned via the labyrinth (which was us) to the rapturous embrace of Ariadne. It was exciting and amusing and it worked on all sorts of different levels, which became evident afterwards when the older people spoke about what it had meant for them. One lady who had been able to follow the plot very closely spoke about the psychological impact of the story. People will often discover different meanings in a story if left to themselves, which is what the work is about: it's about what the experience means to *them*. Some people will just receive it as an enjoyable thing to be part of or just to watch, which is fine. Others will be touched at a deeper level.

That was my first encounter with the Minotaur. Shortly afterwards I chose to use the story in the acute psychiatric ward where I had been working regularly for some time. It isn't the most obvious story for such a setting, but I knew the place well and had built up some confidence in my own ability to handle a situation which was often pretty strange.[1] You never knew who you would have in the session from week to week: it was unusual to have any kind of cohesive group because of the nature of the people and the illnesses they came in with, their various states and medications and the fact that the doctors might suddenly send for someone half-way through a session. Often you would have a client in for just part of the session. For all these reasons, I had developed a way of dividing a story up into bite-sized chunks so that if somebody came in and could only stay for a short while, they were able to take away with them a sense of wholeness because they had been in a bit of a story which had its own beginning, middle and end. This way it didn't matter if they weren't there for the whole thing.

On this occasion, very unusually, a nucleus of a few people had been coming in for a few weeks, so for once I thought 'Let's just go with the session plan and see if by any chance we have enough people who know each other well enough to try it.' As luck would have it, that is what happened. My plan was to start with a general, physical and vocal warming-up, followed by what I call 'heroic moulding' – working with a partner and putting him or her into some kind of heroic, strong pose, then gathering the people into two groups and inviting each group to inspect the other group's tableaux. Then we worked together as a whole group making first the shape of a ship and then the shape of a monster. Then I began to tell the tale. I told it within the framework of the larger story in *The Odyssey*, because I

---

1   See Chapter 18 for more.

think it's important to tell people that it's only part of the myth, but we didn't touch on things like Ariadne being left behind or Aegeus throwing himself into the sea. I just said that we would be doing part of the Theseus story in which he throws his lot in with the men and women who have been taken captive over to Crete, beginning when they set sail from Athens. We had someone being King Aegeus, saying farewell and waving them off. Then we had the ship arriving in Crete and the people from it being taken to the palace of Minos. We had Theseus and Ariadne falling in love – that little part can be divided into three if you think the session is likely to be interrupted. Then comes the part of the story in which Ariadne comes to Theseus and gives him the clue about the thread and he makes the journey through the labyrinth, in and then back out again, having slain the Minotaur.

The way we did it was that we, the prisoners, became first the labyrinth and then the monster, so that we could be slain as the Minotaur and return to being the labyrinth. There was just one part, the monster, that we created *en masse*, which bothered one person so much that she left the room – but she wasn't in role, she had just happened to pop in while this bit of the story was going on. I found her afterwards and she was okay: it had just been a bit much for her in the confined space.

In using stories it's essential to realise that they are not *just* stories: they are so much more than that. If you are doing something in a dramatic way and in a fairly small space, it can be quite scary for some people. I don't think that's bad, but it is something one has to be aware of. Any material, even something apparently innocuous like making jelly on a spring day, may turn out to be something that someone finds worrying.

We actually completed the story that day, which felt like a bit of a miracle. The Minotaur was killed and Theseus made his way back through the labyrinth (which was us) and freed the prisoners (which was us). We had people participating in a general way as well as five clients, myself and an Occupational Therapy student in roles. At one point one of the students was both Theseus and Ariadne, but we managed to keep it going. Somebody who had never been into a session before got very involved and joined in chanting the 'wail of woe' that we, as the prisoners, set up. He also enjoyed being a courtier in Crete and locking up the prisoners. Somebody who had been coming for a very long time was first of all the King of Crete and then Theseus: this meant he was first the King, receiving the offer of these victims, and then Theseus, slaying the Minotaur and setting the prisoners free. This was the last session this man did after coming for quite a few weeks, so it made a satisfying climax to his experience of Sesame. He left the hospital the following week and was well for quite a while afterwards though, as often happens, he did eventually relapse again.

We grounded at the end of the session with a mirror dance, working very quietly in twos and then coming together in the circle. It was one of those things that just happened to work and I felt I had been lucky. At the same time its success owed a lot to the fact that I had been working there long enough to feel safe taking an informed risk.

The third setting in which I worked with *Theseus and the Minotaur* was the hospital annexe of Wormwood Scrubs. I had been working at the prison for five years, so again I was on very familiar territory and felt I could handle the material while working with the people. The hospital annexe is for people who acknowledge that they have a problem and that problem has caused them to re-offend many times. They opt for the annexe because they want to change, they want to stop that pattern, which often involves drug abuse and alcohol abuse: because they need money for booze, money for drugs, they have ended up committing crime. Some people are also there for rape and other kinds of sexual abuse: it's not uncommon for these abusers to abuse themselves, and this comes out over the process of their stay. The annexe is a therapeutic community as far as it can be within a fairly high-security prison setting.

For the session in which we did *Theseus and the Minotaur* we warmed up physically and vocally in familiar ways and then we did something unusual: we made knots and un-knots, holding hands in a circle and physically winding ourselves round, getting knotted together, and then physically unwinding, getting unknotted. Then we made statues of different sorts of creatures. Then I told the myth, using some music to illustrate parts of it. When we came to act it somebody who was quite new to the session chose to be Theseus, which was marvellous. Somebody else, who again was completely new, said that he wanted to be the thread, not being aware of how I worked or anything else. He thought he could just joke and say 'I'll be the thread – ha, ha, ha!' Then I said 'Great, fine, you be the thread. No problem.' Everybody laughed and he looked gobsmacked, but agreed to go along with it.

The enactment began and the man who was Theseus held his thread by the hand, winding through the labyrinth and taking the thread with him. He took us all with him, in a manner of speaking, as he wound his way through the labyrinth we made. Then we turned into a wonderful monster, which Theseus slew with great 'Arrrrhs', roarings and noises. I can't remember if that was one of the times that a prison officer poked his head round the door to see what was happening: they were used to the noises coming

from Bernie's room. Having slain the Minotaur, Theseus made the return
journey with his thread – but this time, because the deed had been
accomplished successfully and he was feeling empowered by it, he picked
up the man who was the thread and threaded him bodily through us, as the
labyrinth, on the way out. Everybody was involved, working at their own
speed and level.

One of the men actually took on the part of Ariadne. This was an
interesting and quite a brave thing for a man to do in an environment which
is, with the exception of some staff, entirely male. Also, many of the men
seem to have difficulties with the females in their lives and with the feminine
aspect of themselves, which is something that many of them find frightening.
People in the annexe sometimes go through a process of coming to
acknowledge a homosexuality they've never recognized in themselves before
and then they become scared about being seen as feminine in an all male
environment. Taking on a role that is in any way feminine is a risk because
of the badinage they may encounter afterwards. But here was this man – call
him Q – being Ariadne and holding on to the thread.

I would like to pause at this point and say something about this very
interesting man, who had spent a lot of time in my sessions and had gone
through a process of learning to use the medium, which at first he found
quite strange. He first appeared eight weeks before we did *Theseus and the
Minotaur*. It was my choice when I worked at Wormwood Scrubs not to ask
about the clients I was working with and the offences they were in for. I
could have looked at their files, but I chose not to. Sometimes another
member of staff in the Annexe would talk about an individual prisoner or,
more importantly, the person himself would talk to me about an aspect of
his crime or his past record or about his feelings in general. Some people
who work there choose to ask for background information, but I didn't want
to do this because I wanted to bring in a sense of freshness, of the world
outside and my non-involvement with the institution and its constraints was
part of this. In retrospect I know that this conscious choice helped me with
the men and the men with me. So I don't know for certain what Q's offence
was, but I think it was some form of thieving connected with alcohol abuse.

At Q's first session I came in with the Australian Dreamtime story about
Tiddalik the Frog who drank up all the water.[2] Q looked interested but a little
baffled. He didn't join in but sat to one side of the room, watching and
making the occasional comment. I wondered, as I often do after a first

2   For more about Tiddalik, see Chapter 29.

session, if he would come back. Next week he was there again and participated more fully. We did what I call a music collage, for which I bring in several pieces of music for the group to listen, respond individually and then create some kind of drama together out of those individual responses. The first piece of music became a defeat in battle. Out of the second piece they created an idyllic country scene. The third turned into a party in which Q was very active, driving a car to the party and getting into a whole issue around drinking at the party, resisting the temptation of the booze while other people got drunk. (It was from things he said at this session that I picked up on his history of alcohol abuse).

The third session was quite chaotic with a lot of people in and out of the session and Q seemed to find it difficult to deal with the changing numbers. This often happened: there would be only three or four people in for a few weeks and then, quite suddenly, it would be crazy with eight or nine or more. When there were a lot of people, the balance of the group dictated what you could and couldn't do and those people who had been coming for several weeks in the smaller group often found this hard to handle.

I was unable to come the following week and that always had repercussions: you never knew how it would affect people, whether they would stay away because you had let them down – but Q was there. We did this session around the themes of group support and individual effort and working from within, enacting a Coyote story. Before the story we warmed up and worked physically, making triangles and other pointed shapes with our bodies, and took turns to hide objects, saying 'warm' and 'cold' as people got closer and further away from them. This week four people were actually able to stay for the whole session and Q did a lot. He was Coyote in the story, taking part in dialogue and remembering the plot. He was also a rock and transformed into other things. There was some friendly banter between him and the other men. It was his fourth session and by now he had learnt the Sesame Method. In this work it's important to remember that when people haven't encountered it before it can feel very strange. It's often a little while before a person feels comfortable with it.

There was another gap before I went in again, this time to do a session using real objects. Again, Q was there. We warmed up physically and played with imaginary objects before I brought out the real objects: a blue and white scarf, a small crystal pyramid, a stone and a pepper pot. Q became very involved and seemed to enjoy the session hugely. He chose the stone and he was off, taking us 350 years into the future. With this stone he became a god, helping to save the Earth from famine. The stone was food for our world. In somebody else's scene, which was more of a fairy-tale, he chose the pepper pot, which became Aladdin's lamp and, coming out of the lamp, he was a wonderful Genie, carrying the Genie's duality for good and ill.

Another man chose the crystal and used it as something that would help you to find the thing that you wanted. In this scene Q said that what he wanted to find was love: he sought love and he found it. The final scene that day was led by someone who hadn't come often and did a whole thing about getting and selling drugs and Q kept his head, quietly doing what he wanted to do with all the stuff about drugs going on around him.

The following week the atmosphere in the Annexe was very strange because people were being asked to leave and be relocated in the general prison service, having been caught breaking the rules. Q came for my session and there was just one other man. Both men shared their anxiety about the situation in the Annexe and then Q took part in an enactment of the Chameleon Myth.[3] The following week eleven people came and Q seemed to have no difficulty coping with the numbers. The atmosphere was quite tricky with a lot of mock aggression and some real aggression mixed in, the 'tough' people versus the 'soft' people. Q didn't let any of this bother him. His confidence and understanding of what we were doing just carried him through.

People at the Scrubs would sometimes ask 'What is this for?' This question comes up surprisingly seldom in most of the work that I do, but in the Annexe they are very tuned in to the idea of therapy as it is what the whole place is based on. Q was interested to know what this was for and why was he doing it. Before this particular session began we had a chat and I could see that he really wanted to understand how dramatherapy worked.

The session itself was based on the idea of shapes and the stories that can come from them. We had a maze for the first story, some kind of jungle for the second and an art gallery for the third. In the first story he was the attendant in charge of the maze, in the second one he was the cannibal chief and in the third one he was an art critic: in all three stories he had given himself a role with implications of status and maturity, people who could take responsibility and be in charge. This was his penultimate session.

He left the Annexe the following week, after playing Ariadne. After the enactment of *Theseus and the Minotaur*, he talked to me about how much the sessions had done for him in terms of building up his 'confidence'. That's a word the chaps used a lot. Though their feelings might have been touched

---

3   An Edo myth from west-central Nigeria, which I found in Pears Encyclopoedia of Myths and Legends.

in different ways by a variety of experiences in the sessions, 'confidence' was something they could understand. Whether you call that a feeling of well-being about yourself or an ability to go up to someone and talk to them, however you put it, gaining confidence was something that meant a lot.

Along with confidence, the other two things they really valued were being able to relax and having a laugh. The times when people were able to say of a session 'Oh, Bernie, we've had a really good laugh in here', I always felt that something worth while had taken place. We were in a situation which could feel very bereft of laughter. The healingness of being able to laugh should never be underrated.

The Jungian analyst David Holt once said at one of the Shakespeare weekends at Hawkwood College, when a group of us were working on *Hamlet* and everybody suddenly began to laugh, 'Laughter and tears come from the same place'. I always remembered that, but it's something I've only really understood since Edward, my son, was born. There were times when I was not at all sure whether he was going to laugh or cry. The sound really does come from the same place. The tears could so easily tip over into a laugh. It was quite remarkable how the tears and the laughter seemed to well up from place really deep down inside him.

As a student of Sesame I was once accused of being a clown, not a therapist. I was a bit shaken at the time — but that was before I had really listened to Mitch Mitchelson[4] and his ideas about clowning. And it was a long time before I met Edward. Maybe mentioning my son is a bit self indulgent, but perhaps he slipped in to help me say the learning may change but it *never stops*.

---

4   See Chapter 14 for more on clowns.

CHAPTER 17

Working with Symbol in the Mental Health Centre

Jo Syz

Like the sick man, the religious man is projected onto a vital plane that shows him the fundamental data of human existence, that is, solitude, danger, hostility of the surrounding world. But the primitive magician, the medicine man or the shaman, is not only a sick man: he is, above all, a man who has succeeded in curing himself. (Mircea Eliade 1988, p.27)

My aim in this chapter is to show how drama and movement can be used as a tool and a language to negotiate with mental disturbance, offering a means by which people are able to discover, or rediscover, lost parts of themselves. The client's journey towards self-discovery is facilitated by the therapist, who has made a comparable journey into the inner world by means of the rite of passage that takes place through training. He/she has an experiential understanding of some of the hazards, some of the landmarks, that are there for the client and is therefore able to meet the patient with some sense of the inner landscape in which both the illness and the cure take place. In this, the Sesame practitioner shares certain qualities with the medicine man or shaman described by Eliade.

I do not believe it is possible to discuss mental health problems without relating them to the cultural and historical context in which they exist, so I propose to talk about this briefly before looking at some ways in which mental disturbance can be addressed through movement and drama. My reason for beginning with the quotation from Eliade was not to romanticize psychological disturbance, but to suggest that the way mental health problems are viewed in our culture belongs to a specific social and historical background. The culture we live in differs from those Eliade is talking about mainly in that it doesn't place much value on relating to the non-rational world: it is firmly centred in external, physical realities. The question of finding a balance between different kinds of psychic reality is perceived as unnecessary.

When people become mentally ill, these certainties begin to come unstuck. They seem to lose themselves, or get overcome by unfamiliar aspects of the self that emerge and take over from the competent, outwardly orientated self that we tend to see as the whole person. At this point it becomes impossible to deny that the self we see from the outside is not the whole story. It becomes a necessity to address their own inner realities to both initiate and facilitate the processes of healing.

If parts of the self are hidden, where are they and of what do they consist? At this point, the term 'psyche' becomes useful. Jung, the analyst whose system of thought informs the basic theory of Sesame, understood the psyche as the whole human organism, body and mind. He saw the psyche as a self-regulating system with a natural tendency towards balance, growth and consciousness. It is in the nature of unconscious material to seek expression and psychological health depends on the integration of this material into consciousness, which is a vital aspect of the creative process.

Jung saw the process of 'individuation', of becoming fully oneself, as an ongoing result of allowing unconscious material to emerge and integrating it into consciousness. This process, in his view, involves bringing into balance the different ways in which people relate to the world – through *feeling, thinking, intuition* and *sensation*. When these four functions are out of balance, the functions which are weakest tend to become repressed and, as a result, the person suffers a diminished sense of self and loss of meaning.

How does one begin to recover the whole self that is lost through breakdown of the healthy processes of the psyche? Lost aspects of the self are difficult to find because they vanish into that unknowable realm psychologists call 'the Unconscious', but the psyche has a way of reasserting its lost meanings through symbols. These arise naturally in art, story and dance, music and dreams. By working with drama and movement as a language of self expression, Sesame is in a tradition as old as human culture itself. The individuation process has been woven into the fabric of society through ritual and sacred art, dance and story-telling and the interpretation of dreams, since the beginning of time. These are all avenues through which it is possible for the unconscious to speak its symbolic language.

An account of the Senoi people who live in the jungles of the Malay Peninsula demonstrates the way attention to the hidden world of the psyche can benefit those cultures that recognize the necessity of listening to its messages. The Senoi have been described as 'the most democratic group reported in anthropological literature'. They themselves believe this is due to the importance they place on dreams and dream interpretation. From childhood they are taught that dreams should be treated seriously. If someone dreams that a particular person harms them, or that the dreamer himself harms someone, the dream is told and some kind of gift is given or received. In Jungian terms, the Senoi are acknowledging that their dreams express aspects of their psyches which normally remain hidden and which, left unconscious, may cause illness or discord. When a Senoi child has a terrifying dream of falling, he/she is told to let himself fall (in the dream) and commune with the spirits of the people he meets in the place he falls to. This often results in the child bringing back, from a dream, a new song or dance or craft form, which he then passes on to the tribe.

Loss of the symbolic in a culture often results in tragic disintegration and decay, which has happened for the Australian Aborigines since the complex web of symbolic relationships between people, families and land was destroyed by Europeans taking over the ancestral homelands and their native belief systems. Before this loss, the Aborigine way of life was constantly recreated and given meaning by singing the songs and performing the symbolic rituals of the Dreamtime across the sacred sites of Australia. If this was not done, they believed that the world would be uncreated and chaos would ensue – and this was exactly what happened. Without access to the sacred sites and with the abandonment of ritual which allowed unconscious libido to be expressed and incorporated into society, the culture lost its soul and meaning.

It would be wrong to suggest that any system of values or healing can be transposed directly from one culture to another, but I do believe it is possible to reinterpret these patterns in terms of what has also, though more slowly, been lost from our own culture in the course of technological advance. This 'advance' has taken its toll of our connectedness to the earth and to one another through a shared sense of meaning and spiritual relationship. In our industrial culture, the rational *thinking* function seems to dominate the *feeling* function, while the *sensate* function (related to what we can perceive with our senses) dominates the *intuitive*. Technological advance has been accompanied by large-scale environmental destruction, fragmentation of family and social structures and an increase in social problems, psychiatric disorders, addiction and violence.

Yet there seem to be signs of a new consciousness beginning to emerge in which the fundamental value of feeling and intuition becomes clearer, mirrored by the new discoveries of physics, which suggest that the deeper we go into an understanding of the world, the closer we come to realizing that the world cannot be understood by the intellect alone. The spread of interest in Buddhism and in the symbolic movement rituals of T'ai Chi Chuan, with their aim of holding the opposing aspects of the psyche in balance, may also point the way to a new spirit emerging in the West.

In T'ai Chi, the movements are felt as a natural expression of the psyche channelled through the body. The meaning of the movement does not depend on how it is perceived from the outside, but emerges as an expression of the person's inner being. Sesame drama and movement have a comparable base. They are not for performance to an audience, for there is no audience: there is only the group that is taking part in the session. Laban's art of movement is employed by the Sesame therapist as a means to work with the inner world of the client as it expresses itself in movement. Thus a client whose movements tend to be sudden and direct, but who has difficulty moving in a sustained and flexible way, may become more focused in himself if he is helped towards movements which involve sustainment and flexibility.

The heart of movement work is spontaneity. A spontaneous movement is one in which there is a sense of profound aliveness and connectedness. It is impossible to create spontaneity, but it is possible to create a situation in which spontaneity can emerge. This can only happen when someone does not feel self-conscious: that is, when he does not feel he is being judged. The paradox is that the letting go of the self-conscious ego results in becoming more dynamic and flexible. In the same way, it is by expressing and integrating unconscious material that the ego becomes stronger and more able to manage what may previously have been felt as overwhelming emotions and experiences.

Another factor that is particularly helpful to psychiatric patients is the structure of the session itself – a clear, recognizable cycle with a beginning, middle and end.[1] A focusing phase precedes the main event in which contact with the imaginative and physical material of the session is fullest and this is followed by a grounding, bringing the client out of physical and creative material that has been worked with and returning him/her to full awareness of the context in which the session was begun. A series of sessions will be planned with an overall format which has this shape as well, with the deepest work done in the middle sessions and the last few moving towards withdrawal and closure of the group. These structures can be very helpful to people with fragile egos who are struggling with, and feeling overwhelmed

---

1   For more detail of the session form, see Chapter 13.

by, unconscious material. The processes of opening and closure, containing within them an experience which brings people close to unconscious material, becomes a model for strengthening the ego's necessary defences. Contact and separation are fundamental processes of the human condition, reflected in birth, death and times of transformation. Each session can be seen as a model for the possibility of being in contact with potentially disturbing unconscious material without becoming overwhelmed by it. The material is encountered and explored, then it is safely closed and integrated. Each time this occurs, consciousness has broadened and, in consequence, the threat from repressed unconscious material becomes less powerful.

The material worked with in the session is also, in itself, an important means of containment as well as expression. By taking on a role, the participant is able to explore powerful emotions within the structure of a story or an exercise. He/she is always given the power of choice, choosing a character he feels drawn to or, if this seems to be more important, one in which he feels safe. The enactment itself will often uncover spontaneous aspects of a character that could not have been predicted, but these are held within the containment of the story or exercise. The story acts as a vehicle. Rather than working with people's personal material, which might feel too frightening or self-revelatory, stories are chosen which contain a possibility of the clients finding imaginative parallels with their experience. In general, the safer and less self-conscious a person feels taking part in a session, the more profound the therapeutic process can be. The sense of safety depends to a large extent on the participant being able to trust that he/she will not be abandoned in a state of vulnerability, but can safely explore his own material at depth, knowing that it can be worked through, integrated and contained within the session.

As an example, I would like to describe some work done with four men attending a psychiatric day centre in Brighton. Their ages ranged from early adulthood to middle age and they also had quite a wide range of needs and abilities, in terms of physical, imaginative and emotional expression. We did a series of eight sessions aimed at providing material that would engage the interest of the client group and allow them to express aspects of themselves that would not find room for expression in their everyday lives, while at the same time supporting them in any weaknesses that might emerge, helping them to develop a sense of confidence and self-esteem.

As Jungian symbolism often equates the unconscious with the under-world, we did some stories that involved journeying into the underworld followed by successful emergence from it. We did stories in which healing came about through completing a journey which involved confronting and mastering fears. This story work produced some powerful moments arising spontaneously out of enactment. We also did a lot of movement work. Some members of the group had very characteristic patterns of movement and we provided movement work to help develop and extend their movement range.

In the fifth session we worked with the traditional African story of *Mella*, in which the daughter of a tribal chief goes on a long journey to confront and seek help from the Serpent Healer for her father, who is sick and dying. Before working with the story itself, the group were invited to join in an exercise designed to stimulate the imagination and, at the same time, enable them to explore a range of movements. Some group members moved almost solely within a rather tentative range of gentle, flowing, flexible movement patterns, so I set up an imaginative situation which would enable and encourage them to explore firm, direct and quick movements.

First we travelled through long grass, pushing vigorously through it with our feet and arms. Then we entered a forest and became covered with ants, helping each other by brushing them off until they were all gone: the aim of this was to introduce very sudden, dabbing movements. After coming out of the forest, we found that our path had been blocked by heavy boulders which had to be lifted out of the way, requiring firm and focused movement. Then we reached a grand canyon with a rope bridge across it, which we had to cross one by one with the encouragement and support of the group. The aim of this was to create a sense of focus and direction in the group. At the end of the story each member of the group was provided with a James Bond-style, single flying machine and we each pushed off from the edge of the cliff in turn with our machines, until we were all flying around the space together. After a while one of the clients indicated a place down below where it looked safe to land and there our journey ended.

The whole exercise felt very much as if we were all working together, helping each other to overcome obstacles. While pure movement exercises may be helpful in facilitating people to identify and work with different types of movement, the use of imaginative material helps people to embody these same movement types more fully as the focus is not on the movements themselves but on what is happening in the story. As people can feel very self-conscious about the way they move, this second approach helps to draw out particular kinds of movement that might not otherwise be accessible.

In another session, I wanted to explore two topics side-by-side: I wanted to look at conflict and its resolution and, at the same time, to explore man's relationship to the natural world and suggest a different perspective on it. With everyone sitting in a circle, I read part of a speech by the Native American leader, Chief Seattle:

How can you buy or sell the sky, the warmth of the land? This idea is strange to us. If we do not own the freshness of the air and the sparkle of the water, how can you buy them? Every part of this earth is sacred to my people. Every shining pine needle, every sandy shore, every mist in the dark woods, every clearing and humming insect is holy in the memory and experience of my people. The sap which courses through the trees carries the memories of my people... We are part of the earth and it is part of us. (Steed 1988, p.68)

The group then became imaginative seeds, planted in the earth, and slowly grew into mature trees to the sound of the didgeridoo – an instrument which has very specific cultural associations but which felt appropriate in this context. The participants became deeply engaged in this part of the session and it felt very powerful. By embodying a process of nature which is reflected in the human organism itself, people can feel themselves to be experientially reconnected with the fundamental process of growth – a process from which they may have become dissociated and their psyche is attempting to redress, manifesting itself as illness.

After this exercise I set up a scenario in which some people chose to represent trees and others represented tree cutters. Then two groups were formed, one of trees and one of tree cutters, and each was asked to create out of themselves three sculptures representing possible functions of living or dead wood: we would take turns to witness each other's group sculptures and then come to some kind of resolution. The sculptures which emerged from this exercise were very powerful and imaginative. In the course of the whole exercise, it became clear that man-made objects could only exist within the context of the natural processes that the tree sculptures represented: the man-made objects were not an alternative to nature, but were derived from nature. For this reason it was decided that a certain number of trees must be allowed to be cut for human use, but only on the condition that the natural world upon which humans depended was kept safe and not overwhelmed.

The final tree sculpture gave seeds to the humans, who then spent some time scattering and planting these seeds around the space for future generations. At the end the whole group came together in a unified tree sculpture symbolizing the universal Tree of Life. Having explored some powerful material through the session, the coming together of the group in that final sculpture felt very rooted and secure. After they had separated, the final grounding brought them gently back to their present lives.

The symbol of the tree runs through many cultures, representing the manner in which the universe manifests itself with the human being as a reflection of the process. The seed is the germ which contains all the information that is needed for the tree to emerge into maturity. The tree is often seen as that which connects heaven and earth, its roots reaching deep into the ground and its branches into the sky. In Shamanic cultures, the healer must climb through many levels of the Tree of Life until he reaches the Otherworld, where he looks for the lost soul he has come to recover. The tree is, archetypally, a useful symbol to work with in the area of mental health. The unconscious is sometimes symbolized as the Ocean. People who become mentally ill often seem to be flooded with unconscious material which is experienced as overwhelming and which they are unable to integrate into consciousness. One physical property of a tree is that it can act as a pump, drawing water out of the ground and pumping it into its capillary system so that, eventually, it evaporates from the leaves, the vapour returning to become water again. So it becomes possible to recognize how symbolic work with trees may help clients with the process of integrating unconscious material which may have felt as overwhelming at some point: the natural process in which they become imaginatively involved parallels the process that the psyche is struggling to achieve.

The Sesame approach in this setting involves using a very powerful, symbolic medium, which can help aspects of ourselves which have been repressed to be recovered, contained and integrated. The act of allowing one's creative spontaneity to emerge and be held within a character, story or movement, can encourage the emergence of parts of the self which may not be accessible to an intellectual, analytic approach. Since verbal therapy engages more fully with the thinking function, it follows that Sesame has a unique kind of contribution to make within a wider framework of treatment that includes the analytic and the psychiatric.

References

Eliade, M. (1988) *Shamanism: Techniques of Archaic Ecstasy.* London: Routledge.
Steed, J. (ed) (1988) *Thinking Like a Mountain Towards the Council of all Beings.* Philadelphia, PA: New Society Publishers.

CHAPTER 18

The Shared Feeling
Sesame in Acute Psychiatry

Bernie Spivack

I started working in the Acute Psychiatric Admissions Ward of a London hospital in 1986 when, as a recently qualified Sesame practitioner, I was attached to a branch of the Manpower Services Commission. They had a dramatherapy project in which unemployed people received some training and were then sent to work in various different placements. My task was to run the training group and arrange the placements. I made it a rule that people had to be in the training group for at least five or six weeks before going out on to placements and I also insisted that there were two other Sesame practitioners on the team. No one ever went out to a placement without a Sesame practitioner helping to plan the session and going with them. Mostly this combination worked, but when it came to the Acute Psychiatric Admissions Ward I quickly discovered that this was a place where a session plan didn't get you very far and there was really no substitute for in-depth training.

It was clear from the first day that the people who came in with me were uncomfortable working in that setting. I felt strongly that there was no reason why they should stay with it, since they weren't at that point Sesame students: they were still at the stage of deciding whether to do the Sesame course. One day, when another Sesame practitioner from my year was in the group, we were told on arrival that someone we had got to know over the past few weeks had been allowed home and had gone over the balcony. Whether he fell or he went over on purpose was not known for certain because of the drugs he was taking at the time, but he had died as a result of the fall. We were supposed to do a session immediately after hearing this news, which we did. The non-Sesame person couldn't cope because she was so distressed and I just said 'Don't worry. It's okay. We understand. You go. Don't feel too bad about it. Why should you be able to cope? You haven't had the training to make you able to absorb this kind of information and be available to do the job in hand, which is to do a session if there is anyone on the ward who feels that is what they want.'

Quite often in this kind of situation people on the ward will actually come. They may talk a little bit about the sad thing that has happened but, in essence, they haven't come to chat. They haven't come in to worry and get into their heads. They've come in to be part of something which is different from the news that has been surrounding them. That is one of the big things you have to know and be able to give. How you deal with it afterwards is your business.

Sesame trained people can manage a situation of this kind because they are used to creating boundaries. Boundaries don't exclude you from connecting with other people's feelings and being able to be close to them, but an understanding of boundaries means knowing what we can do and, maybe, what we can't. You are there at the time you are there. You hope to help the clients achieve what they want to achieve within that time. You have to accept those limitations and work within those limitations. If you can't work within those limitations, then don't be there. Learning to accept that there are limitations to what we can do about really distressing situations and at the same time be there and do what we *can* do is a large part of what the training and the work are about.

Having said that, this particular setting is not for everybody. There are people who work well in other settings but who are not happy, not able to be content, with this. There is very little continuity, very little sense of working with people to achieve objectives over time. In the Acute Ward you have to be able to seize the moment and settle for working with that. Some therapists need the continuity and the satisfactions that go with having contact with the same clients week after week. But there is also being able to grasp the moment and what happens in the moment. It may be a matter of temperament – either you feel comfortable with it or you don't. Or it may become a possibility after a few years of practice in the medium, if not now. I think I may be a bit of a grasshopper, so this is something I haven't found difficult – possibly because of my theatrical training, going back to being a child in a theatre school. I'm used to the idea of grasping the moment and the moment being sufficient. When you work with a group of actors you are together for a relatively short span of time. You have to be able to make relationships, work together and be creative together very quickly. You do that for a short spell of time and then you've gone. But that doesn't make the connections you make with the other people any less real or valuable. You acquire a facility for doing that without actually thinking you need months and months to get to know someone. You become very open and accessible to that quickness of meeting.

On the Acute Ward you do occasionally have the same person for four or five weeks and then you will see development, but it won't be for months. You may just see the person breathe more easily, you may see them relax, over one session. You have to be able to leave that situation and never see the person again. You have to be able to accept this. I found I could accept it and it felt all right. Then, over time, I began to find another kind of continuity. Because I was in the same hospital, on the same ward, over a long time people began to come back and say 'Oh, you're still here doing the drama!' The faces changed, then, over time, some of them came back. This actually helped me to feel that what I was doing mattered. I could see that in the person's internal state something had happened. I had made a connection which meant that next time it was easier for that person to think 'Yes, this is a place I felt safe in' or 'creative in' or 'different in' or 'not mad in'. They arrived looking for something they had found in the sessions before.

There's a big difference between what people do in Sesame and other things that happen on the ward. The focus is in the body and not in the head. Also, somebody may arrive and say quite aggressively 'What are you doing here?' I will reply, and really mean it, 'You don't have to do anything if you don't want to.' Often for the first half of the session, or for the whole of the first session, a person may do nothing or seemingly nothing but listen to the music. Then you notice a certain difference in their way of watching what's going on – there's this semi-reluctance, but okay. And all of a sudden the person gets up and joins in the final circle. Then you realize that the person who was seemingly passive was actually part of what was going on. Reminding people not to have to *do* is so important. For very good reasons, people on the ward often get encouraged to *do* and quite rightly so: people who just lie on their beds and do nothing are understandably encouraged to get up and do things. But when it comes to Sesame sessions, it makes a refreshing change to be told you don't actually have to join in: you can *choose* how much or how little you put in. This is always the base line of Sesame work, because you don't get anything of value happening unless people are able to come to it in their own way and time – but on the Acute Ward I really emphasized 'You don't have to do anything' in contrast to what went on for those people most of the time.

Another key factor in this setting is unpredictability, which means that any session plan you come in with may have to be binned because of what is happening on the ward that day, or just because the atmosphere doesn't feel right. Again, I am aware of a theatrical parallel: in performance, things happen which require the cast to improvise, sometimes in quite difficult circumstances. You can't stop a performance because a prop isn't there or someone has forgotten their lines. Something has to happen, so you improvise.

There is just a brief period after you arrive at the hospital, before you are 'on', in which to discard and rethink. This is the half-hour staff handover, when you hear how things are on the ward. The theatrical parallel would be that you are giving a performance and noticing, before you go on, how the lighting is and what is happening with the other actors. You sit in the staff conference soaking in information and at the same time another part of your mind is going 'The plan I had for today is unsuitable. Think again.' It isn't just 'Oh my goodness, PANIC!' You have this time to prepare yourself before you go into the room, see who arrives and what kind of state they are in and do some more thinking on your feet. If in doubt, I would always begin by grounding things with some well-focused body work. If everyone was whizzing around all over the place I wouldn't attempt the imaginative – though if one of the group themselves brought in something imaginative, fine. This does happen. You do a movement and somebody says 'Oh, it's like picking flowers.' Then you say 'Oh, well, we could do that!' That's often the way a session goes. A lot of material you wouldn't think of as suitable becomes suitable when it's brought in by a client.

There was one occasion on this ward when somebody came up with a plot line in which a little girl opened a story book and said a spell and up came Satan. Now there is no way I would have brought in a story with the Devil appearing in it, but it came from a client and I went with it. I was the little girl because the client wanted to be Satan coming out of the book. At the same time I wanted, within the terms of the dramatic reference, to make sure we got rid of the Devil before the story ended – but not by saying in a heavy way 'Well, you can stop being the Devil now!' Still speaking in my little girl voice, I said 'Oh my goodness, I really shouldn't have played with my Uncle's books – I'm sure there must be something I can do that the devil won't like to make him go away.' And the person playing the Devil said 'Oh, you mean the Green Monster?' 'Yes, that's it! I'll make a spell and the Green Monster will come.' I said a few words and then, as I was the only other person there, I became the Green Monster and frightened the Devil horribly. Then, as the little girl again, I said 'I won't play with Uncle's book ever again' and then the person who had been the Devil said 'I'm terribly sorry, I won't touch any of your books ever again, they're too powerful and important and I won't do it.' She became funny, so the scene ended with humour. Never underestimate the use and value of humour. It can be a great safety valve and saving grace. If anyone could and should be ridiculous from time to time it's the practitioner who should be. If there's going to be egg on anybody's face, let it be your face. If anyone's going to look a fool, you're going to look a fool — *never the client.*

That was how the Devil scene ended. Of course we had a very, very, very lengthy grounding: a physical, vocal, stompy, rhythmic grounding which went on for about 15 minutes. In the Acute Ward my groundings were often 10 to 15 minutes. A typical session would consist of a 15 minute warm-up and bridging time, about half an hour of doing and a 15 minute grounding. Even in the less acute psychiatric settings, it's very important to make sure you have a good chunk of time at the end because you need to be sure that when people leave you at the end of their time with you they are in a state to cope and orientate themselves in the real world they are going back into. If you need to take longer on grounding, you take longer — until you are satisfied they are no longer within the imagined world but firmly in their own bodies, in their own time and space, here and now. Until you feel sure of that you don't let them go. If by chance they do go to the toilet or something, you make it your business to find them if you have any doubts on this score. Having said this, there will be occasions when people leave a session in a worrying state and then it is comforting to remember that they are in a therapeutic environment, so they are not going to be on their own. If you ever feel that someone may be in a grey area at the end of a session, you make sure you tell someone on the staff who will be there after you have gone.

A question I sometimes get asked in relation to work with psychiatric patients is about the use of imaginative work with people who may be confused already about who they are and who may already think they are someone else. The question is whether playing a character other than themselves would make them even more confused. My answer, based on working over the years in several different psychiatric settings, is that in practice this problem doesn't seem to arise. If a person was very, very disturbed, he or she wouldn't want to, or be able to, do imaginative work because he would be in places in his own head to such an extent that he wouldn't be able to orientate himself with any other form of reality but the one he was living in. Coming away from that, I would argue that if you are well enough to manage it, entering into imagined states in something which has been given the boundaries of a story with beginning, a middle and an end – along with the concept of 'You are not actually being the person – you acting with me, or with us, and we are entering the story together as the king and the servant and maybe one or two courtiers and then, importantly, we all leave the story and come back into the real world' – seems to be experienced more as a way of reaffirming of what is real. The imagined place is an agreed, shared place, which makes it very different from the lonely, involuntary imaginings of mental illness which are in your head alone and hold on to your thoughts and which can be very frightening. I have seen people who were quite deluded go into playing a part in a story and suddenly come together in a very sane and eloquent manner, both in role and interacting with other people. I remember a man who used to think he was various biblical characters taking on the part of King Midas and performing it beautifully, interacting with the other characters and having all the details of the story in place.

At the same time, it's important to remember that in a therapeutic setting excellence of performance is not what it's about: it's about what the clients actually end up doing. Sesame students sometimes find this quite hard to come to terms with when they come into clinical settings after having done all sorts of beautiful things in the studio with a peer group of like minded souls. They have to learn that they can't afford to have that kind of focus when they go into clinical settings. It just isn't pertinent and if you look for it you are on a highway to nowhere. It may eventually begin to happen in certain settings where you have a chance to build up a feeling for the work over time, but you won't get it happening with people you see for a maximum of six weeks. There the focus has to be that the clients who come will be able to find themselves participating in something which will be, for them, first of all creative and then a healing experience: to set up a facilitating space and in it to kick-start something so that the session ultimately becomes the client's own. Going along with clever ideas is all very well, but what you really hope will happen is that your ideas, however wonderful, will fade as the clients gain confidence and the session becomes theirs. The cleverest thing is providing a container which will enable clients to use the session for themselves. If I had to define in one phrase what happens in good session work, I would say that it's a *shared feeling* – the title I've given to this chapter. By this I don't necessarily mean the practitioner's feeling being shared with the client, but that they should feel comfortable to share theirs with you. Then if you feel comfortable enough to let them know that you are also sharing with them, it makes for a two-way traffic. So long as there are boundaries and you are aware of what you are giving them, it helps to have the feeling reciprocated.

So a good session grows out of how you manage to meet the client group on the day. To give an example: that day we came in after the man had died jumping off the balcony, I improvised, on the spur of the moment, what I felt the group needed. An idea came to me and to give it the kind of distance I felt we needed, I lied. I said 'There's an ancient Greek custom about harvesting the crop of the vine.' We all got into harvesting grapes and making wine and, in symbolic terms, channelling our own growth. It was a healing image but used, in Sesame's favourite term, 'obliquely'. Something was going on in the country with warmth and life and laughter and people treading the grapes – lots of 'firm' action, in Laban's language, and the ritual of welcoming the first fruits of the harvest. I told the story about how this thing goes on in a certain little village somewhere in Greece. Afterwards my colleague asked 'Where did you read about this?' I replied 'I didn't – I made it up!' He said, 'So you lied?' I said 'Yes, well, it could go on for all I know!' The point was that I felt this was what the situation needed and the group really responded. We didn't actually drink the wine, as there is more than enough booze and other substances around in people's lives, but we ended with a feast. A lot of eating goes on in drama sessions, which has a symbolic side because people are eating the experience. People often left the sessions saying they felt hungry, which was all right as the sessions were always just before a meal.

Because the other people at Manpower didn't feel comfortable in the acute setting, I would often find I was doing it on my own. I went on doing it until the funding for the Manpower project stopped. Then I didn't go for a while until the hospital rang to say that the activity was missed on the ward and offered to fund it themselves, so I went back in 1989 and worked there for another three years.

As I got to know the setting better and became familiar with the different climates and moods of the place, I gradually became a little more adventurous until, after several years, I did something that felt very bold: I went in with the myth of *Theseus and the Minotaur*. It was bold because the story has very strong meat in it. Of course that can be said of any material: you can go in with 'The cat sat on the mat' and it can be 'iffy', as there may be someone there who has some association with cats and/or mats. But thinking about this myth, you have people being taken captive, a monster that has to be killed, a lot of strong images and symbols. There's poor Ariadne being dumped on the island, which is how it ends. You have to be careful how much of the story you use. But I felt it could be of positive benefit for the client group at the time, so I got round to thinking 'I'll go in with it in mind and if the atmosphere is such that it feels all right, I'll try it.'

As ever on the Acute Ward, I was prepared to feel the atmosphere and bin the plan if necessary. I had so often gone in and found that what I planned felt so inappropriate that I ended up doing just a movement session. I would have to see the mix of people that came in and gauge the concentration level to see if they could take being told a story.

I had by then developed my own way of dividing up a story when I told it, because often a client's concentration span could only handle so much at a time and then they would have to leave the room. Rather than have people leave the room at a point in a story that might not leave them in a very good state, I would divide what I was telling into chunks so that people could live just one part of the story and it still left them with something of value. This way of working also gave people a chance to de-role if they had to leave and get some sort of grounding, even if it was just a quick shake before getting their jackets on. We would do a bit of the story and then I would say 'Now we have an interval, a commercial break, like in Coronation Street!' That would put it into the a sort of non-theatrical context people could understand.

As it happened, luckily, the atmosphere felt right on the day I went in with *Theseus and the Minotaur*. I decided to go for it and the result was rather splendid. I set it up carefully so we had the option of either having an imaginary monster or – this was the idea we actually stuck with – we were the labyrinth, the labyrinth became the Minotaur and was slain and then the Minotaur became the labyrinth again. So we had the process of the monster being killed, destroyed and separated and then Theseus had to make his way out with Ariadne hanging on to him with the thread. The labyrinth then became the prisoners who were set free by Theseus and Ariadne. The story as it worked out within the laws of the drama was dramatically and artistically impressive and at the same time, from the Sesame point of view, we were creating a space in which a client could experience quite a lot, and not be stuck with it but be able to grow and move on.

One of the tricky things about working on your own with a group of people who may be very disturbed is that while you're holding everybody, you may have someone who's a bit on the edge. You don't want to negate their needs, but at the same time you're having to carry everybody else. It can be tricky, but you have to do it. There are a number of physical, hands-on things you can do, but if you are in a situation where you can't physically connect, what can you use? Nothing but the sound you make and the feeling that you get into your voice. There are so many ways the voice can be used to good effect. For instance, you can suddenly whisper and people will stop and listen. This is another thing from my theatre background that helps me and that students in training could learn more about. It's not easy to teach, partly because people are actually more touchy about their voices than about their bodies: you can tell someone that their movement is awkward far more easily than you can say 'Have you thought what you're sounding like?' But this is a tool of our trade. It has an important place in the dramatherapist's tool box. To be able, when it's needed, to firm up your voice and make it a little louder or vary its tone is a great asset.

If I'm having to lead from the middle, which is very often the case – I may find myself having to be a character in the story as well as being the story-teller – then I will use a different, story-telling voice to say what happened next in the story; I'll be using something more like my talking voice to play the character. I can't be two people, I can only be the unit I am, but I can make my voice work for me so that I can then be in the other role.

When, as sometimes happens, someone suddenly decides to come into a session with their own material, going off on their own planet in the middle of something we are all doing, I will say in a firm voice 'That's a splendid thing, maybe it's something we can do some time, but IT ISN'T WHAT WE'RE DOING NOW!' You have to make sure that whatever was said isn't rubbished, that it is honoured in its own terms, but at the same time be firm about the fact that 'It isn't what we're doing now'. You can't let one person's disintegrating stuff take over because it isn't good for that person, and it certainly isn't good for the other four or five people who are trying to be part of what is going on. Usually the person will then either drop what he is doing and be part of what is happening or he will drop out for a while. He won't usually leave the room, but he may just drop back a bit and the action moves on and then somehow he will find himself getting caught up in it again. It's as if you've given him a little boundary. The message is 'If I want to come in and be part of what's going on, fine. If not, okay. But this is not the space where I'm expected to be crazy.' And 'If you're crazy, fine, but in this space we're going to be creative if you can handle it.' 'Oh yeah, fine – and if I can't handle it, I'll leave.' In essence, people stay because you're not focusing on the unwell: you're focusing on this as a space where there's a possibility to do something creative if you want to, if you feel able to. Or if you just want to be in this space because it's different from what's going on out there on the ward, fine.

Having said a lot about my way of working and how it reflects my personal experience in theatre work, it feels important to say as well that it is just one way of working. My hope is that readers of this book will learn from the different voices represented in it not only the theoretical base and pattern of what we all do as Sesame practitioners, but the equally important fact that how you work in this medium is always shaped by who you are and the experience that you, personally, bring to it.

Students may take a year to absorb and understand the basis of the work, but at the end of that time they won't just have one way of working – they'll discover five, maybe six ways of working, because although the rules of the game are the same, how they are framed will depend entirely on individuals and how they work from themselves.

CHAPTER 19

Dramatherapy in Forensic Psychiatry

Rodger Winn

Forensic psychiatry is simply aspects of psychiatry that concern themselves with the law. One facet of forensic psychiatry, the Regional Secure Unit, was established in the early 1980s to meet the needs of serious offenders with mental health problems in areas of assessment, treatment and rehabilitation. These offenders usually come from difficult family backgrounds and have a history of mental illness that has culminated in a serious offence such as assault, rape and even murder. Part prison, part mental health unit, part rehabilitation hostel, the Regional Secure Unit has to strike a balance between security and therapy. It provides an array of treatments including psychotherapy, occupational therapy, art therapy, key nursing and neuroleptic drugs. As the ones who wear the keys, the staff, including myself, can be seen as both therapists and prison warders. We literally unlock doors, while also trying to open up the client to himself and to his or her relationship with others. In this rather unusual setting I have been working as a dramatherapist for the past three years. In this chapter both I and one of the dramatherapy participants will be addressing the use of dramatherapy and, more specifically, the uses of role in such a setting.

As those clients who choose to work with dramatherapy progress through the unit, so they will move on from the Acute Dramatherapy Group to a session known as the Rehab Dramatherapy Group, which takes clients from all the other wards. Although similar in many respects, including the format and length of sessions, the Acute Group actually takes place on the Acute Ward and can be seen as concentrating on an invitation to play, encouraging initiative and confidence and offering an opportunity for self-expression in a safe setting.

The Rehab Group takes place in a larger room and is more expansive generally. There is a greater emphasis on improvisation, including free improvisation, as well as myth and story. The chance to experiment with role is central to the work done in this group. The ability to take on a persona or character and then be able to separate from it is a sign of a healthy psyche. It gives clients a chance to transcend themselves, exploring hidden aspects of the unconscious self or amplifying and exploring aspects of personality that are always near the surface. This is particularly appropriate for clients in a secure environment as they are very much in a state of limbo, often being unable to return to the lifestyles and the people they once knew. The future, including a place to live, is often little more than a vague concept. All these issues need to be addressed while people are in the unit. Being in a total institution in which many of the clients' rights are taken away, it can be seen that the old roles of, say, husband, or daughter, or provider, have been superseded by those of criminal, patient and outcast. In this context it can be seen that a chance to experiment with roles in a safe setting is invaluable.

To put the dramatherapy sessions in this setting in perspective, it also needs to be emphasized that at least two-thirds of clients in Regional Secure Units are still suffering from some form of psychosis. Following this chapter is a client's first-hand account of his own psychotic experience, which he has instinctively described in terms of role. Through such illnesses, clients experience, among other things, a dramatic change in role – perceiving themselves as being severely persecuted, or acquiring a grandiose view of themselves to the point of believing themselves to have special powers, religious connections or connections with royalty. After such an experience a person can feel very confused in terms of identity and can be left untrusting or very dependent, often feeling unable to present any role at all – either to themselves or to the outside world.

In contrast, many people in the unit are still involved in the painful process of struggling with their old beliefs and delusions, addressing them and attempting to change them through therapy, which includes medication. The dramatherapist can help the clients to rebuild a sense of identity by developing basic skills around improvisation and play, helping them to express themselves by tapping into skills which may have been dormant for many years, or may never have been consciously used before. As one client said, the sessions helped him to rediscover himself, drawing on skills he had forgotten he possessed. In this way the individual's healthy side is being drawn out and strengthened.

The concept of role can be explored in a variety of ways in dramatherapy. The classic Sesame approach is through story and myth, in which clients are encouraged to choose roles and are able to explore aspects of themselves through enactment. It is very much in the Jungian tradition for the experiences of life and death, the rites of passage that every culture shares and the archetypal roles we all have within us, to be explored through the safe containment of the myth. For example, the roles of the Hero, the Monster, the Trickster and the Mother can be chosen and explored to reveal aspects of the clients' personalities which are normally unseen, giving them a chance to be writ large. In this way the introverted client can show the nobility and strength of the hero; the controlled, 'bound' client can experience the spontaneity, wit and deviousness of the Trickster; the intellectually 'bound' client can slip into the innocent, carefree role of the Child. The selection of roles can also reveal any block in the personality that needs to be worked on – such as, for example, the client who always chooses the angry, aggressive role, may decide to play a submissive character. The dramatherapist can sometimes see roles not readily shown elsewhere expressing an underlying, deep-seated problem and showing an aspect of the personality that needs to be drawn out and strengthened.

The choice of myth or story is obviously influenced both by the needs of individual clients and the direction that the group as an organic whole is taking. Having said that, the group's response to a myth can never be predicted. It is often the most unexpected aspects of the story that provoke interest and inspire the imagination. The great Hero myths of Greece, the Arthurian quests and the Hero myths of the North American Indians have worked particularly well in this setting. Like the clients in the unit, the Hero must draw on hidden personal qualities (more often than not also accepting help from others) in his struggle to overcome seemingly unsurmountable odds.

Moving away from myth, another way of exploring role can be developed with more experienced groups through improvisation. This can be structured in various ways. An improvisation can, for example, begin with one person and be built up with others joining that person so that the group develops a story line together. The new person coming in often acts as a fresh impetus for the scene, enabling the group to take it further. Another stage on from this is taking a whole new scene with a new role into an existing scene, so that those already improvising have to adapt to it. This form of improvisation can be very fast and very freeing: it can be likened to the concept of stream of consciousness, where unfettered individual and group issues can rise to the surface. Over the weeks familiar patterns can be seen emerging as clients go in an arc and are, for example, constantly authoritarian, or undermining, or scapegoated. It is useful to enable clients to recognize these patterns and to widen their repertoire, as the characters played can be psychologically linked to the people playing them. In accordance with the Sesame tradition, this process is allowed to progress and develop without recourse to verbal analysis of the behaviour that is being exhibited. The emphasis is on providing a variety of experience in which the individual can unconsciously, alongside the development of confidence and trust, progress towards an enrichment of self-expression through role. One becomes aware of one's internal set of characters through the doing and the being and the sharing.

Alan, one of the clients in this dramatherapy setting, has given a vivid description of his mental illness and the work he has done, specifically in terms of role. He has also highlighted other benefits of dramatherapy for those suffering from mental illness, emphasizing the isolation imposed by mental illness and seeing dramatherapy as attacking alienation and disunity, while also enabling people to practice skills and spontaneity. This is a very important point as without roles there is no drama, but without relationships there can be no shared dramatic experience.

It is clear from Alan's contribution *To Act or Not To Act?* (Chapter 20) that many aspects of the Sesame tradition are distilled within his description. Apart from details I have already mentioned, he recognizes the importance of the warm-up and exercises leading up to the demands of the main event and the need to let people get involved at a level they are comfortable with. He also emphasizes the need to develop trust within a group before anything significant can take place.

Here it can be seen how dramatherapy sessions are about coming together, sharing and leaving with a sense of achievement, enjoyment and well-being. I am constantly amazed at the difference between the group at the beginning of a session: isolated, shy, stubborn – and the same group at the end: warm, friendly, connected. To enable this transformation is not an easy process with this client group, as it is often easier to remain isolated and withdrawn than go through the sometimes painful process of moving, imagining and sharing. The basic Sesame principles enable this process, since their emphasis is always on developing session material that is gentle and non-threatening.

Alan's ability to articulate his experience is a rare and valuable insight into how dramatherapy is received and perceived by a client. I would like to conclude by thanking him for his contribution. Most people I work with as a dramatherapist would be unwilling and unable to articulate themselves in such a way and this is entirely understandable. By and large the response to dramatherapy is emotional and aesthetic and it should be in no way considered inferior to any other form of therapy because of this. It is in the doing that the therapy takes place. I sometimes ask clients what they get from dramatherapy and I am told a variety of things, including 'It gets me out of bed' and 'It's a laugh' and 'It's an escape.' I find the latter particularly interesting as I have also encountered a great reluctance to deal with issues directly in the unit: generally speaking, the more fantastic the story or scenario, the better! I feel this is a very appropriate and necessary role for dramatherapy in such a setting. It is something of a truism to talk about freeing the imagination, but I believe this is the dramatherapist's most important task. The imagination can enable a client to escape into another role, another world and another shared experience, coming back enriched and hopefully changed. Without a well developed imagination, how would we be able to contemplate a future outside the confines of our past and present experience?

CHAPTER 20

To Act or Not to Act?

In the Secure Unit

Alan[1]

I was 23 and at London University when I first began hearing voices (auditory hallucinations) and slowly these came to dominate my life. I left college and eventually my bedsit and ended up living rough on the streets. My paranoia first attached itself to those directly around me: landlord and family, friends from college, my family and others who were close to me.

Then my mental pain attached itself to people on the streets. Eventually I came to believe there was a world conspiracy against me, that all could see inside my mind. In an attempt to escape all personal contact, I tried to isolate myself completely from everybody. I was able to steal food and clothes and believed I was 'allowed' to do this: if I didn't survive, 'they' would have a victim.

So for three years I didn't talk to anyone except when (after stealing money from bags which had been deliberately, so I thought, left lying around in offices or wherever) I had a little money and was able to buy food or pay for public transport. I was convinced not only that everybody could see inside my mind, but that they were actually 'transferring' into it the mental pain (emotions and feelings) and ideas that I was experiencing. I viewed this in terms of an individual or small group of individuals who personified the desires and wishes of the whole world, who were persecuting and torturing me.

My disturbed mental condition then, and my eventual crime, were, for me, part of a forced, temporary role – not *me*. All play roles in life, consciously or unconsciously, or both: life now is historical, not absolute. There are two

---

1 Written while detained in the Regional Secure Unit referred to in Chapter 19.

main aspects of an actor playing different roles: identification and poetry, which are a crucial part of everybody's lives. When people can identify with, or relate to, the suffering and trials depicted by the actor or actress in his or her role, it's a psychological release.

The 'poetry' is the need and desire to aspire to an unalienated, whole and harmonious state of things – an escape into some sort of ideal life (Utopia, proper Socialism, Heaven, Elysian Plains or whatever). It is something we cannot experience in reality under present conditions of individual and social division and conflict – except occasionally, in a limited way.

Drama can be a kind of training in social skills. It attacks alienation and disunity. Acting roles with other 'actors' or participants and presenting these to an audience – even if it's not social, but a monologue right through – is confidence building and an exercise in communication. It is worthwhile if only it combats the *isolation* of the mentally ill – like my own previous isolation, as I have described it.

The relationship is dialectical, but isolation is an ingredient of most mental disorders and in the most extreme cases almost total isolation is the result: there is no, or very little, struggle against these conditions. Since dramatherapy helps to fight this, it can make an important contribution in getting sufferers to build relationships with each other and to look outward instead of withdrawing into themselves.

If only through the various roles, patients interact with one another. The common interest is crucial in the case of forensically (mentally) ill males and females. Dramatherapy with improvisation can lead, hopefully and eventually, to the therapeutic practice of identification and coincidence of experience. This is central to patients gaining insight into their illnesses or disorders and is relevant to all good therapeutic pursuits.

Often 'improvisation' can aid a natural spontaneity to develop in personal relationships. Learning how to ad lib and improvise is something many people would like to do in everyday life. Life is far more satisfying if the individual can socialize easily and communicate both seriously and humorously with other people. Improvising on stage or in a drama session can help the individual function in outside, 'normal' society.

To be specific and look at our drama group, Rodger, our dramatherapist, uses some original ideas – for instance, in the group's 'warm-up' exercises. These act as a gradual introduction or induction to the more demanding tasks of the session. Although sometimes 'eccentric' or 'unorthodox' or, in the opinion of one group member, 'childish', I think they help bind and cement the group together. They are also good fun and vehicles for the group members' sense of humour.

Recently we had a stretchable cloth, roughly the size of a sheet, for the six patients and two staff, who comprise the group, to hold. Each person held the cloth on the edge until it was stretched like a trampoline cover, then a small ball was produced which we had to, collectively, bounce on the piece of material. If the ball could no longer be kept going up and down on the cloth but went over the edge, we started again. This is just one example of an interesting warm-up.

Getting members of the group to contribute ideas for the sessions is freeing for both patients and therapists. This kind of group participation is a step towards greater independence or interdependence. The latter two are not necessarily contradictory, since being able to trust others is paramount. To work progressively as, or with, a team is a positive measure and even a gauge of an individual's independence and 'stability' (and vice versa). This challenges institutionalization and dependence, two aspects of the patient's general condition.

Further shared planning of a scenario (i.e. a basic story line and a few different scenes), then enacting it, can to an extent fuse ad lib and a proper, structured script, resulting in a satisfying combination. We do this in Rodger's group to beneficial effect. It's surprising how everybody joins in and enjoys this form of therapy. Yet it is essential in this type of group that involvement by individuals should not be forced but nurtured in an organic way so that progress is not stifled. These are some thoughts that occurred to me after attending Rodger's Drama Group for over a year.

CHAPTER 21

Moving Through a Block in Psychotherapy

Mary Smail

Marilyn was a woman in her mid-thirties who was referred to Sesame by her doctor. She had been talking and talking to her doctor and had also been in psychotherapy, but got nowhere with it. She went into times of very dark depression and didn't understand why. She also had a stammer that was so severe she could hardly speak when I first met her. She said she wanted to do some form of dramatherapy because she felt that it would involve less talking and more movement and that this might free her to find out what was wrong. It was an exploratory meeting. We talked a little about the different kinds of dramatherapy and about psychodrama. She thought psychodrama sounded too confrontational for her. The idea of a Sesame group felt equally frightening. What she wanted was to work one-to-one, more with movement than drama. This was her idea, not mine. She explained that in psychotherapy she could never 'get it out'. Her actual words when asking about movement were 'Will this work for me? Will this get my feelings out?' I said 'I don't know. We can only try.' Eventually we agreed to start by having four half-hour sessions working with movement and sounds. By sounds, as I explained, I meant not talking or singing but just making sounds the way a small child does. She seemed to feel very happy with that. She asked if, within that half-hour, there could be five minutes set aside for talking. I replied that of course we could talk at the end of the session, but I was careful to explain that I was not an analyst or a psychotherapist, so there would be no analysing of what was said or done. This was in keeping with the Sesame Method, in which we contain what comes up in sessions and make sure people are grounded before they leave, but don't analyse what comes up because that is not our job.

She didn't arrive for the first session: her sister rang to cancel. I did wonder if she would turn up at all, but then she arrived for her session the following week. We were working in a very large room. We began with a physical warm-up. First we took turns to beat different rhythms on the drum. Her movement was very light and flowing with no weight at all. Similarly when we did some stamping, trying to make contact with the floor, there was no feeling of contact with the floor: her movements remained light, floating and ungrounded. We did some stretching to get the body moving and she was quite happy to stretch. I suggested she might like to stretch in a direction – above, forward or behind. She said she really wanted to stretch into the past. She brought that in herself, saying 'I'm stretching behind me. I'm stretching back.' When I wondered what she was stretching back to she didn't want to say anything more, but kept on reaching behind her. So we worked together with 'back' and 'behind'. The session was mainly about looking back and looking forward and being here. We worked with those three things and finished with a very gentle hand massage.

The next week she arrived looking very cheery and bright. The room we were working in was cold, so I put on some fast tempo music and we moved quickly around the place to warm ourselves up. She copied a lot of my movement and didn't seem to be able to find movements of her own. She commented on how large the space was and I said 'I wonder what we can do about that?' So we began to explore the space around our own bodies, exploring whether we wanted to come close to one another or keep our distance. It turned out that we wanted to come closer to one another and share space. We talked briefly about how it felt to be close to each other and far away. Then we exchanged spaces and experimented with being each other: she took on how it looked to be me and I took on how it looked to be her. After doing this in movement we spent some time sculpting one another, adjusting each other to look the way we ourselves felt that we looked now. There was a lot of fun in all this. At the end she talked a bit about closeness, since we had been quite close to one another. She talked about not being close to her mother, saying that she felt no bonding had happened between her mother and her. The depression had first started 15 years ago at the birth of her own son, her first child, when she felt there was a lack of bonding: she related this to the lack of bonding with her own mother.

In the third session her movement was lighter than ever. She could hardly stay in one place but whizzed around all over the place in a way that felt quite manic. So we did some stamping, really working on the feeling of being big and very heavy and how exaggerated could we make this? Eventually she was beginning to get the feel of really getting the feet firmly into the ground. Having done that, when she was more centred and more still, we began to do some call and echo work with our voices, across the room. I would do a call and she would echo it back. At first she found this embarrassing. I would make quite a large calling sound and what came back was almost a whimper. Then she began to copy and after a while I asked if she would like to lead with some calls. She started to do this and then suddenly suggested, completely out of the blue, that we go paddling in the Scottish North Sea. I thought 'Go with it', as this kind of inspiration, coming out of context, very often turns out to have come from a deep place in the psyche which needs the experience for some reason of its own – so we began to test the cold water, making the kind of noises you would make on entering a very cold Scottish North Sea. Having this image seemed to help her into the voice. She made some strong, sharp, 'hoohh' and 'hihh' noises as we went into the cold, cold water. We went in up to the waist, no further, and then hurried back out. Then, at my suggestion, we tried going into a warm Mediterranean sea with lovely 'Ahhhh' sounds. I had had enough of cold Scottish seas and, being also aware that the session was coming to an end, I didn't want it to end in the temperature of the North Sea. She then said she had found something lovely at the bottom of the sea: a silver bracelet with diamonds in it. She wanted to keep it and suggested putting it inside her bra, as she didn't have a pocket.

At the end of that time she talked again about early rejection. I reminded her that I was not a psychotherapist. She said that all the same she did want to talk to me about the depression but she wasn't ready yet. I said 'All right. We'll just keep going.' I put on some music and we finished with some massage.

There were a few more sessions rather like that. Basically we experimented with sounds and movement, just getting the body and the voice more used to working. Then we came to session seven, in which we started moving to the Van Gellis *Earth Sounds*. She moved quickly into a position in which she was holding herself in, holding her tummy, with one hand hiding her face. She then began to cry. I moved to her and put one hand on her and said 'Just let it out.' She cried for a minute or so. I asked if she could put what the tears felt like into a movement. Then she began to move really heavily and to say for the first time 'I'm angry!' I went to be beside her and said that I was with her and we could both face the anger. Still to the music, we crossed the room using slashing movements and sounds, loud sounds that she had never made before. When we reached the far side she began to weep and moan. I said again that I was with her and it was okay to cry. She began to address the wall, calling it her mother, saying how she felt she had been rejected and telling her mother how she felt. I asked her if she wanted to answer as her mother and she did this. She didn't get into any feeling when speaking as the mother. After a few minutes we moved away and began to come back to the present. She was then very shocked at the sounds and what had happened. She just wanted to be quiet and she asked me at that point to hold her. Then we did some massage work, which had become ritualized as a way of ending a session. She would sit on a chair and I would kneel behind her, so there was no eye contact and very little physical contact – just my hands kneading the shoulders, helping them to relax, and then brushing down the arms to try to shake off the kind of things that she had been experiencing.

Nothing happened after that session was over. She didn't want to talk about it at all and obviously I didn't press her to do so. The following session was relatively uneventful. Then, for session nine, she arrived in a way I hadn't seen her arrive before – no smile, no lipstick on (which was her usual way of presenting herself). She immediately came into the room and asked if she could smoke a cigarette. I said yes to this, which normally I wouldn't have done, because I felt she needed it. Then she said that she felt very heavy. I said 'Okay, let's move as if we are very heavy.' She began to move in a stooped position that I hadn't seen before. It reminded me of *Pilgrim's Progress*, as if she was carrying a great burden on her back. I said 'It's as if you are carrying something. Is there anything we can do to unpack this load?' She said 'Yes, there is something heavy on my back.' Then, with intense concentration, she lifted her hand over the top of her head, over to her back, and pulled something off, which she handed to me. I put it down on the floor about a foot away from us. We were both kneeling on the floor, side-by-side. She then sat for a while again and I said 'Is there any more?' The same thing happened. It happened three times, so that three things were on the ground in front of us. I asked her 'Is there anything else?' She said 'No more now.' The implication was that there was still more in that burden, but 'no more now'. I said 'What are we going to do with these?' She said without a thought 'Burn them'. I asked 'How are we going to burn them?' She immediately got up and began to gather wood for a camp fire. I went and got sand and water as a precaution, so that if the fire got out of control there would be something on hand to keep it in one place. (In this way I was able to tell her, within the symbolism of the drama, that I was on hand to help her contain any strong feelings that might be about to come out.)

We lit the fire together, both of us blowing the flames, then just sat and watched it. It was quite a big fire. After a while she burst into tears. I had been sitting on the other side of the fire from her and I just went round to her and held her hand as we sat watching the fire. Gradually it died down but it didn't go out. The session was about to end, so I said to her 'Shall we put this fire out?' She said 'No. I don't want the fire put out.' So we banked it up with sand, surrounding it very firmly so that it was a contained fire. It was left burning: that seemed to be important. Then she said 'The things that I have burnt were betrayals.' That was all. We left the fire and ended the session with the massage ritual. She said 'I'm going to tell you about these things, but not this week.'

In session ten she made no mention of what had happened the week before. We just had a movement session which was quite light and breezy. For session eleven we did a story called *The Healing Herb*, which she enacted with me and seemed to enjoy. When she arrived for session twelve she said she didn't want to do any more drama and movement: she wanted to talk. We sat down on the floor and she began to tell me about a domestic accident when her child was very young, which she had felt so guilty about that she never told anyone. She was still carrying the guilt of this. She was also carrying the pain of knowing that her husband had affairs with other women. She had blocked these things off in her mind and hadn't been able to talk about them to the doctor or to her therapist. These were the betrayals she had been carrying in her burden.

After she had told me these things I said 'Do you think you could get your husband to go with you to Relate?' Her first reaction was shock, horror, but then she said she would suggest it. For session fourteen she turned up as bright as a button and said they had made an appointment with Relate. We both recognized that our work had achieved what she wanted, so we finished off the session with some movement reaffirming what we had done and who she was and that there was a future for her. In movement terms, she was reaching forward now.

Looking back over the fourteen sessions, I feel some amazement at the speed and clarity with which she moved towards the discoveries she needed to make. Working in the body she was able to recognize that she had a burden on her back, first to bear it, then to talk about it, and finally to discover a way forward. Finding the burden was the turning point. It is a very clear illustration of the way drama enables us to symbolize deep psychic wounds in an immediate, physical way. Having found the burden, she was able to unpack it in a physical manner and to acknowledge its contents as real, without having any pressure on her to say what they were. She was then able to take her time before sharing her painful recognition of the sense of betrayal that she had been blocking off – betrayals involving, in immediate terms, her husband, and in the long term, some very deep feelings around parental betrayal, both by her own mother and by herself in relation to her son. When, with her permission, I gave some feedback to her doctor, he was astonished about the marital problem as there had been no hint of it in her conversations with him.

Another interesting development in our sessions was that when she arrived and we said 'Hello. How are you?' the stammer was always very pronounced, but by the end of each session the stammer would be gone. I said one time 'Have you noticed that your stammer isn't there?' She said 'Oh no, I hadn't noticed at all. You're right.' I realized I might be taking a risk saying this but even then, when I pointed it out, the stammer didn't come back! I sensed that possibly her stammer could be connected with her resistance to the pain of the things she feared to name. It's interesting that it was Marilyn herself who had the intuition that drama might help her to get past the block. In learning to use the medium, she found her way bodily into places she couldn't bring herself to talk about. Once there, she was able to find, in a way that felt absolutely real, the things she had not managed to find words for. Having done this, she was then able to find a new direction. What happened after this I don't know. Having unpacked her burden and discovered its contents, she now wanted to talk about them. It felt appropriate, therefore, that she should return to some form of talking therapy. The movement we had done was a bridge to the talking.

It feels important to say in conclusion that when I began working with Marilyn I had no idea how it was going to work out: initially I just went with her feeling that movement was what she needed. There were times when the situation seemed to be utterly stuck and I didn't know what to do, so I did the only thing that's possible in such a situation: I stuck with it. The change, when it came, came very quickly. Fourteen weeks is really a very short time in which to have such a change take place.

CHAPTER 22

A Place Called Sesame
Dramatherapy with Disturbed Children

Jenny Pearson

The intensive treatment of children who have been physically and, in many cases, sexually abused, is the ongoing work of a small therapeutic community in South London, which I shall call Beech Lodge.[1] Once a week, in term time, I walk up the stone steps of a tall Victorian house in a leafy road with my Indian drum under my arm and join two colleagues for a mug of tea and a half-hour briefing from the resident child psychotherapist – and then we're on. As we arrive, the children can sometimes be heard calling in excited voices 'It's Sesame. Hello, Sesame!' I noticed a long way back that they seldom use our names or relate to us as individuals, which feels significant. In their minds, we seem to be a kind of place where they can go once a week and experience themselves in new ways, a place where they are able to imagine and follow where imagination takes them. This way of playing, which Peter Slade calls 'dramatic play', is easier for less damaged children: these very disturbed children find it difficult because their disruptive behaviour tends to cut across any creative endeavour. So it helps to have the encouragement and protection of adults who can simultaneously hold the boundaries and be with them in their play. The child in us plays with the child in them, while the adult in us is there to guard the boundaries and make sure no one gets hurt.

Within the art form we hold for them, the children are able to find and express aspects of themselves that may not find room to emerge in their everyday lives in a residential home which is, of necessity, geared to contain

---

1   The name and location of 'Beech Lodge' and the children's names have been altered to protect confidentiality.

and address the violent rage most of them naturally feel at the way life has treated them. Over time, we have noticed that a child who is being particularly violent and difficult outside drama sessions, will frequently enter the world of story with relief, as though shedding a barbed and angry mask, to choose a role that enables him/her to be quiet and gentle. The gentle, loving aspect of the child has been split-off and rejected by the child himself, partly because it feels dangerous to be vulnerable and partly because of angry feelings that seem to push more urgently for expression. In drama, paradoxically, the child has a chance to take time off from being his angry, everyday self. He can choose to be a kind person, or a quiet, lazy person, rediscovering these aspects of himself without having to own them, because everyone knows that this is drama and he is only acting in role. With the Sesame team holding the boundaries and our firm rule that 'nobody gets hurt in Sesame', the child is in a space where he knows that his vulnerability will not be exploited. Drama provides opportunities to express anger and hostility through strong movement and battles with man and beast in safety, because of the 'no hurting' rule. Small boys who feel bullied and downtrodden outside often choose to be heroes and giants in a story, while even the toughest Jack will behave in a gentle way towards Daisy the cow as he leads her to market. Again and again we have noticed how the child who is being particularly violent and destructive outside will come into drama looking for a part in which to express the more peaceful and loving aspects of the self.

This is just one pattern we have observed over more than five years in which I and a series of colleagues from Sesame have been privileged to be part of an extraordinary unit, set up to work intensively with these very damaged children. They also have an art therapist who comes in, as we do, once a week in term time, and a full-time child psychotherapist, who sees most of the children for individual sessions two or three times a week. The age range of the children is from seven to twelve and the average length of stay is two years, at the end of which the child's progress is assessed and arrangements are made for the child to be adopted or fostered by a family, or to move on to special boarding school or adolescent unit. Many of the children have been removed from their original families by court order and do not return to them. In theory, the house is run like a large family unit, with no more than nine children in residence and a high ratio of care workers to children, allowing for a lot of individual attention. There are moments when the group does feel like a large family, but this impression is frequently disrupted by outbursts of fairly extreme behaviour. Most of the children go to local schools, ranging from the local primary through various special schools, while the occasional child who can't manage school has private tuition. The room we work in is a large play room which is cleared of all objects for our use.

The children come for their sessions either singly or in small groups, never outnumbering us. This arrangement came about in response to the needs and reactions of children we worked with in the early days, when Sesame and Beech Lodge were new to one another and looking for an optimal working pattern. At first we divided the children into two groups: the older ones and the younger ones. There were two of us to begin with, so we were outnumbered in both groups. The children would arrive very excited and fly around the room like peas in a drum, bouncing off the walls, their energy completely unfocused, lashing out at one another as they went. Drama, as such, was a non-starter in this situation: first we had to find ways of catching and focusing this wild, angry energy. I was fortunate in that the person who came with me to help start the project was none other than Marian Lindkvist, known to us as Billy – the founder of Sesame and originator of a way of working that we call Movement with Touch. It was this that harnessed the mythical wild horses of the house and had the children, in due course, focusing their energy creatively through drama.

Using Movement with Touch in work with children who may have been sexually abused requires great certainty and know-how on the part of the therapist. Once you see it working, the rationale for it is so obvious that there is no room left for doubt. A sure-fire winner, with girls as well as boys, is the very basic exercise that Billy calls 'pushing'. I have described how we used this exercise in our training in a placement with people with autistic tendencies: how it channelled and focused the diffuse, over-excited energy that was always around (see Chapter 7). When we introduced 'pushing' to the children it had exactly the same effect: the energy that had been all over the place instantly became focused as they pitted their strength against ours, one-to-one. The difference from the autistic placement is that there, the therapist offers resistance for a relatively tentative assertion on the part of the client, whereas the children at Beech Lodge go for it with all the physical strength and determination they can muster, hand-to-hand and eye-to-eye, striving to win the contest. The action absorbs their need to assert, to fight, to make their presence felt. Over time, as they grow, the struggling therapist finds him/herself beginning to lose ground, laughing and congratulating the child 'No, no, this is too much, you are getting too strong for me!' After this initial plunge into action, it may gradually become possible to turn the 'pushing' into something more contained or, as the Laban terminology has it, 'fine touch': the two people balancing, leaning their weight against one another, hand-to-hand, and forming an arch between them for the others to pass through. Pushing remains a popular opener for sessions, particularly with the boys. Some children who have worked with us have become aware that 'pushing' makes them feel better, calmer, more focused, instead of flying around out of control. One boy, Damien, whose surplus energy and aggression got him into a lot of trouble outside, would sometimes ask 'Can we push?' when he felt a need for it. Variations include pushing shoulder-to-shoulder and back-to-back. Another alternative is 'pulling' – either simple pulling, face-to-face and hand-to-hand or, as Billy suggested to the squealing delight of the smaller children, having children lie on their backs and dragging them around the floor by their hands or ankles. The physical contact with the floor has a 'grounding' effect as well as being fun: the child's body gradually relaxes into the movement. Some may remain straight and tense to begin with, heads lifted anxiously off the floor, but the general hilarity usually gets to them and laughter leads to relaxation. We will encourage this, saying 'See if you can go floppy! Let your head down on the floor!' Dragging a child by the ankles in a wiggly movement adds to the general absurdity as well as encouraging the body to bend and relax. These exercises tend to end with the adults exhausted and the excited children screaming 'Do it again! Do it again!'

None of this would seem to have a lot to do with drama, but it is movement with a therapeutic rationale and, within the format of the session, it serves as a 'bridge' leading from the wild, unfocused movement of the children on arrival into a quieter, more focused place where it becomes possible to tell and enact a story.

There is no better example to illustrate our way of working with this client group than the now classic story of 'The Bad People', which Billy created specifically for Beech Lodge during our first year working there. It is a story which combines an element of fun and play with a symbolic theme which both acknowledges and works on the central issue for this client group. It has become a tradition for us to use this story when we work with a child for the first time. Also, we often begin the year with it after returning from the summer break. The children never seem to tire of it.

The warm-up, as specified by Billy, is a game of 'Grandmother's Footsteps' in which everyone in the group creeps towards the 'Grandmother' along the floor 'on their tummies'. The person leading the session is 'Grandmother' and warns everyone sternly that he/she is going to be very fierce, no quarter given and 'no cheating'. Much is made of this. Because the 'Grandmother' is already seen to be in role, this fierceness is part of the game and the rules are enforced with exaggerated rigour. Again, the fact that the game is played on the floor has a grounding, reassuring effect which is physical and is therefore absorbed unconsciously by those taking part. The game leads into the story, which is told by the original 'Grandmother' with the group sitting in a circle:

Long ago and far away there was a village.

The people kept a precious sack of gold and other treasures deep underground.

Sometimes they would take something out of the sack and have a feast. There was always plenty left. Nobody knew all that was in the sack.

One day all the men of the village went out hunting and when they got back the treasure was missing.

The theft had been seen by the old grandmother. She said it had been stolen by the Bad People who lived through the woods, over the river and through the deep, thick grasses.

They had hidden the sack in a small cave at the foot of the hill. It was always guarded.

The hunters decided to get it back.

The journey was long and when they reached the river they had to build a bridge before they could cross it. There they met an old person. The person told them how the guard of the sack marched and that he always stopped for four seconds before he turned round and marched back: this would be the moment when the hunters could slip into the cave.

They had to creep through the grass and not be seen or heard by the guard, only moving when his back was turned. Then when two or three were in the cave they had to take the sack, run out of the cave, and fall down in the long grass while the guard's back was turned. To get safely away, they must lie in the long grass and move only when the guard's back was turned. Bit by bit they got to the river and once they had crossed it they were safe.

When they got home with the sack they celebrated its return with a feast. Then they put the sack in a safer place.

The parts are put on offer. Invariably the children opt to be hunters (though one boy, Simon, liked to play one of the Bad People in tandem with one of us. He somehow managed to create his own version of the tale, adding in part of another, Native American story about the Wolf People, so that he and his partner guarding the stolen treasure were also wolves in an exciting 'alternative' world away from the village – but that, as they say, is another story!) Other parts are the Hunters, the Guard, the Grandmother and the Old Person by the river: the last two can be played by the same person if the cast is small.

The relevance of 'Grandmother's Footsteps on Tummies' as a warm-up is immediately apparent when the hunters come to approach the cave through the long grasses. The excited tension generated by the need to move while the guard's back is turned and keep completely still while he marches across the cave entrance, peering into the long grasses for signs of movement, always takes me straight back to childhood games of 'hunters and hunted' and 'kick the can'. I find myself back in the fields and woods, a hunted animal trying not to breathe in my hiding place as the 'hounds' go by. It is at points like this that drama and imaginative play overlap, as Peter Slade observed. By setting up a dramatic space and introducing this kind of situation, it seems to me that we are simultaneously creating an inner space in which the children have a chance to experience a form of imaginative play which is common to healthy children, but which their troubled lives may not have allowed room for until now.

I also feel there is something going on between us and the children that resembles Winnicott's description of the 'potential space' or 'area of illusion' set up between the baby and mother. It is an area of paradox in which the child is able to enjoy a sense of being alone because he/she is not really alone: the mother's presence is taken for granted and becomes the basis for a sense of security, within which aloneness and adventure can be experienced in fantasy. The child's world is protected from intrusion by forces more powerful than him. At the same time, these enemy forces are repeatedly imagined, opposed and overcome in fantasy: knowing the secret of the Guard's routine four-second pause or, in another story, the weak point in the dragon's underbelly, enables the young hero to triumph repeatedly over forces more powerful than himself. The therapist's function within the drama, as well as holding the story and playing minor roles, is to bear witness and mirror the achievements of the hero – reinforcing these achievements in a manner comparable to the mirroring role of the mother, for whom an infant's small achievements are momentous steps deserving of acknowledgement. In fact we work with stories of different kinds, not just hero stories – but the principle holds good that whatever form the story of the day may take, our presence as holders of the story and the space puts us in a mirroring role in relation to the children.

It is, of course, impossible to draw accurate conclusions about what is going on for these children in the course of dramatic experiences in which they seem to be deeply interested and engaged – but aside from the sheer fun, it does feel as if something important is going on. We are talking about children with histories of being repeatedly overwhelmed in frightening ways where they should have been protected. Some of them have never known the ordinary experience of playing safely under the watchful eye of a parent. Yet within the drama, something of this kind seems to happen – enabling them to drop their guard and really play.

It was not always so. We had to work hard in the beginning to gain the children's confidence and esteem, being subjected by the them to a whole range of tests and challenges until, quite unobtrusively, we became absorbed into the tradition of the place and new children began to arrive for their first sessions with the pre-formed view that Sesame was a good thing. The first negotiations took place around Billy's African drum, a wondrous object made especially for her by an African out of the skin of a sacrificed goat. While deeply suspicious of us, the children could not, and did not, resist the lure of drum with its furry surface and deep, powerful resonance. Our first communications were in the form of drum rhythms exchanged and imitated. A boy called Andrew, being contrary, scratched at the fur and likened the sound to nits. He went on to take part in a series of exciting one-to-one enactments with Billy, involving her in setting up barricades against attacking armies and wolves. A drum still features in most of our sessions at Beech Lodge, mainly for purposes of de-rolling and grounding at the end.

For most of the children, the golden key that opens up the world of imagination and dramatic play is story. The stories we enact with them are mainly traditional fairy-tales and myths from different cultures around the world. These stories – as Jung (1940), Joseph Campbell (1949), Marie Louise von Franz (1970) and Bruno Bettelheim (1976) have variously pointed out – originate and resonate in a very deep part of the psyche, calling up energies and feelings that seem to be universal and straight from the heart. It is invariably through involvement in these stories that the children are able to move right away from the painful emotional turmoil within, finding an alternative world in which they can be someone else for a while, setting aside the bizarre and violent behaviour that makes life so difficult for them and for their carers. This may sound like escapism, but I don't think it is as crude as that. It feels more as if story is giving them an entry to places within themselves that they didn't know were there, so that they begin to surprise themselves and us with powers of imagination and communication that no one knew they had.

An eight-year-old boy called Jason who came to drama shortly after arriving at Beech Lodge was very absent minded, seeming to drift off into fugue states in which he couldn't always hear what was said to him. He could neither read nor write and didn't seem to be able to learn. At this time his frame of mind was being described as 'borderline', though it was also felt that his symptoms could be the result of severe trauma. One day, when the small group in his drama session was embarked on a ship, Jason suddenly came out of his trance and took command. He continued to engage in the drama sessions that followed, usually contriving to seize a part in which he could exercise control – a sensible precaution for someone needing to protect himself and his feelings. When he required someone to carry out his orders, one of us would quickly get into that role and be exaggeratedly subservient, so that even he could see and enjoy the humorous aspect of what was going on. Then he began to suggest original twists to some of the stories, revealing an active imagination at work. A day came when he announced that he had a story that he wanted us to enact. As it is our practice to make way for suggestions from the client group, we encouraged him to tell his story (not making any promises about enacting it, as we didn't know at this stage how actable it would be). Jason asked us to sit in a circle around him and told the following story:

> There was a boy called Jack who found a stone with a dark hole in it. He looked inside and found two snakes, a Mummy snake and a Daddy snake, who began to chase Jack. They moved very quickly, but he managed to get away because he could move at the speed of light. After he got away he came to the woods and a Woodcutter looked after him. One day the Woodcutter and Jack were in the woods and they saw a brown thing and a spotted thing in the shape of trees. The Woodcutter saw eyes in the trees looking down at them and he realized that they were the snakes. He grabbed a very sharp axe and cut the snakes in half. After that Jack was safe and went home to his parents.

We were all amazed at the story. It was beautifully crafted with a clear beginning, middle and end, set in the familiar landscape of traditional stories with the classic figures of Jack and the Woodcutter. It also showed an original imagination at work, representing some quite personal and frightening material in symbolic form. This child might not be able to read or write, but he was a natural for the oral tradition. As we prepared to enact it, choosing parts and assuming Jason would take the role of Jack, he spoke firmly to Billy telling her 'You be Jack!' (It was a frightening story and a bit close for comfort, so perhaps he felt it would be safer to have Jack played by someone else.) Billy said 'I can't run fast enough. I'm too old.' 'You don't have to,' said Jason. 'You can pretend, like this!' And he showed her. Clearly we had a director in our midst as well as a story-teller! In fact, Mary took the part of Jack and Billy chose to be the Woodcutter: it is a basic rule that people choose what parts they play. We enacted the story for Jason while he sat on a table and watched. As the Woodcutter, Billy contributed an important detail: after cutting the snakes in half, the Woodcutter skinned them and asked Jack to help her make something from their beautiful skins. There is a therapeutic rationale for this repairative ending. (Winnicott observed that children can feel bad inside after an aggressive action.) While Jason's story gave his aggressive feelings a necessary outlet at an unconscious level, something else needed to happen to ensure that he would not be left feeling bad inside. As Winnicott says: 'a child values finding that hate or aggressive urges can be experienced in a known environment without the return of hate and violence from the environment of the child.' (1964) Jack's environment didn't retaliate: instead, the Woodcutter asked for his help in making something beautiful. This kind of resolution through making, or growing, at the end of a story that has expressed angry, even murderous feelings, is a form of containment frequently used in Sesame.

The session with *Jack and the Snakes* wasn't a flash in the pan. Jason went on constructing stories with shapely plots and traditional imagery for the rest of his time at Beech Lodge, not every week, but frequently. Coinciding with this development, we were informed he had begun to make progress with his reading and writing. In cases like this there is no way one can prove cause and effect, but it has been noticeable that other children who have found a unique, creative voice in drama and movement sessions have simultaneously begun to change and blossom in their lives outside. Sometimes a breakthrough in drama has coincided with creative developments in art therapy or some significant movement within the very different context of individual psychotherapy. I wouldn't want to seem to be claiming that we have necessarily led the way in these changes, but we do seem to play an effective part within the context of a broader programme that seems to be able to reach these very damaged children behind their well constructed barriers and defences.

Another child to whom I was close enough to witness profound and interesting changes over a period of more than two years was Philip. He was eight when he arrived at Beech Lodge, physically small and educationally backward to a degree that he attended a special school for children with learning disabilities. His thought processes seemed to be quite chaotic and when he spoke it was often difficult to understand what he was saying. He was sometimes affectionate, not always in appropriate ways, and often physically abusive – a fairly typical behaviour pattern in children who have been subject to sexual abuse. At the time we were doing a lot of individual sessions and, to make optimum use of Sesame time, it was decided that I would work one-to-one with Philip in the 'soft play room' – a small room filled with giant plastic-and-foam building blocks in different shapes – while Mary and Pam simultaneously worked with another child in the big play room.

The arrangement worked well as Philip was quite violent at that time and the soft play room provided him with objects he could safely hit – a detail that influenced the shape and direction of our work from the beginning. We had already established a working relationship during a brief spell when he was in a group with two older boys. Because he was smaller and younger than the other two and they were inclined to bully him, the Sesame team had adopted our strategy for containing disparate individuals within a group: each of us giving concentrated attention to one child, containing and joining in whatever that particular child did. In a story called *The Cloud Eater* (about a monster who eats up all the clouds so that there is no rain) the other two boys chose to play the part of heroes who slay the cloud eating monster while Philip, in his bizarre way, went for the part of the cloud eater. He seemed happy for me to share it and there were some enjoyable moments in which we dived greedily from the mountain top with cries of 'Look, here's another one!' Gobbling up the clouds put us in a class apart from the heroes and other people in the valley below, setting up a natural alliance which carried over into our one-to-one work.

Philip arrived with a slightly sheepish expression on his face, unsure what to make of having a session to himself. I sat on a building block and offered the drum, a 'transitional object' that few children can resist. By this time Billy had moved on with her famous African drum, but Mary and I had both acquired upright African drums with fur surfaces from Oxfam. Philip struck the drum a few times, but his heart wasn't in it. I asked what he wanted to do. 'Fight!' he said. 'I want to be Karate boy.' 'Okay,' I said. 'Who are you going to fight?' 'My enemy!' he replied. By now he was standing up, looking around him with the a fierce, cross-eyed look that was to become very familiar over the sessions that followed. I stood a rectangular block on its end and said 'Here's your enemy. Let's see what you can do!'

The sessions that followed all began in the same way. Philip would rush headlong into the room, stand a block of soft play on its end and lambaste it with cries of 'I'm going to punch him! I'm going to break his legs and his arms! I'm going to kill him!' I said 'Okay, I get the idea, but this is a bit boring. It's always the same. We're here to do drama. Why don't we make a boxing ring? That's your corner and this is your opponent's corner and you're not allowed to start until I ring the bell. I'm the umpire!' 'Yeah – right!' he said and went straight to his corner. From then on our sessions became formal fights with Philip decreeing whether it was karate, judo or boxing. One time I rang the bell for the end of a bout and he went on beating up his opponent. I became extremely angry, in role, raising my voice and ordering him to stop immediately. 'You have broken the rules by fighting after I rang the bell,' I said. 'This time I'll give you a warning – but if it happens again you'll be disqualified from the competition and you won't be allowed to fight here again for six months. Do you understand?' He bowed his head and replied, in role, 'Yes, Sir. Of course, Sir. Sorry, Sir. I won't do it again.'

Time and again I have rediscovered the advantages of exercising authority in role (see Chapter 6). The children will respond to over-the-top discipline *within the drama*, whilst they would probably defy or ignore a bid for control from outside the dramatic form. The beauty of this manoeuvre is that fierce commands issued in role are invariably obeyed and enjoyed as an authentic aspect of dramatic play. At the same time, this gives us an acceptable means of holding boundaries and avoiding stuck situations.

For many weeks Philip remained single-minded in wishing to spend all his sessions fighting. On two occasions when I introduced stories that other children had enjoyed, he went along with this in a half-hearted way but returned us firmly to the boxing ring the following week. Then a story came my way which was to take over the space for two whole terms. It was a Japanese story of a Sumi wrestler who encounters three strong women and trains with them at the top of a mountain, wrestling with the grandmother and eating uncooked rice for a year: at the end of this he defeats all the champions in the land and receives a bag of gold from the Emperor, returning with it to the mountain and marrying the youngest of the women – the granddaughter of his wrestling coach.[2] Philip leapt into the part of the Sumi wrestler, in which he tickles the youngest of the women as she is carrying a pitcher from a stream and she traps his hand under one very strong arm, marching him up the mountain side to meet her mother and grandmother. We left the story at the point where he has been training for a year and is about to go down the mountain to fight in front of the Emperor. I said 'We'll finish the story next week.'

---

2   For a version of this story, see James Riordan (1984)

He arrived for his next session with a change of plan, declaring that he wasn't ready to go down the mountain yet: he wanted to stay with the grandmother and do more training. This went on week after week. There was evidently something about the situation of the Sumi wrestler learning to fight and growing ever stronger on a diet of raw rice in the home of three strong women that satisfied the needs of this very troubled child. I knew from our weekly briefings that he was having a difficult time outside our sessions, getting into trouble for violent behaviour at school and struggling with fantasies about murder and suicide. The place up the mountain seemed to be both a refuge and a source of hope, possibly with the idea that if he trained hard and long enough he might eventually have the strength to defend himself against the enemy. The story held some kind of healing symbol for him and he held on to it with a healthy determination. In place of the cross-eyed, fighting look with which he used to arrive, he would walk in, look me firmly in the eye and state his intention of remaining at the top of the mountain for a very long time. At length this communication was reduced to a kind of shorthand: he would walk in, look at me and say 'Ten years.' All our sessions began and ended at the top of the mountain. I sometimes brought in other stories, which he was prepared to entertain so long as we began and ended them in the place where he wanted to be. At his suggestion we even had an excursion from the mountain top to eat clouds.

Never at any point did we discuss the symbolism of the story or its relevance for Philip. To have done so would have felt like an intrusion into a kind of sacred space, for the story had a power and a reality that both addressed and transcended any personal associations that might have attached themselves to it. There was just one occasion, significantly in the moments after we completed our work on this story, when Philip found a need to talk about it: even then he stayed quite naturally within the boundaries of Sesame's oblique approach, talking about what had happened in terms of his role in the story – though it was clear from the way he talked that he was connecting with it quite deeply and in a personal way.

The end came about in a manner that felt quite natural. We were coming to the end of the summer term. I said there would be quite a few weeks when we would not be doing drama together and then I asked him 'Do you think the Sumi wrestler could go down from the mountain and have his big fight in front of the Emperor on the last day of drama before the holidays?' He thought for a few moments and said 'Yes. All right.' After two more sessions up the mountain, he arrived on the last day ready for the big event. The women in the story gave him their cow to sell and buy a big, beautiful belt. Wearing it, he entered the Emperor's palace and defeated all comers,

returning to the mountain top in triumph with his bag of gold. As Grandmother, I told him he could marry my granddaughter and they could live in
our house. The Mother and Grandmother moved into another house nearby.

'Is that the end?' he said. 'Yes. He stayed there and helped the women to
farm their land.' 'And I lived in the house with my wife?' 'Yes.' 'And if
anybody tried to hurt my wife, I could fight them and protect her?' 'Yes, of
course you could, because you are the champion, stronger than anyone else.'
'So no one could hurt her?' 'No.' That seemed to satisfy him, but then he
started to look bit lost and said 'What am I going to do next week?' I said
'There won't be drama for a while – but after the holidays we'll be back.
Then we can do some more stories.'

When we met again in the autumn he didn't request the Sumi Wrestler:
apparently it had run its course and he was ready for new experiences. We
worked one-to-one for another year, in the course of which he would
sometimes request a particular story: he knew *The Wizard of Oz* better than
I did and asked me to play Dorothy while he played all the other parts in
turn. He was gaining height and strength: gone were the days when the
strong Grandmother could carry him around under one arm. Then I was ill
and missed a whole term, during which Philip worked on his own with Mary
and Rodger. They kept me in touch with news of all the children and I was
very interested in what they told me about Philip. When they told him I
wouldn't be coming for a while he showed no obvious reaction to the news.
However, he made immediate and dramatic changes in his use of sessions.
He had always looked to me to bring in stories and lead his session. Now
he took over the role of story-teller. He also taught them the rules of drama:
how you don't actually fight, because although you can punch and kick you
don't make contact with the other person's body: 'You do shadow boxing.'
he said – and demonstrated. My unplanned absence seemed to pitch him
into a big developmental step and he was able to use the situation to work
with Mary and Roger in a new and creative way, simultaneously holding on
to me and what we had done together as part of his inner world. In
psychological terms it could be said that he had developed the power to
symbolize. Interestingly, a short while after this big shift in his work with
drama, it was discovered that Philip could read.

The stories he told to Mary and Rodger had, like Jason's, a strong flavour
of tradition with recognizable themes and motifs from stories he had worked
on with me, including heroes and monsters and helpful old people in the
background teaching you how to fight. When I returned the following term,
I had the pleasure of hearing some of these stories and taking part in their
enactment. There was no reason for him to go on working one-to-one as he

was now well able to work in the art form and even share a session with another child for his last term at Beech Lodge. One day, shortly before he left, he suddenly said to me at the beginning of a session 'You were here when I arrived, weren't you? You know me very well!'

Perhaps Philip is a special case, as we really did work through a lot of things in his solo sessions, but in a sense this observation could be extended to include all the children who have taken part in Sesame work during their residence at Beech Lodge. Working with symbolic material over that kind of time-span, we get to know them at a level far deeper than ordinary, outward interactions allow. Interaction in drama and story is an experience akin to stepping into one another's dreams. When a child chooses a story and chooses a part to play in that story, those of us who stand beside the child in that place are privileged to share in a personal fantasy world. It is a sharing that requires tactful handling. Simon was a boy who showed little interest in combative roles and eventually said that what he really wanted was to be Cinderella. His request led to a very enjoyable and satisfying session: *Cinderella* is the world-wide transformation story with which boys, in their heart of hearts, seem to identify as strongly as girls – though few have the courage or opportunity to enact the fantasy. Simon also asked for *Hansel and Gretel*, a harsh story of abandonment which at that time we would have thought twice about bringing in ourselves, and *Pinocchio*, in which he showed a sensitive awareness of needing to soften his defended, wooden persona and become 'a real boy'.

So far I have written only about boys, who have outnumbered the girls throughout the five years that Sesame has been at Beech Lodge. It so happens that I have personally led more session work with boys than with girls, on whose needs Mary has tended to focus more attention. The way we work is for each of us to take responsibility for leading a particular session for a whole term, during which the person in charge of the session carefully monitors the progress of the child or children in it and chooses appropriate stories and movement work, while the other two therapists join in the session by playing parts in the story and generally supporting the action. I have therefore been present in a lot of work with the girls, though not necessarily shaping and leading it. We worked with mixed groups to begin with, but soon gave this up because diversions, including violence and sexualized behaviour, interfered too much with what we were there to do. We also recognized that there were some sexually-based differences in the use that the boys and the girls made of their sessions, which we could meet more easily by separating them. As time went on and the level of disturbance in the children coming to Beech Lodge seemed to increase, we also found that most of them did better if we worked with them in pairs and sometimes individually. For these reasons we now do more sessions, but the sessions are shorter than they used to be. This means the children all get prime attention in a situation where we are able to be more open and playful than we could be if we were constantly having to keep a larger group in order.

To generalize, the girls we have worked with have tended to be less violent than the boys, expressing their anger and pain in less physical ways, including bad language and subtle projection, goading the boys to act out in their vicinity and looking on with quiet, satisfied smiles. Having said that, the first girl we worked with was famously violent. Alison, at 11, had the look of a sophisticated 17-year-old: she would arrive for her sessions smiling broadly and embrace you, but might at the same moment hit you over the head with a hairbrush. She seemed to love drama and always arrived with her own ideas for the session – something we usually encourage, but with her it was a manic bid for control and she sometimes needed to be brought down to size. In *Grandmother's Footsteps* one day, she insisted on a turn as Grandmother and stood dangerously over our recumbent forms, shouting at point blank range: 'You moved! Go back to the start!'

After we had endured this bullying for a few moments, I said 'Grandmother, we are your grandchildren and we are tired. Could we stop this and come and visit you, in your house?' It was a long shot, but it produced an instant and surprising transformation. Alison walked to the end of the room and arranged some covers over a table, creating a makeshift 'house'. She then disappeared inside and was silent. We approached the house and Liza knocked on her door saying 'Grandmother, may we come in, please?' A voice from inside answered rather quietly 'Yes, all right, you can come in.' She pulled aside the entrance cover and said 'Look – I've got presents for you' We said we had brought a picnic. She thanked us in a small, gentle voice we had never heard before. After the picnic she started to produce individual presents for us from inside the house. 'Here's a ring for you and a bracelet for you and a beautiful scarf for you. There!' she said, draping the scarf round Mary's shoulders. 'That looks lovely. It suits you very well.' As she gave us our gifts, each of us said 'Thank you, Grandmother.' Mary asked if there wasn't something beautiful for her to wear as well, but she replied (significantly, for Alison) 'No. It's all for you. There isn't anything for me, but (here her voice became more cheerful again) I've got some strawberries for you to take home. There you are!' We hugged her and took our leave, all very gentle, and she waved us off before disappearing back into her house. Seconds later she burst forth, brash and noisy as ever and well out of role.

Brief encounters with the sensitive, split-off side of Alison continued to be an occasional feature of our sessions. Each time, the transformation brought a marked change to her voice and facial expression and she became unrecognizably different from her usual self. At these times we all felt painfully protective towards her, sensing a vulnerable, loving nature that had been so severely abused and exploited that, to protect herself, she had buried very, very deep. We always had to establish a real connection with the hurly-burly of her usual disintegrated mode before she would take us with her to that other sane and gentle place. The fact that both modes could be held within her sessions indicates a hope that one day she will find it possible to own and integrate the gentle and loving side of her nature in the self that she presents to the world.

Some of the girls have become very fascinated with movement, taking it way beyond the warm-up work I have described and sometimes choosing to interpret stories with expressive dance movement. There was one small girl, Annie, whose creative gift was initially apparent through the versatility and originality of her swearing. She was a natural for drama and movement, but it took a while to work through the phoney American accent and pert, hip-swaggering manner that she felt she had to put on when playing a role. It was on her down days, when she was too depressed and defeated to strut the stage, that she began to respond in a more natural way when we just stayed with her, rocking her with gentle movements or telling a story while she lay curled up in her sleeping bag. On these days she liked to relax with us, shoulder-to-shoulder or back-to-back. In the course of almost three years of sessions she came to understand the worlds of story, drama and movement at a deep and satisfying level. She sometimes asked if she could lead a whole session, showing a sensitive understanding of the medium as we use it, down to checking if we were happy doing what she required of us. In one of her last sessions she brought in a story we had never done with her – Hans Anderson's *Little Mermaid* – and told it right through before we all enacted it in movement with her (naturally!) in the title role. A while back, an event like this would have been quite an ego trip for Annie, but on this occasion the art form seemed to take over and we were all touched by the poignant beauty and authenticity of what she did with the story, which mirrored something of her own sorrow and sense of betrayal. She also liked to work with movement in an abstract way, conveying humour and fun, as well as darker feelings, through pure movement without a story to lean on. When she moved on to an adopting family, Annie was planning to go on doing drama in a new setting.

I have written about seven of the eighteen children we have worked with intensively over the five years we have been at Beech Lodge. The others were just as interesting in their unique ways of homing in on Sesame and taking from it what they needed. My purpose in describing some interactions in close-up has been to show the Sesame approach in action, working through symbol and the art form, without any need for interpretation, to relate it to the children's personal material. We simply provide a place called Sesame for them to come to and discover different aspects of themselves within the art form. If they have anything to say about their discoveries we, of course, listen. But we leave the business of making links with their personal experience to their psychotherapist, whose proper task it is.

I would like to conclude by acknowledging that the ongoing work in this challenging setting depends to an extraordinary degree on the trust and openness that exists between individual members of the Sesame team. As initiator of the project, I am fully aware of the extent to which its success rests on the support I had from Billy at the start and on my colleagues taking an equal share of responsibility in the session work. All those named in this chapter have worked at Beech Lodge for over a year, while Mary was there within a few weeks of me and is there still. The work has become an important part of our long-term friendship. In acknowledging my colleagues, it feels important to give their names in full, in order of appearance: Mary Smail, Elizabeth (Liza) Gall, Pamela Marshall and Rodger Winn. And a special acknowledgement to Marian Lindvist (Billy), who came to help launch the project and stayed for a year!

References

Bettelheim, B. (1976) *The Uses of Enchantment*. London: Thames and Hudson.

Campbell, J. (1949) *The Hero with a Thousand Faces*. Princeton: Bollingen.

Jung, C.G. (1940) 'The Phenomenology of the Spirit in Fairy-tales.' In *Collected Works* Vol.9. London: Routledge.

Riordan, J. (1984) 'Three strong women.' In *The Woman in the Moon and Other Tales of Forgotten Heroines*. London: Hutchinson.

von Franz, M.L. (1970) *The Interpretation of Fairy-tales*. Dallas: Spring Publications.

Winnicott, D.W. (1964) *The Child, the Family and the Outside World*. London: Penguin.

CHAPTER 23

Children Without Words
Sesame in Romania

Barbara Goossens

In December 1990, following the overthrow of the dictator Ceaucescu, I was among many horrified readers of newspaper reports about the discovery in Romania of houses full of children, abandoned by parents who could not afford to rear them. The background to this was a political one. Ceaucescu had decreed that every couple should have at least five children. The resultant poverty was so dire that people began to look for ways to get rid of children they could not support. One obvious, though terrible, answer was to dump children in government-funded homes for the 'irrecuperably' disabled. If the child was not disabled, there were doctors who could be persuaded to find 'something wrong' and supply a report to this effect. In this way, large numbers of children, many of them quite healthy, were abandoned to their fate in the state homes.

After Ceaucescu's overthrow, people entering these 'homes' discovered children who had been crowded together and subjected to extraordinary neglect, many of them kept in bed round the clock and unable to walk, talk or respond to attempts to communicate with them. This was in the news shortly after I completed the Sesame training and something deep inside me reacted very strongly. I thought 'I must go to Romania and see what I can do to help.'

In retrospect, I think I may have been influenced in my response by something quite specific and personal. My experience of Sesame, as a student-in-training, had brought me in touch with other people in a way that felt quite new, reaching a part of me that had felt isolated throughout my life – on account of the fact that I am hard of hearing. Though I managed my education – including quite a tough training in drama at East 15 acting school, because I can lip-read and use invisible hearing aids – I have carried from childhood a sense of being shut-off in a world of my own. But my experiences within the group at Sesame, having contact with people at a very deep level within an art form, had me feeling 'in touch' in a new way.

Now here were children so out of touch, so alone in their neglect, that no one seemed to be reaching them. Their situation was worlds away from my own, since I was fortunate to grow up in a close and loving family – and yet, because of my particular experience of feeling shut-off from people by hearing impairment, I felt a possibility of understanding something about them. I felt I could reach them by using what I had learnt on the Sesame training, so I joined a group of volunteers who were going out to Romania to work with the children. I went for three weeks and then returned later for another three weeks. In between the two trips I went to Billy for some intensive supervision.

The situation in which I found myself with those children was such that I had no choice but to work, as Sesame enables us to do, from myself – from the gut, rather than any theory about what I should be doing. I was confronted with children no one knew anything about. Most of the files contained incorrect information because of the dishonest transactions around their admission to the homes. The word that came up most often was 'irrecuperable', implying that the child in question was disabled beyond recovery, though there were no details as to what this disability consisted of. Since the original diagnosis was most likely to have been a lie to justify abandoning the child, there was little point in pursuing the history any further.

In most cases, all that was known about a child was what met the eye. The fact that I didn't speak Romanian was not a disadvantage, since most of the children couldn't speak at all. I quickly realized that here was a situation in which I would have to rely on intuition, combined with two basic tools of Sesame that I knew to be reliable from my training placement with people with autistic tendencies: Billy's Movement with Touch and Laban's analysis of movement.

I was with a group of workers consisting mainly of nurses and students. There were plenty of volunteers helping to look after the main group of children in the Children's Home to which I was assigned, so I decided to concentrate mainly on those children who did not come rushing and cling on, but crawled away to hide or found it hard to make contact with anyone. All the children needed individual attention, but these were the hardest to reach. Being rewarded with a glance, a smile or any response at all after long hours of trying to reach them told me that my efforts were worthwhile.

I helped to look after 63 children on a daily basis. All were psychologically and/or physically disabled, but by no means 'irrecuperable' as their
files suggested. The sad truth was that many of them would have been normal
children if they had stayed with their families, instead of being shoved into
crowded homes with the minimum of care just to keep them alive. Our task
now was to provide human contact and stimulation, to let the children know
that someone cared. Even in the home where I worked, which was one of
the better ones, the staff didn't have the training or the time to give the
children the attention they needed.

This was my first experience of working on my own. Looking back on
it now, after nearly five years as a drama and movement therapist on the staff
of a psychiatric clinic in my home city of Zurich, I recognize that I had only
just begun to have an understanding of the complex theoretical base upon
which Sesame work is grounded. What I did have, which enabled me to go
about my task with confidence and achieve real results, was a capacity to
work from the gut, to use myself as a resource for making contact with the
inner world of the other person. I still believe this to be the central strength
of the Sesame approach to dramatherapy. The fact that we had a full year of
experiential learning as a group, allowing time and space for aspects of
ourselves to find a voice through the art form, puts two very precious tools
into the hands of the Sesame therapist: a real awareness, born of observing
other members of the group, that in all our clients there are hidden,
unexpressed feelings and energies waiting for a chance to come out and,
closely linked to this, a grounded confidence that comes of being in touch
with my own inner world, which enables me to encounter the inner world
of the other with recognition and fellow feeling. The fact that we are used
to working in a non-verbal way means that these attitudes can be brought
into any situation, including work with children whose language we do not
know and who, in most cases, do not communicate through language at all.

This was the base from which I worked. It provided me with a structure
that supported me, where others often had difficulty even beginning to
bridge the divide between themselves and the children. The descriptions that
follow illustrate ways in which the Sesame approach enabled me to push
open the doors behind which some of the children had become shut away
and apparently unreachable. What I did with them was essentially the same
as what I now do with patients I work with in the psychiatric clinic – reaching
them not through any knowledge or theory about what is 'wrong' with them,
but by making contact with the healthy part of them and giving them an
impulse to make the essential move towards me, towards life, towards
whatever is going to give life a meaning for them. The patients I work with

are mostly in the clinic for only three months. I don't believe you can heal someone who is mentally ill in three months, but I do believe you can give them an impulse that will help them towards healing themselves. A lot of the work I do here is non-verbal, as it was with the Romanian children, because that way you get a direct expression. If you don't use words, things will happen which come straight from your guts. You may not like it to begin with, it may be quite a shock, but it comes from deep within you. This means that it comes charged with energy and meaning. It's real!

In many ways, the work I did with the children in Romania was like this. I had even less time with them, but my hope is that some if the things we did together helped to start a movement, an impulse, that was useful. I will give some illustrations. There were three children I worked with quite intensively. All three were non-verbal, so we communicated through Movement with Touch and I relied a lot on what I knew from Laban to help me interpret and work with what was happening.

The first child, Anna, was 12 years old. She was physically normal with normal eyesight and hearing, but she was non-verbal. She communicated with sounds – usually a very high, screeching sound, which she made when confronted with anything she didn't know – or just when she wanted to say 'I'd like some milk'. You had to guess from her communications with hands, feet and facial expression what she wanted to say. She was small for her age and skinny, but very strong. She expressed a lot of anger and frustration through sudden attacks of jumping on top of people, trying to hurt them, lashing out, banging her head and screaming. She wasn't good at interacting with other people, preferring to do things on her own. It goes without saying that she was emotionally disturbed.

Once I had decided to concentrate on working with Anna, I set about creating quite a formal structure for our work. I drew up a list of aims in relation to her needs, as I saw them: to build up her trust towards me, encourage initiative in making contact with others and to encourage her to dress herself and become toilet trained. I also aimed to increase her sound vocabulary by encouraging her to communicate with me through a variety of sounds, taking this towards words when I could. All these aims were to be combined with lengthening her concentration span.

It was several days before I could get anywhere near her. She would see me coming and have a quick look at me, but if our eyes met she would run away. It felt as if I was constantly invading her space. I tried to win her interest by doing things that were fun, like playing with the other children and occasionally make an inviting gesture towards her. This eventually worked. She would come and sit with me for a few seconds and be off again. The time she spent with me increased bit by bit.

The space we worked in was a big, uncarpeted room with a concrete floor, equipped with a physio ball and two mats. This we shared with ten other children who were also in need of individual attention. When I started rolling on the mat with the other children, which seemed to be fun and made them laugh, Anna would jump on top of me to make herself heard. I would scrape her off my back and explain with gestures and sounds that she was hurting me, after which she would sit next to me and watch me playing with the others. One day, after she had been watching me roll with the other children, she came and sat looking at the mat. Eventually, she took a turn at rolling with me. We made a low, rhythmic 'Hwuum – hwuum!' sound together as we rolled back and forth. This went on for quite a long time. In that moment, the sound seemed to be about our shared identity.

I kept repeating this sort of thing with her. One morning she came towards me with her usual screeching sound, gave me a big hug, and then ran away. It felt as if we had broken through a huge barrier. After this I began to work with her in a room by ourselves, playing on a mat. We developed our own games, rolling and establishing contact in various ways or just sitting and playing with our hands, dabbing fingers together and saying 'hello' with our feet. This kind of playful, affectionate contact was entirely new to her. I continued to avoid eye contact, as this still seemed to scare her.

During this time Anna began to make progress in her daily routines. She also took an interest in my appearance: if my clothes were not as neat as she thought they should be, she would tidy me up. When I first tried to do the same for her, she ran away – but a time came when she would allow me to straighten up her socks and trousers the way she did mine. She was learning to give and take.

Anna, like the other children, was constantly seen as being 'naughty'. The children tended to get punished for everything, so that they didn't really know the difference between having done something wrong and having an accident. To help Anna to discover this difference, I resolved never to react to her with anger: to set firm limits, but not to punish her or any of the children by hurting them. If they hit each other, I would stroke. If they yelled, I would whisper. I tried to do the opposite to what they did and gave them a hug if they allowed me to. This seemed to work with Anna: she seemed to realize that somebody meant well towards her.

She became very affectionate. When I had time for her we sometimes cuddled up, not making a sound. Sometimes I would rock and make sounds, which she would sometimes join in. Sometimes we just dabbed our fingers.

When she had one of her fits of anger, I would go and sit close to her and often she would come and cuddle up quietly in my lap. She would put her hands over her head or my jumper over her head, making it clear that she didn't want to see anyone: it seemed that she just wanted to feel.

By the time I left, Anna could dress herself properly – though she wasn't quite toilet trained. Her concentration span had increased a lot. She was interacting a lot more with the other children and screeched a lot less. She still would not answer if I spoke to her in words, but her sound vocabulary had increased. We had a special way of communicating with gestures, glances and sounds.

One interaction stays in my mind as a good example of the way I worked with Anna, which also has a clear rationale in Sesame terms. We were at lunch and Anna, disliking the food that was set in front of her, began to screech. She screeched non-stop. Even when I turned her chair around to look her in the face, she went on screeching. At that point I did the one thing that I knew would work: I screeched back! I did it because I knew that it would reach her, being a communication in her own language. For a few seconds we sat there screeching at one another and then, quite suddenly, she burst out laughing. I had called her bluff and she knew it. After that, Anna's screeching ceased to be an unpleasant means of getting her own way. It turned into a joke between us. She knew that if she screeched, I would screech back – and I did. Sometimes we would take the screech down and end up making a different, lower sound – a kind of 'Boo boo boo!' Thus, in Sesame terms, the chorus of screeches had become a 'bridge' towards a new situation in which sound was a shared communication.

Through the way we worked together with sound and movement I tried to give Anna an experience of the mirroring that she was deprived of by very early separation from her mother. My echoing and responding to her sounds meant that she had a sense of having an identity and an effect on her surroundings. The fact that she could be naughty and still receive warmth and hugs meant that there was more to life than a concrete room and a mat. In finding me, she also began to find herself.

The second child to whom I gave close attention was Anton, a boy of nine with normal eyesight and hearing who was also non-verbal. He had only learnt to walk in the three months before I met him. He walked with sudden, indirect movements – a bit like a robot – and always in straight lines. He was small and skinny and his head looked too large and seemed to feel heavy to him, as though he was not in full control of it. Being so thin made his body look more fragile than it actually was. He was full of tricks and avid for attention, making it clear that he wanted play, not cuddles. He was quite unable to dress himself and was not toilet trained.

My aims with Anton were to encourage a mutual trust, greater response and greater concentration, to improve his ability to interact with me and the other children and to encourage him to feed and clothe himself and become toilet trained.

Though able to walk, Anton was still not very safe on his feet. He had been moved from living in a small room to the big Home, where he suddenly had lot more space and made an important discovery: a ball, which was his favourite toy. He chased this ball for hours on end and it was the perfect therapy for his physical development. Within a month, Anton could walk without problems and within two months he was running after the ball.

Because he loved the ball, I often used it in my interactions with him. This felt obvious, though I was also following the Sesame way of starting with the material that the client brings in. I hid the ball under my jumper, which at first he found very confusing. He would try to find it without success. I would eventually point out where it was, but not give it to him: he had to lift my jumper over the ball and get it out. At first this was too complicated for him and I had to help: it was several weeks before he could get it out himself. When he became frustrated with his efforts, I made sure there was plenty of laughter to maintain his concentration.

To channel his rather wild energy, which had him throwing the ball up into the air all the time and in every direction, I tried to teach him to give it to me by placing it in my hand. This was very hard for him because he often shook a lot and couldn't hold his hands still. At first the ball would end up on the floor, always to my left. We practised playfully until he was able to put it into my hands. The first time he achieved this, a very big smile spread over his face – clear proof that Anton was intelligent. He hadn't just repeated the action: he had understood its importance. Towards the end of my stay he became able to throw the ball towards me, which was another big achievement for him.

I have said that Anton tended to walk in straight lines. He did this in the 'perky' way that was characteristic of him, often cutting a ninety-degree corner in the middle of the room. To introduce round movements, I did a lot of 'turns' with him – swinging him in the air, turning a pirouette and running races in a circle. These games were energetic and his energy, which had been repressed up till now, came bursting out. He particularly liked 'See-saw': we would sit on the floor facing one another, holding hands and taking turns to lie back and pull the other one up, with a regular rhythm like a see-saw. Anton had little sounds with which he communicated and we gradually extended his 'tune', which he kept repeating, by bringing in new sounds. Next to the ball, the greatest therapy for Anton was laughing. He never made a serious business of anything.

In my notes, shortly before I left, I wrote:

> Working with Anton has been great fun and he is a much more contented and happy child... He has grown a little and is much stronger physically on account of his constant movement and running after his ball. He seems to have put on some weight as well... He now relates to me and recognizes me: he comes up to me and gestures for specific games and actions... To start with he would not share anything with the other children. Now he will join hands with others and sometimes even play with them, sharing his ball. He remains a bit of a loner: I often find him by himself, amusing himself perfectly. He now feeds himself, which is a great achievement for him... Dressing and toilet training haven't yet been achieved. His sound vocabulary has increased: he makes a lot of different sounds and laughs and giggles often. Words still don't mean a thing to him. His concentration has increased a little: the ball games have been going on for longer, as have the movement sessions. Basically, as long as there is excitement he shows interest. If I had more time, I would continue to increase his control of his movements, with which he has already made lots of progress. I would try to develop round movements, sustainment and stillness, alongside grounding his energies.

The third child was John, a boy aged 11 or 12. His eyesight seemed normal (though he had one lazy eye), but his hearing showed a slight loss and he sometimes seemed to be lip-reading. He would focus his attention on my mouth and seem to be imitating mouth movements, without making any sound. He was non-verbal but made a lot of sounds. If talking to someone for a short while, he would change his mechanical sounds of 'guh guh guh' and 'djg djg' into round sounds of 'mah mah' and 'bah bah'. He was fully mobile and looked younger than his age.

My aims with John were to encourage mutual trust and greater response and concentration; to ground his swinging moods and his fidgety energy by centering him with challenging and channelling exercises, and for him to learn to feed himself.

I discovered that he was musical. In the course of two months I worked with him on rhythm and beat, to gain his attention and channel his energy. I would clap my rhythms against his hands, arms and thighs and he would often join in. To begin with he took my hands and repeated the motion. Then he started to shrug his own shoulders to the beat. After that he used his own hands. In this manner, and through other games, he slowly began to communicate with me.

I also brought in a lot of 'centering' work as he got frustrated and fidgety sitting about all day. I would sit him on my lap, spread his arms out by holding his hands, and then bring them in onto his tummy, saying his name as I did so. This is an exercise we learned on the autistic placement with Billy. The action always made him smile. I also worked with 'fine touch' stroking and dabbing movements[1] with his hands and feet, feeling the contrast between these gentle movements and his rather harsh surroundings. He had little awareness of his feet, but was constantly busy with his hands. If they were not in his mouth they would be grabbing something. Stroking and dabbing were new sensations for him. At first he pulled back, but gradually he consented to remain seated, playing with my hands.

We sometimes conversed in *gobbledegook*.[2] When I used real words I would speak slowly and make sure that he could see my mouth. He often tried to shape his mouth after mine, but couldn't manage to speak.

To bring fresh stimulations into his life I began taking John outside. We would listen to different sounds – tapping the wooden landing, tapping a tree, tapping a metal pole, tapping the wall. We would listen to the wind and the water or just touch the surface of a tree, a wall, or the smoothness of a leaf. These sensations were new to him and he just melted when we did these things, becoming calm and happy and relaxed. The tension would leave his shoulders and face and he would start to smile.

He was a very fidgety and energetic child as well as very strong, which may be why no one had taken him outside the grounds of the Home before. I found him much calmer outside. After about ten minutes he would calm down and begin to relate to things. I always held his hand because he didn't know the dangers of the outside world and he would pull my hand as a sign

---

1   'Fine touch' is a Laban term for movements that are gentle, flexible and sustained, of which 'stroking' is an example. When using Movement with Touch with people who have a lot of energy, it becomes possible to achieve 'fine touch' movements, which are poetic and rather dreamy in quality, only after the energy has been channelled and released through engagement in strong, direct movement.

2   Gobbledegook – improvised nonsense language – can be very expressive, whether it is spoken or sung. It is often used in Sesame drama and in vocal exercises, such as improvised opera, since it frees the user to express feeling without needing to remember, or construct, a verbal script. For exactly the same reasons, it can be useful with non-verbal clients.

that he wanted to go running. He loved running and it made him laugh. The colourful markets were of no interest to him. If he saw an apple he might just grab it and eat it. His greatest joy was the big lorries: he would stand still in awe as they passed by, and for about a minute after they had disappeared, wondering what that great big thing could have been. He ignored cars. Now and then he would shriek and giggle with joy. I was embarrassed one day when he demonstrated his joy by rolling on the pavement.

There were a lot of quiet moments when we simply sat together with his head lying against my chest, holding my hands, and maybe fiddling with my fingers, just relaxing and gazing into space. If I put him on a swing he would giggle with joy. I could see him lapping up the sun's rays as they touched his face. These were the most important moments of all. John was experiencing the sunny side of life.

One evening, as I walked into the room to say goodnight, our eyes met and a big smile spread across his face. He stopped what he was doing and headed straight towards me. He had never done such a thing before. He was a very introverted person and I was still under the impression that I was only an object to him – but for some reason it seemed to have clicked with him that I was someone who cared about him. We had a little conversation in *gobbledegook* and his hands kept touching the jacket I was wearing. He just sat beside me, making it clear that he wanted me to stay. If I turned my head to another child he would place his hand on my shoulder to get my attention. Several days later I was the first person he ever hugged.

As well as working one-to-one with individual children, I established a nightly ritual for the group which was known as the 'special session'. It took place at 6 pm, just before they went to bed. This was a time when the younger children were on the toilet or brushing their teeth. The older children were always dealt with first, so they would be all ready for bed when they came to our evening session. This was a short Sesame session on the lines of Billy's sessions for people with autistic tendencies, a familiar ritual with some mat work interspersed with rocking and singing songs. The children loved it and it calmed them down before going to bed, which was otherwise a difficult time because they were so full of energy. John had an amazing experience during a special session: after spending some time doing his favourite 'rocking ship' movement, we did some mat work to release energy and he was amazed to find he had done a backward somersault! For him in particular, this chance to release the energy that was still bursting out of him at the end of the day made it possible to relax and have a more peaceful night.

In my report on John, I wrote:

> I never thought I would be much more than an object to him, but he now comes up to me, I get big hugs and he stays with me. These to me are signs of safety, trust and recognition... He always responds to me, even if it is just by observing my actions. He translates them in his own time. His concentration is improving: 35 minutes has been the longest so far. His mood still swings and the energy is still there, thank God! Outings to the market have calmed him a lot. Best of all, in terms of grounding, was the 'special session' after supper. He now feeds himself: it's still a bit messy, but a great achievement... If he gets the chance, he will tell stories in *gobbledegook*! They last for ever. He recognizes his name, for he smiles when I say it – but he does not speak it yet.

The three very different children I have described taught me a lot about life, for which I am deeply grateful. We seemed to achieve a lot together in a little time. I knew when I left that they would need a huge amount of help if they were to go on and find an acceptable degree of that quality we call happiness in their lives. My hope was that by beginning to push open the door I might have given them a glimpse, an incentive, to help them on their way.

CHAPTER 24

Poetry in Motion
Drama and Movement Therapy with People with Learning Disabilities

Jocelyne James

Much of this chapter is concerned with the territory of non-verbal experience. Translating this into a comprehensible text proves quite challenging in itself because, to understand such experiential processes, more than just our rational, intellectual functions must be engaged. We need our senses, our feelings and our intuition. The written and spoken word occupy a prioritized position in society and have grown to be equated with our notion of communication. However, my work as a Sesame Practitioner very much inspired by the Sesame Course, involves the exploration and development of other, often somehow lost, forgotten or abandoned languages – those of the arts.

Amongst the many verbally articulate people with learning disabilities I have worked with, there have also been some who have found it practically impossible to express themselves in words. Because the way in which we speak and the content of what we say informs our sense of self and relationship to others, for these individuals there is a danger that life may become meaningless and isolated. I am very much aware that discovering the ability to talk without words, to speak through the arts, can have a profound effect, and I am amazed at the 'dramatic movements' I have witnessed in people. For many, gaining access to other forms of self-expression – including, in particular, drama and movement – has been a powerful and transformative experience.

I cannot do justice to the range and depth of theory and philosophy which underpins this work in the space of a single chapter, but perhaps I can capture something of its potential in practice. Therefore I would like to consider the significant relationship between the creative and healing processes in this context, focusing on specific moments in my own working experience to illustrate the connection.

It is clear that the psyche finds natural expression through images. They form the vocabulary of our dreams, which Freud termed 'the Royal Road to the Unconscious'. Bettelheim (1982) celebrates the symbolic quality of art: 'Because poets speak in metaphors about the contents of the unconscious, Freud insisted that they and other great artists knew all along what he had to discover through laborious work'.

An example of such poetic consciousness in action in the therapeutic context was offered by a young woman who, when I first met her, though able to use words effectively, rarely spoke. She was extremely quiet and shy, but gaining confidence in her expressive freedom. One morning she arrived in the session to announce:

> My aunt has a garden.
> It is full of red roses,
> and pink roses.
> They are growing,
> And I am growing.

The simple and clear identification with the blooms described the essence of how she was experiencing herself. Another young man, aged 22, had been told by doctors that he would die before the age of 16. He shared with me the defiant metaphor 'Well, I beat the sell-by date on that can of coke!' Jung conceived of imagistic perception as psychological vision, suggesting that to see through the literal to the symbolic is to glimpse soul.

The arts facilitate the emergence and development of imagery – whether auditory, in the case of music, percussion and voice; visual, in the case of art mediums such as paint, pastel and clay; or kinaesthetic, in the case of dance and movement. Poetic and dramatic forms may combine any and all of these sensory functions.

Music can capture specific moods, atmospheres or feelings so that complex and intense emotional states can be expressed where words are either unavailable or futile. During enactments, individuals might choose an instrument to act as their voice, allowing percussive conversations to emerge between people who literally cannot otherwise speak. Also, for those who are verbally fluent, a musical instrument can sometimes provide the opportunity to express the essence of what is being communicated more poignantly than words.

Dance and movement awakens and deepens the connection between psyche and soma. My work is body-centred, and particularly so with this client group. Jung claimed 'the symbols of the Self arise in the depths of the body' (1940). Before training at Sesame I felt very cut-off from my body and much identified with the thought patterns and processes in my head. As a result of the course I experienced a deep initiation through movement into self-discovery. I have witnessed a similar process take place for 'people with learning disabilities' as movement speaks to and through the body, giving shape and form to experiences that are beyond words. Acknowledging our physicality to this extent allows clients to discover hidden languages for self-expression and contact.

Stories, myths, fairy-tales and legends from many countries and cultures provide a wealth of imaginary stimulus and are an infinitely rich source of wisdom, knowledge and understanding. Exploring world mythology and literature through drama in this context has led to both the acknowledgement and the celebration of cultural differences. Archetypal patterning in figures, themes or narratives can represent roles and relationships within the individuals or the group's psychic order and development. Through experiential identification with and/or enactment of symbolic material, very real and valuable insights can emerge and specific conflicts can be explored, expressed and potentially resolved, metaphorically, through the dramatic medium. The same room within an adult education centre, once invested with the power of the imagination and the integrity of the dramatic illusion, can become the site of unlimited inner and outer journeys.

An integrative multi-sensory approach which actively stimulates the IMAGE-ination for self-exploration can promote extraordinary growth, development, healing and change. This is particularly relevant for individuals who may suffer from differing forms of sensory impairment. There are many different structures and frameworks through which individuals can experiment with their abilities to both initiate and respond, greatly strengthening their sense of self in the process. As Winnicott suggests, 'It is in playing that the individual child or adult is able to be creative and to use the whole personality, and it is only in being creative that the individual discovers the self' (1971).

Each member of a group might individually offer an image in sound and/or movement for what their emotional state is at that time – what is happening inside them. One person may close the body and cower away, allowing a tiny whine to emerge. Another my bounce up and down, grinning and shrieking with delight. These movements are dependent upon the spontaneous freedom of the individual in that moment. Sometimes a specific verbal image is added: 'a frightened mouse' or 'a strong, free horse'. After each contribution, the rest of the group will copy and reflect back the precise quality of gesture and sound. This provides essential insight and an opportunity to both empathize and identify with each other's different energies and moods.

One woman who joined a group was particularly withdrawn, with no language to say how she felt. During this work she put her hands to her head and screamed long and loud. Sharing this very poignant truth, and having it acknowledged and understood by peers, seemed to provide significant relief. The very act of giving shape and form to her feelings was transformative in itself, and from here she began to build bridges.

We might play a mirroring game in pairs, where both individuals initiate and respond to each other as though they were the reflected counterpart in a looking glass. There has been an enormous amount of psychological research concerned with the role and value of mirroring in healing early problems of child development. My experience of movement has proved that this simple act has an extraordinary effect in strengthening the sense of self.

There are numerous individuals who may have begun this exercise with a slightly reluctant inflection in the fingers. When a partner imitates this movement exactly, it is as though a light goes on in the person's face. The fingers become a waving hand and the other waves back. Both arms begin to sway and, yes, the partner's do, too. Feet tap, legs lift, and before long both are using their whole bodies and taking risks together. They are indeed dancing!

Recently some group members brought along a new client to an ongoing session. 'His legs are in callipers and he doesn't speak,' they explained, 'but he could watch us.' I offered this simple mirroring exercise to music, inviting him to participate. The woman sitting opposite him whispered to me 'How are we going to do it? He can't do it – he doesn't understand!' I invited her to go ahead and try. She put up her hands, palms facing him, and he did exactly the same. She extended an arm and he followed her. She mapped a circle through the air and he copied. From here, the two performed a beautiful piece of improvised, synchronized dance work. When they had finished, both their cheeks were wet with tears, having been so 'moved' and 'touched' by their mutual self-realization. *A Gift of Healing* suggests that:

> Healing is a thought
> by which two minds
> perceive their oneness
> and become glad. (Walsh 1988)

There was a great sense of celebration and occasion in the group, who applauded and cheered the event. A new sense of himself and of this man's relation to others had emerged and the memory of the immense joy on his face will remain with me for a long time.

This work might be extended to involve the whole group when, in a circle, someone enters the middle, leading everyone else in improvised movement. In the centre, people share their idiosyncratic movement patterns whilst those around the edge pick up new ones through observation and imitation. This expands the potential movement vocabulary of each person within the group, providing more freedom and choice. The process involves both supporting and depending, trusting and taking responsibility, holding and being held.

A similar framework can be effective for exploring voice, which is an integral part of the body. Instead of reflecting movements, we might call and respond, or chant and echo. Removing the emphasis from words eliminates the pressure to construct meaningful sentences. This, added to an atmosphere rooted in unconditional positive regard, can allow whatever sound is present to flow freely. I notice this is particularly liberating for people with hearing impairment who might otherwise rarely use their voices due to the constant signing of all dialogue. For them it can prove enormously satisfying to experiment unselfconsciously with their ability to create sound. Some have been inspired to really sing out for the first time in their lives.

One man I worked with had no voice at all when I first met him. In exercises of this nature he seemed unable to produce sounds of any kind. It was during a dramatic enactment in which he played the role of a dragon that he first discovered his voice. Whilst using his arms and hands in a gestural display to demonstrate fire-breathing, out from his mouth emerged a penetrating noise that stopped us all in our tracks. This was a very surprising and extraordinary moment for everyone involved. It was the embodiment of the image of the dragon that empowered his voice, which continues to grow in volume and definition to this day.

As well as self-generated sound, pre-recorded musical stimulus is a regular feature and can have a powerfully evocative effect, allowing us to reach within and unleash hidden impulses. We have all experienced the effects of pieces of music which perhaps encourage us to cry and feel nostalgic, to be uplifted or full of grief, love, joy or pain. It inspires and affects the emotional world.

One lady who had no words and was notably tense, withdrawn and tightly bound, was very responsive to music. When I first met her she was somewhat stiff and immobile and demonstrated a unique behavioural pattern which involved sticking both fingers in her ears, while at the same time making a loud buzzing sound. The volume of this sound increased if anyone approached her. On hearing Vivaldi's *Spring* one day, she began to weep. The streaming tears seemed to unblock waves of intense feeling and sensation. The release of such deeply held emotional tension allowed her body to soften and relax, liberating energy for movement. While still crying, she began to breathe more freely and flow quite naturally to the rhythm of the music. Staying in close physical touch and moving empathically with her, I noticed that she was completely aware of her self, her own presence, whilst being open and willing to engage with me for the first time. This emotional thaw marked the beginning of the end of her isolating behaviours, which had defended her from contact both with herself and with other people. I imagined a block of ice melting.

Touch can be an integral aspect of group drama or movement. I encourage the development of confidence in this area through many different activities, including games, massage and relaxation. Many people with limited vocabulary have also inherited the physical inhibitions and reserve renowned in our culture. Understandably, they gain immensely from being given the opportunity and permission to touch. It can be a valuable and direct route to enhancing the quality of relationship and communication.

I am reminded of the controversial experiments that Harlow and Zimmerman carried out with Rhesus monkeys in 1958. Given the choice of two artificial surrogate mothers, one made of wire and loaded with milk and the other of soft cloth but with no accompanying food, the monkeys repeatedly chose the latter at the expense of nourishment from the former. From this it might be deduced that for human beings, too, tactile experience could be as necessary and crucial as feeding. Within the context of therapeutic work it can be a source of reassurance and comfort, a demonstration of unity, care and support, where words are inadequate. Touch has always been a healing art in its own right.

Experience has led me to have great faith in the art form's inherent power to facilitate expression whilst simultaneously containing it. This is very apparent in constructing rituals that channel so-called 'negative' emotions creatively. These can be very effective when working with people with challenging behaviours who may need to understand and integrate difficult feelings. One technique is to ritualize aggression in the form of choreographed or enacted fights, with firm boundaries suitable to the needs of each group. One way of doing this is to restrict, or even ban, actual physical contact: the blows must stop short of their bodily target. Then, when both trust and dramatic distance are established, physical contact can be encouraged. Partners can improvise and perform their own unique dramatic fantasies through mime: examples have included boxing matches, duels at dawn, archery, shoot-outs, fencing, Kung-fu and other martial arts.

This not only allows interpersonal conflicts to be expressed safely: it also evokes the archetype of the Hero or Warrior, the 'fighting spirit'. I do not underestimate the psychological 'battle' that has to be fought by individuals who struggle against not only physiological problems, but also social, political and ideological factors.

One very anti-social woman, who rarely interacted with others and had been fairly uninterested in dance and movement, suddenly discovered an enthusiasm for body-work as a result of these rituals. Characteristically, she insisted on working alone and gained a compelling pleasure from acting out karate-style gestures, kicks and shouts. They seemed to articulate the essence of her personal energy, mood, rhythm and feelings. I had never seen her so lively and engaged as when she began executing these movements with great skill and commitment. A few weeks later she rushed in to show me a book on martial arts which she had discovered in the library and promptly demonstrated some of the illustrated moves. She was researching and perfecting her style.

Applying Laban's terminology, we might suggest that in the early stages of her experience in the group the 'firm, sudden, direct and bound' movements enabled her to express anger and fear. For many weeks, through movement and music, she repeatedly enacted symbolic attacking and defending procedures. Initially this was in solitude, but later with a partner and then, by invitation, with myself. Having satisfied this need, she began to change the pattern. I noticed her observing others and exploring in herself 'fine touch, sustainment, flexibility and flow', giving shape to more joyful and lyrical qualities in dance.

During group massage and relaxation, she began to make physical contact with others. Through touching and being touched, a gentleness, sensitivity and awareness evolved and, with these, the ability to give and receive – which is necessary for relating. There have been undoubted and observable repercussions concerning the quality of her relations with self, other and the world. This is psyche and soma healing creatively together.

While developing this work I often introduce a cushion as a third object, familiar in Gestalt therapy. Individuals punch, kick, throw, hit and stamp on it with surprising vigour and enthusiasm, releasing very natural, deeply felt frustrations and resentments. It is not unusual now for group members either to use a cushion spontaneously for this purpose or to offer one to someone else at an appropriate moment. It has become an established convention for letting off steam.

Another ritual which acknowledged very painful and difficult emotions was invented through improvisation by a group when a young member of staff died unexpectedly. Many of the complex array of feelings associated with grief were expressed through the dramatic ritual they created. Two older men using drums led the group in a lengthy, sombre procession of mourners. This eventually reached a climax when they created an arch to represent, as they said, 'the gateway to heaven'. Two others sat as guardians at the entrance, receiving symbolic gifts and last words for the deceased. Each member of the group came to pay respects and share messages in the form of images, words and feelings before passing through the arch. As well as being impressed by their creative and imaginative competence, I was very moved by the depth of sadness and love expressed in this unique funereal ceremony or rite of passage.

I have found this client group particularly responsive to masks, both neutral and archetypal. The masks evoke powerful and ritualistic qualities and can unleash primal energies. One example of this occurred with a man I had worked with for eighteen months, who had not yet been able to tap his creative resources. He was rather heavily built and generally quite motionless, lacking in language and showing little interest in the art mediums on offer. I was beginning to question the value of therapy in meeting his needs before the introduction of mask work.

As soon as he saw a mask he stood up and intimated that he should wear it. I offered him musical accompaniment and he entered the space. He immediately became animated, his limbs carving patterns through the air with a greatly heightened sense of body awareness, improvising and exploring a variety of mysterious and wonderful gestures, reaching out and then withdrawing, lifting up and then sinking. He then visited each member of the group and gently stroked their cheeks. They, like me, were astonished and in awe of the graceful balance and co-ordination with which he moved, and in this sudden, surprising change in 'character'. The mask acted as a key to unlock floodgates of expression, inspiring the actor in the previously passive spectator. When he had completed the piece and removed his mask he appeared deeply affected, vulnerable and open. I imagined a child waking from long sleep. After this his participation and involvement in the group increased significantly. Petruska Clarkson claims 'People need to begin to allow themselves to conceive of being different from the way they are. Thus a bridge is created between the current reality and the conceivable self.' (1989)

Another way the dramatic medium has accessed conceivable possibilities is through the enactment of idealized cult figures and pop idols. My groups have ranged in size from four to fifty. In the largest we would sometimes create an atmosphere and set the scene for a rock concert. Each person had the chance to be their favourite star on stage, miming to the music they had chosen. Here the strength of the art form is clearly apparent. Through a process of identification, people owned qualities ascribed to their heroes. Bob Marley, Elvis Presley, Madonna, Cliff Richard, Witney Houston, Jason Donovan and Michael Jackson were just a few of the legendary figures selected on such occasions. One man very capably accessed the powerful and charismatic energy of Gary Glitter and provoked his audience to chant and salute their fists at him...'Come on, come on!... Come on, come on!...' in true Glitter band style. In this group culture I saw people re-inventing their sense of self and relationship with others in the light of uncovering their expressive power and freedom. They discovered within themselves new and exciting attributes which might otherwise have remained projected out onto another. There was an enormous amount of energy and enthusiasm for this work and I was constantly inundated with tapes.

Peter Brook describes the essence of theatre: 'I take an empty space and call it a bare stage. A man walks across this empty space while someone else watches him and this is all that is needed for an act of theatre to be engaged'. (1968). I like this definition and believe that the dramatic integrity of any theatrical illusion lies in imaginative commitment. I find the life-blood of drama, not in any complex tricks or devices but rather in the nature and quality of the relationship between actors and spectators. To create drama is to embody the imagination. It is the natural magic of the psyche.

This client group have been the most intuitive teachers in how to transform play into drama into theatre. They get right inside the art form and breathe it into life. Their ingenious use of simple props exemplifies this gift. I have often used hats to introduce role play and characterization. Hats are clear and simple signifiers which can be interpreted by their wearers in infinitely different ways:

> The space is empty. Sharon picks up a brown, floppy hat and, having bent over, she walks slowly and tentatively, leaning on her imaginary walking stick. She introduces herself as an old lady on her way to the shops to buy cat food. Pausing for a moment, she tells us about her life.
>
> Graham puts on a cap and settles down in an armchair. He is our grandfather. It's late in the evening and we sit around the fire. He has

a tale to share...Stephen decides to join him in the role of Grandmother.

Donovan has found a policeman's helmet. He starts to point and assert authority. He gets out a notebook to write down names and marches two people off to the police station.

Alan covers his face with black velvet. Silence... Stillness... 'I am the dark,' he whispers mysteriously. Total focus and concentration... Eventually he removes it, very carefully, and we breathe again. An atmosphere of respect pervades.

Lilly rushes for the witch's hat and already her face is grinning. Stirring a cauldron, she casts spells, pausing now and then to stroke her cat.

Kevin selects a flamboyant lady's hat and parades the catwalk with style and grace.

Dramatic portraits of this kind allow individuals to step out of their habitual patterns of behaviour and to experiment with other possibilities. The young can glimpse for a moment what it is like to be old, while the shy try out what it is to be sociable. The vulnerable may gain access to an experience of power. The light can meet its counterpart, the darkness. The kindly get a taste of being wicked. Cross-gender casting allows men to get in touch with 'the feminine' and women to make contact with 'the masculine'.

We might also work with embodying the imagination through the dramatic enactment of different animals. The visual stimulus of vivid colourful photographs, added to appropriate vocal or percussive accompaniment, have led to the most extraordinary, dramatic representations of lions, tigers, dogs, badgers, wolves, butterflies, etc. One ostensibly reserved and gentle man who suffered from repeated, violent behavioural outbursts chose to become a wild bear. This gave him the opportunity to claw and snarl in role, thus acknowledging and channelling his vicious impulses creatively. Afterwards he expressed sincere gratitude and relief. Similarly, individuals who were characteristically quiet, sensitive and obliging, became sharks, crocodiles and gorillas, which enabled them to explore their more noisy, challenging and anarchic qualities.

Opposites become integrated through the art form as conscious and unconscious aspects of the personality unite. Fears are played out and potentialities rehearsed. Energy is mobilized and engaged, leading naturally to changes and shifts in relationships and perceptions. Hillman (1983) suggests that 'a healed consciousness lives fictionally'.

In recent years we have been witnessing enormous changes and developments in the attitudes and values relating to this client group. Normalization philosophy is filtering through health, education and social services concerned with re-defining the rights and responsibilities of 'people with learning disabilities' so that they can be integral and complete members of society. There are many excellent community integration schemes in operation and clients are, to put it too simply and metaphorically, making the transition from being 'insubstantial objects' to 'societal subjects' in society. The therapeutic application of drama and movement in this context provides an opportunity for people to come to terms with the psychological, emotional, physical and intellectual and spiritual changes involved in this process.

I have often worked in this context with the powerful imagery of Oscar Wilde's famous fairytale, *The Selfish Giant*. Central to the story is the building of a huge, impenetrable wall by the Giant to prevent people from entering his garden. Within the surrounding protective walls, the Giant spends many years in isolation and the garden is stuck in a permanent state of winter. It is a painful and lonely period which changes at last when a few people manage to climb over the wall. In the trees where they have climbed, blossoms emerge. When the Giant realises what has happened, he chooses to knock down the bricked-up barrier, and as the people return to the garden, so does the long-awaited spring.

Many clients have made symbolic connections between the wall in the story and the barriers between themselves and other members of society. The story reverberates metaphorically in many different directions: it is both unnecessary and inappropriate to make definite or concrete interpretations. The symbolic relevance of such a story will be different for everyone each time. However, the winter in the garden seems to resonate for this client group with barren years of alienation excluded behind institutional walls. Historically, the expectations from these individuals may have been limited and individuals themselves have often experienced profound poverty in the areas of creativity and communication. Clients have identified strongly with the forgotten and misunderstood giant trapped inside the walled garden.

I have sometimes felt, in the course of our drama and movement therapy sessions, that we, like the children in the story, were trying to climb over bricked-up walls of defences and barriers which have cut people off and prevented their potential from flowering. (The so-called 'normal neurotic' population, which amounts to most of us, undoubtedly has its share of these, too.) The energy, enthusiasm and vigorous determination demonstrated by clients knocking down the wall during enactments might be indicative of

Figure 24.1. Mirroring in pairs (photograph by Rebecca Mothersole)

Figure 24.2. The expressive movement (photograph by Rebecca Mothersole)

the strength of feeling involved for them in overcoming these obstacles and restrictions to growth.

One elderly lady I worked with for a number of years described a memory from her youth, when she discovered she was so-called 'mentally handicapped'. She shared some of the rage and agony this had wrought within her. It had meant, she said, that 'I couldn't do any of the things I wanted to do. I wasn't able. I wasn't allowed.' She was aware that after this moment she stopped trying. She didn't take the same risks and ceased to 'strive for' or 'attempt to'. Her self-image was characterized by limitation.

The theatre, in contrast, is a place where anything can happen and everything is possible. The 'empty space' is a forum of opportunity. Jung claimed 'the urge and compulsion to self-realization is a law of nature and thus an invincible power.' (1940). I notice my clients laying claim to this space these days, as by right and responsibility it is theirs. In much the same way as a splint is employed to heal a broken leg, the dramatic illusion can be employed to mend the damaged self-image of a human being. The individual struggling with real or imagined inabilities can make use of a willing suspension of disbelief to transcend limitations. Once translated from the context of our work into the world, a new landscape of possibility emerges.

References

Bettelheim, B. (1982) *Freud and Man's Soul*. London: Penguin.

Brook, P. (1968) *The Empty Space*. London: McGibbon and Kee.

Clarkson, P. (1989) *Gestalt Counselling in Action*. London: Sage Publications

Hillman, J. (1983) *Healing Fiction*. New York: Station Hill Press.

Jung, C.G. (1940) 'The Psychology of the Child Archetype.' *Collected Works 9*. New York: Bollingen.

Walsh, R. (1989) *A Gift of Healing*. London: Arkana.

Winnicott, D.W. (1971) *Playing and Reality*. London: Tavistock.

CHAPTER 25

Sharing the Space Inside
One-to-One Work with People with Profound Learning Disabilities

Mary Smail

The work I am going to describe was done within a few months of completing the Sesame training. It was my first piece of work in the field of Learning Disability, so that it was very much a learning experience for me as well as for the three clients I worked with on a one-to-one basis. However, far from my newness to the work being a disadvantage, I feel, in retrospect, that the clients gained from the fresh energy I brought with me. On my side, this working experience was important, both personally and professionally, because of the way it grew out of my experiences on the Sesame Course.

Over a period of 20 months I went to a residential home for people with profound learning disabilities once a week, where I did three half-hour sessions with individual residents – mainly using movement. The people I worked with were all extremely withdrawn, so that what they were able to do in sessions was minimal. I am going to concentrate on one of the three, a woman in her early twenties whom I shall call Nancy. She had been in a residential home since childhood and had worked with Sesame practitioners before, including the founder, Marian Lindkvist.

Before we met I was told that Nancy had a history of abuse and rape. She had lost a lot of people who mattered to her, so it was particularly important to make no promises that couldn't be kept. She walked with a stooped gait, understood a lot of what was asked of her and enjoyed singing and dancing, especially to the Beatles and other sixties music. I was warned that she found meeting people difficult and it might take some time to get to know her.

That warning was something of an understatement. Nancy didn't just find it difficult to meet people, she made a great performance of not doing so. Invariably when I came to work with her she would say 'I don't want to work with you.' The starting point would be just to get her into the room where we worked, and often I didn't even manage that. Because she had been raped, even though this was some years back, the drawing away became even more pronounced around the time of year when it had happened. She would see me coming and shoot off to her room. I talked to the people at the Centre and we agreed that it would be right for me to follow her to her room and see if I could negotiate to do some gentle massage work with her there, often with some singing – just rubbing her gently and saying she was all right.

Before that could happen there was often quite a long procedure to be gone through before she gave me permission to enter the room. My entry was usually preceded by negotiations which went on for some time and were not always successful. I would knock gently at the door and say 'Nancy? It's Mary! Can I come in?' There would be silence. Then I would say 'Nancy? Could I just come in for a minute?' That could go on for five or ten minutes. Eventually she might come to her door and open it a little way and we would have some kind of conversation. Sometimes I would be allowed in, sometimes not. If not I would say 'That's all right' and go downstairs to make myself a cup of tea. Very often she would then reappear downstairs and watch me making my tea. I soon abandoned all idea of a session being something that took place in the room designated for it, realizing that, in Nancy's case, these to-ings and fro-ings between the session room and her bedroom *were* the session. They formed a kind of dance, a set of movements going on between us.

Sometimes when I followed her to her room she would just fling open the door and lie on the bed. I took this as a communication along the lines of 'You can come in but don't expect me to do anything.' It was then up to me to work out what she wanted to do and how far I could go in this session. We always started with having some kind of playful body contact. I would go and sit by her and if there was a finger in sight I might touch it and say 'Nancy's finger – Mary's finger. Oh!' That might get a little response, or it might not. It might get the finger withdrawn. I might try a conversation of elbows, which might get a response or not. Quite often the thing that would work would be noses which, I am aware, sounds quite crazy. I would touch my nose and her nose and say 'Mary's nose – Nancy's nose'. That would often get a smile. Every session that took off at all would finish with saying goodbye through the same little ritual, this time initiated by her touching first her nose and then my nose, saying 'Nancy's nose – Mary's nose!' She would refuse to leave a session without touching noses.

Through my initial 'body parts greeting' I was testing, getting her permission, seeing if she responded. I wouldn't pursue any line of action unless I got her permission to do so. A 'body parts greeting', Sesame shorthand for this routine, is a very simple and effective way of initiating a non-verbal greeting that isn't threatening. It's playful and it often leads to a lot of laughter and fun. It worked with Nancy because she was somebody who really didn't want to use words. She *could* use words, but usually she didn't want to. She would fall into these sullen silences. The body parts greeting appealed to her sense of humour. Her first response was often a smile and the nose routine could lead to gales of laughter: she would often collapse on the bed and roll about laughing. There were other times when she didn't respond at all but remained silent and withdrawn as though I wasn't there.

For the first few weeks I was always greeted with 'I don't want to work with you Mary Smail.' Then, very gradually, she became more free until one day when I followed her to her room she turned to me and said 'Journey' – just the one word. I said 'Shall we go on a journey?' and she said 'Yes'. She did something else she had never done before: she reached for my hand and began with her characteristically slow, stooping gait, to walk around the room. I was amazed because this was all quite new and initiated by her. I asked 'Where are we going?' She wasn't giving anything away: she just said 'We're going on a journey' and we travelled on round the room. After a little while I asked her 'Do you see anything?' She said that she saw a mountain. I asked 'What does the mountain look like?' She raised her hands and I raised mine with her and together we made this mountain. We had never done anything like this before. Having created the mountain, she decided to climb it. She was still leading me by the hand, but now we used various things as props to get us up to another level. She led me towards the bed and at first I thought she might be going to lie on it, face down, the way she sometimes did when she wanted to indicate that she had had enough and wanted the session to end – but no, this time the bed was a prop in the drama. Suddenly she took a step up and she was standing on the bed, tugging at my hand and expecting me to follow her. We walked over the bed, the chairs, the dressing table, down on to the floor and then up over the chairs again. I said 'Are we climbing the mountain?' She said 'Yes, we're climbing the mountain.' After some more of this I said 'How far are we going to go up?' She said 'We're going to stop here.' We stopped and I said 'What are we going to do now?' She said she wanted to make a cup of tea.

A cup of tea was another characteristic way of stopping the session: she would leave the room saying 'tea' and go downstairs to put the kettle on.

But this time she didn't leave the room. She was still in the drama and we made a cup of tea together within the drama. First we lit a fire, then we filled a kettle and put it on the fire to boil. As we sat on the mountain top drinking our tea I asked her what we could see. She didn't seem to be able to see very much, so I suggested a lake. She said yes, there was a lake down there. Because I was aware the session time was coming to an end, I said 'Shall we go down and look at the lake?' There was no answer. She just sat with her head slumped forward in her usual position, but still holding the cup of tea. Then she said 'I've been hurt.' There was silence. I said, keeping within the art form, 'What, climbing the mountain?' And she said 'No. Inside. Inside.' Her hand was thumping her chest. This went on for quite a while. She had mentioned being hurt in earlier sessions and then we had always done some massage work. I said 'Shall I do some massage?' But she replied very firmly 'No'. It was clear that at that point she didn't want to be touched at all. Then she put down her cup of tea and took my hand and began to lead me back down the mountain, over the same route. On the way she suddenly remembered the lake. As we came to it we stopped and she said first of all 'Lake' and then 'Daffodil'. She picked the daffodil and I said 'Oh, it's beautiful!'

We talked a little about the colour and said how lovely the daffodil was and then I said 'Well, Nancy, I think it's time to go back to your room. What shall we do with the daffodil?' She said 'I want to take it back to my room.' So we made the journey back, just walking round at ground level this time, until we came back to her room. She was still holding the daffodil and I said 'What shall we do with this now?' In response she let go of my hand and, completely on her own, went over to an imaginary vase by her bed and put the imaginary daffodil in it.

That was the first time she had done any kind of drama in nine months of working with me. I had tried bringing in stories, but she had shown no interest in them. She was much more interested in movement and sometimes in sound. What she had wanted up to that point was holding and singing: she would voice things back to me, like a little song that went:

> Rocking, rocking, gently rocking,
> Nancy and Mary gently rocking.

She would sing along with me and sometimes, if I stopped in the middle of the song, she would put in a word or two herself, echoing and joining in. This journey up the mountain was the first thing she had initiated.

Nothing like it happened again. The journey up the mountain was our prime time. I tried to go with the same kind of thing in the following sessions, to recover the journey, but she wasn't interested and backed off. We had just one other visit to the lake a few weeks later. It was on a day when she had been quite resistant to me. I had tried everything – singing, journeys, the lot – but she just lay on the floor making no response. At length I said 'I wonder if our bodies could make a shape together?' She seemed to respond to that. I was lying full-length on the floor in a kind of semicircle and she came and lay opposite me, making her own semicircle shape, so that together we formed a kind of circle. Suddenly she said 'Oh, a lake!' I said 'Oh, there *is* a lake. I wonder what's in it?' She looked in the lake and she found a silver shell. Nothing was done with the silver shell. This was the only other time we had any kind of imagery coming in. It happened about six weeks after the journey up the mountain. It was clear then that she remembered.

Nothing of the kind happened again. Our sessions became very changeable with no connection from week to week and no reference to the place we had visited together. Yet there seemed to be a difference in her way of relating to me. When we got into the stroking and the massage, she would sometimes say 'Nancy's hurting – Nancy's hurting.' She would make those movements with her hands on her chest that she had made when we sat drinking tea at the top of the mountain and she told me about being hurt. Otherwise it was as though that session had never happened. When I came to work with her it was often like starting for the first time. She could still be very rejecting, saying 'I don't want to work with you' and going off to make tea. However, the Centre told me that during the week she would often say 'Mary Smail is coming to see me on Monday!' On the day itself she would keep repeating right up to the time of my arrival 'Mary Smail's coming to see me today!' Then, as soon as I turned up, it would be 'I don't want to work with you Mary Smail'. The anticipation, the feeling that someone was going to turn up especially for her, was probably my most important function in her life. This was particularly important for her as she wasn't someone who could go out and do things in the centre, so that my coming in was the big event in her week. I worked with two other people there, but Nancy was the person they asked me to come for initially because she had so little else.

Even on the days when she was at her most rejecting, I came to feel that a lot was happening and that this was important. She was testing out how much would I take and still be there for her. At one point I changed my tactics. I decided that I would only follow her to her room for two sessions in a row and after that I would go and make tea for myself during her session time. Again, I took this decision with the support and agreement of the Centre. Her reaction was to become very interested in my going and making tea for myself. She would come into the room and hang around watching me. Then she would come very close, to within an inch of our faces touching, and say 'Are you going home now?' I would say 'No, I'm staying on because I work with two other people after you. But this is your time and you said you don't want to work with me.' She would find this quite disturbing and wander off, but then she would come round the other side of me and say 'Aren't you going home now?' I'd reply firmly 'No. This is your time.'

In these exchanges there was a real feeling of 'Are you here for me? Are you going to stay? What are you going to do with my time?' The feeling behind her questions seemed to be quite intense, as though she were wondering 'If I send someone away, will they go away? Am I the powerful one?' I was trying to show her 'No. I'm here. It's your choice if you come and go, but this is your session.' In other words, I was telling her she had a choice about what she did, but she didn't have power over me. If I had gone right away when she said she didn't want to work with me it would have made her feel too powerful and that would have been very frightening for her. It would have meant she had won a battle that she didn't really want to win, any more than a small child who tells her mother to 'Go away!' The child wants the Mother to withdraw a bit, not to disappear completely. It was important that I was still there holding the time for her and she could have changed her mind at any point. In fact, it was a joint decision with the Centre that I would stay around for her session time whether we worked together or not.

The work I did at this centre was often quite minimal with all three clients. I had to learn to accept this and still honour the work as being something of value. I also learnt a lot about focusing on the specific needs of these clients, recognizing that a lot I had learnt in training had to be dropped to make room for their needs. In my first session with Nancy I remember her sitting huddled up in an armchair and me sitting on the floor to one side of her. I had some music going in the background and we did a very little movement with fingers tapping on her knee in time to the music until gradually, towards the end of the session, our hands came together and touched. That was all we did. The music I used was gentle and flowing, a track from Van Gellis's *Antarctica*.

I found very quickly in these one-to-one sessions that the music was more for me than for the client. One day I realized 'They're not hearing the music. It's doing something for me, but it's not reaching them.' I then began to feel that the music could be getting in the way, taking up space that I would do better to keep free for our interactions. So I stopped using recorded music and used my own voice and hands and feet instead to make making sounds, singing and making a beat. This got more response. I didn't actually sing songs, but I would make up things to sing around their names and what we were doing and sometimes, if it felt appropriate, around something the person seemed to be feeling. I would try to take up the feeling tone of where they were in the session and make that into a melody, so that they could identify with it. If you can do that and get it right you can tell because the whole body posture will relax. You get a feeling of the person relaxing back into you. If you get it wrong you soon know because the person just becomes more tense and rigid and stiff and you think 'Try again. This just isn't right. This isn't where they are.'

I realise that this way of working with song has a lot to do with the kind of person I am and the person I was before doing Sesame work. It comes easily to me to work in this way because I'm at home with song, having sung and recorded music a lot in my life. If someone didn't feel at home making up tunes it might be difficult for them to work in this way, though with the Sesame training and background it is something that most people can probably learn to some extent. It comes down to how you work reflecting the sort of person you are. I would say that because song comes naturally to me it would be something I would use, in the way that a dancer would be more at home with dance and more likely to use dance movements as a means of communication and play. I wouldn't feel so much at home playing with dance movements, so I would have to think more about it.

This question of how you work and what you use in the work has to do with coming from an intuitive, inner place, that is all the time trying very hard to keep itself empty enough to hold the same space that the client is holding inside him or her self. Before going into a session you need to be able to make yourself empty so that you have space for the other person, an inner space that they can come into. You can then use your own feeling to give them something from that space. I would naturally do that through song and a tune.

The process of making that space, for me, and by extension for those I work with, was the central thing I learnt from the training. I remember it from the session with which we used to begin the week, which was called 'Focus'. Coming in from whatever we had been doing over the weekend, we would be taken through a lovely process in movement which brought you to an awareness and a stillness. I soon realized that this was an essential thing to have before starting work. That's why it is important to attend to the simple matter of getting to a session in time, not going in a rush. I always tried to use the walk from the station to the Centre as a time to find this place of stillness. The term I came to use for this process was 'shelving myself', by which I mean letting my own personal stuff slip away so that I could be as empty and as open as possible for the other person. I think of the words 'Open Sesame', from which our work takes its name, as being about this. You are not bringing your own rubbish into the space. You are trying to open up the place and find their riches – in the same way as the training allowed you to find your own riches within.

This has wider implications. I have, personally, always felt society to be restrictive in many ways, putting laws and rules on us. By contrast with society, Sesame is permissive in that it gives permission to be. That is what I try to pass on to Nancy and anyone else I work with. In the training you work first of all to get free in yourself – free, for instance, of those voices that say inside us 'That song won't do. It's not good enough. You've got to do better than that before you can sing in the choir' and so on. Fighting free of these persecuting voices that we all have in our heads is an ongoing process, but it gets a good start on the Sesame Course when you are thrown in at the deep end with the art form and find that you can do it, you're okay, the group accepts what you do and it not only works, it's beautiful. Having worked through that with the other people on the course, it follows that you are then strong enough to take this sense of being accepted and accepting others into working with your clients. Working with them is also a matter of sharing and passing on that feeling of 'Yes, it's okay!'

Carrying this through in the face of the client's rejection, as I had to do with Nancy, is far from easy. The first few times I was met with 'I don't want to work with you Mary Smail' I took it very personally. I remember thinking 'I'm no good at this. I'm not doing the right things. I haven't got it in me to do this work.' It took a long time to be able to accept that this was Nancy's decision, it didn't have to reflect badly on me. I gradually discovered that it was possible to take my bad feelings to supervision, leave them there and go on being present for when Nancy did want to work with me. I also learnt from the people at the Centre that this behaviour was part of Nancy's pattern and not specially to do with me. Training can't arm us against these vulnerable feelings. In one sense, we have to be open and vulnerable in order to do the work. Having that open space inside you for the client actually opens you to feeling the rejection. What you need for survival is a place to off-load these feelings and recover. This is why dramatherapists are required to have regular supervision when they come out of training and start to work in clinical settings.

This chapter would be incomplete if I didn't describe how my work at the MENCAP Centre came to an end. It came about quite naturally after I began to notice that I was doing the same things over and over again. The sense of moving forward in the work had gone and it had turned into repetition. I felt we had done quite a lot of work, and it was good work, but what I had to offer had reached its end and it was time for somebody else to take it on. I went in and said this to the people running the Centre. There was some sadness at the end, but there had been other Sesame people working there in the past and others would no doubt follow me. I just felt that what I had to do there was complete. I think you know these things inside.

Looking back, I feel grateful to have worked there. It had brought me up against a whole lot of difficult issues that it is sometimes tempting to avoid. When I first went in I often found myself up against big and difficult questions. Trying to work with people who are never going to get better – in the sense of recovering and returning to life – can feel very discouraging. Sometimes you go in and find yourself thinking 'What is the point?' The results were so small. The story of Nancy and the journey to the mountain is the prime story, almost the only story to emerge from 20 months of work. In all that I did with the other two members of the community there was really very little to see. Sometimes it would be as little as the fact that, after six months, somebody who wouldn't hold your hand at all in the beginning would hold your hand. There was no avoiding the thought that, in the eyes and language of the world, 'So what?' The achievements were minimal. And yet there would be an occasional breakthrough. Somebody who had sat in a corner with her back to you would suddenly let you hold her and rock her and have gales of laughter and fun and enjoyment, just from the sheer joy of being held and tossed around – fun, pure fun! At moments like that you think 'Yes, it's worth it. It's really worth it.' But you've worked hard to achieve that one session.

My feeling both here and at another Centre where I worked with people with multiple disabilities was 'Yes, it is worth doing, just for the occasional breakthrough – a new movement, a smile, a laugh. After all, for these people, it's their lives you are talking about. That's all they have. If you can extend their experience of life in some way, then it's worth doing.'

The capacity to work with people as severely withdrawn and disabled as those I encountered in these two Centres is a direct product of the Sesame training. Previously I would have had no way of making contact with people so deeply withdrawn and damaged. There was no way I would have been able to enter their reality and stand close enough to experience what it might feel like to be them. I was frightened of people with learning disabilities and I avoided them because they frightened me. But on the training I chose the option of working with adults with autism. Going right into my own fear, I found that there was something very lovable about those people. So I learnt how to love them. The lovable thing about them is their simplicity and the lack of demand on you. They make absolutely no demands. They are quite unashamedly who they are. There's no sense of ego and their lack of ego allows you to let go of your own ego feelings. You don't have to pretend. Through working with them you can find permission to be yourself. They have a gift for this. There's no judgement. It's a bit like working with young children before they have reached an age when they begin to make judgements. I realized then that I had found a way of being that took me away from the things I dislike most about society. Having discovered this, I was happy to stay with it.

CHAPTER 26

Baba Yaga and Vasalisa
Myth Work with Challenging Behaviour

Elizabeth Gall

A therapeutic approach to challenging behaviour assumes that anger is a natural energy essential to our survival; that it is a positive impulse to master the external world and to affirm one's identity and purpose. Only when its development is hindered does it become associated with aggression and rage. Alternatively, it may be turned towards attacking the self, contributing to various diseases, depression and lethargy. We all need positive and constructive outlets for our aggression.

Much has been done in recent years to enable people with learning disabilities to affirm themselves and have creative outlets by way of community housing, jobs, education, leisure and creative activities. Aggression, however, is not only linked with current difficulties: anger expressed today may have been stored in the mind and body for many years, having its roots in much earlier experiences – experiences of early abandonment or a time when someone else made all the decisions in an individual's life, blocking his or her development and self-expression. In addressing the person holistically, dramatherapy connects with history and memory as well as with more immediate feelings arising out of present circumstances.

The story of *The Snake of Vedas* is a useful metaphor in thinking about some of the people referred to me for dramatherapy:

> In Vedas there was a snake that was terrifying the village. The snake was biting, kicking and even killing people. A sage came to town preaching a philosophy of love and spiritual understanding. The snake heard one of the lectures and was so moved by the sage's teaching that he vowed not to be nasty any more. For the next few months he displayed the manners of a saint. When he next encountered the sage,

the snake was downtrodden and beaten and demanded his money back, lamenting 'I tried your philosophy of spiritual understanding and now look at me – I'm half dead!' The sage replied succinctly 'I never told you not to hiss!'

Some of the clients who come my way are literally kicking and biting and, though not actually killing people, they demonstrate a murderous rage towards others, or themselves, or both. By contrast, there are also clients who do not display any anger but are passive and unable to assert themselves, with little confidence when they find themselves in social situations. Between these two extremes are those who tend to be passive most of the time, but will surprise their carers by, for example, throwing a television out of a window or suddenly attacking other residents and staff. The incident may be reported as 'out of character', but it is the other side of the very same coin. The task of the dramatherapist in all these cases is to support the clients and help them to channel their aggression into creative self-expression: in other words, to find a metaphorical hiss.

To illustrate how this can be done, I would like to present a case history.[1] Mair, as I will call her, was referred for drama and movement therapy in June 1993. She was hitting trainees at the Adult Education Centre she attended as well as throwing furniture around and smashing things. She had a long history of hitting out at people and it had recently intensified so that staff were concerned for her safety and for the safety of other trainees. Mair has autistic tendencies and over the previous year she had become increasingly withdrawn, to a point where she had virtually cut herself off from all social interaction. Staff said that she would not co-operate even on simple tasks unless she was offered food as a reward. Yet she enjoyed painting and music.

After an initial assessment, I set a plan for our work as follows: Aims – to encourage a feeling of safety through a supportive, non-judgemental approach; to set boundaries in relation to inappropriate behaviour, such as hitting, by using clear and consistent verbal and non-verbal messages; to allow her to lead the pace of the work, setting demands at a level she could manage in order to achieve a positive experience for her; to empower and develop her sense of self by encouraging self-awareness and allow her to set boundaries regarding her own personal space. Objectives – to use drama and movement to develop creative self-expression, so as to improve self-awareness and confidence and encourage co-operation; to use movement and touch to develop a positive sense of self; to use drama, movement and voice work,

---

1   I would like to acknowledge and thank Marina Jenkins for supervising this piece of work.

both to develop communication and as a positive and creative way of releasing emotions and tensions.

When I began working with Mair she was unresponsive to most communication. She would come into the room and sit down on the same chair with an open posture, remaining virtually still and silent and gazing into space throughout the session. Her facial expression was passive, giving the impression that in her mind she was very far away. She occasionally said the word 'crisps' or made non-verbal sounds. If I came closer to her than four feet she drew back physically, as if in fear. It was important to allow her to define her own physical space and assure her that I would not try to enter this space. I did this verbally and non-verbally. For example, if I wanted to pass her something I would offer it from my chair; if she gave any indication that she was interested, perhaps by a look, I would move tentatively towards her, monitoring her response. If she began to withdraw, I would move away; if not, I would continue towards her. Over time, she allowed me to be nearer to her. Eventually she initiated the physical contact of hands during drama enactments and movement sequences.

When working with people with challenging behaviour it is useful to encourage them to be physically aware of their own bodies: if energy can be channelled and dispersed through the body, it is less likely to erupt in bursts of aggression. As Mair moved very little, I began this process by asking her to be aware of body sensations, drawing attention to different body parts and asking her to notice which parts felt warm or cold and what the textures of her clothing felt like against her skin. I asked her to notice her breath and when it changed from an 'in' breath to an 'out' breath. All of this she could do without physical movement. I also encouraged small physical movements, though it was a while before this met with any response. I always stressed that it was fine for her not to do anything she didn't want to do – this was to encourage a feeling of safety and, at the same time, to avoid creating any feelings of failure.

As well as becoming physically aware, it is important for people to be grounded in their environment. This helps them to stay connected with physical reality. Also, if a person becomes violent, the environment gives one something to draw their attention to in order to stop the behaviour. I asked Mair to be aware of colours, shapes and objects in the room, and of sounds inside and outside the room. Again, she could do this without having to make any visible response to me. I never knew how much attention she paid to any of this, but it seemed a possible way in, so I persevered.

It was important to make eye contact with Mair, as this establishes contact with a person's adult self. When people are violent in this kind of situation, they abandon the adult self and behave like a child without responsibility. I used non-verbal sounds, monosyllabic words, clapping and simple rhythms on instruments to achieve this. Occasionally Mair would respond with non-verbal sounds or repeating the word 'No' and this sometimes resulted in moments of eye contact. It was also developing a small level of communication. Gradually she became more involved and would tap rhythms on the tambourine and respond in other ways to the sounds I made.

These activities became an opening ritual to all our sessions. Having familiar rituals encourages a sense of safety and is particularly important when working with people with autistic tendencies.

After the opening ritual, I would introduce brief drama enactments, which would often relate to a myth or story I was going to tell. Mair was sometimes unresponsive, but usually she would engage quite fully in these activities. I might create a market scene and Mair would go shopping, moving around the space, carefully choosing items she wanted to buy and putting them in her bag. In this way she seemed to be demonstrating a liking for dramatic enactment. She was able to communicate through the use of her imagination.

I would then tell a story. Mair would turn her head towards me without making eye contact and stay in this position until the story was finished. It seemed that she was interested in the story, though I didn't know how much she was understanding. I would then invite her to enact part of the story, but this gained little response.

After two months of meeting once a week, Mair began asking to paint. After telling a story I would invite her to paint any images in the story that interested her. For the first few weeks she just covered the paper with one colour – black, red or orange – and then, in a quick burst of movement, she would suddenly begin putting colour on the carpet, walls or furniture. I would quickly take away the paint and then bring a cloth for her to clean up, which she did thoroughly. I would explain that if we were to use the room it was important that we left it as we had found it and if she put paint on things I would immediately remove the paints. This routine went on for several weeks. Sometimes she would put just a tiny spot of paint on the wall, but I still removed the paints because people with challenging behaviour are constantly challenging boundaries and it is important to be clear and consistent – even about the smallest boundary infringements, as small infringements lead to larger ones. After two months this behaviour stopped. Mair continued to paint in our sessions, but over several months this behaviour was only repeated once.

Then Mair began to paint several roundish shapes on the paper, which she called 'crisps'. She would paint several pages of A4 paper, each one in a different colour. In the next session she would carefully select the paintings she wanted to take home. That she repeatedly painted 'crisps' suggested that they were of some emotional significance, possibly of emotional hunger. The sessions continued in this way for some months before I told a story that appeared to resonate very deeply with Mair. It was the Russian myth of Vasalisa and her doll:

> On her deathbed a young mother gives her daughter, Vasalisa, a doll. The mother tells her that the doll will help her if ever she is in trouble; she is to keep it with her at all times and feed it when it is hungry. After the mother's death, the father re-marries and Vasalisa now has a wicked stepmother and two stepsisters. The stepmother and stepsisters are jealous of her, so they conspire to get rid of her. They let the fire go out and send her into the forest to get more fire from the witch Baba Yaga, in the hope that Baba Yaga will eat her.
>
> Vasalisa sets off into the forest, being overtaken by three riders along the way. The doll, which she keeps in her pocket, guides her to Baba Yaga's house. Each day Baba Yaga sets Vasalisa horrendously difficult tasks before she flies off, and threatens to eat her if they are not completed by the time she returns. First, she must separate the good corn from the mildewed corn; second, she must separate poppy seeds from a large pile of dirt. The doll completes both tasks while Vasalisa sleeps. Baba Yaga is surprised and invites Vasalisa to ask her questions. Vasalisa asks who the three riders are. 'They are my day, my sunrise and my night,' Baba Yaga replies, inviting her to ask another question – but the doll jumps up and down in her pocket and Vasalisa knows from this that it is not wise to do so. She says 'It is not wise to ask too many questions.' Baba Yaga, shocked at the girl's wisdom, hands her a stick with a skull on it and tells her that this is her fire.
>
> As Vasalisa sets off for home, the doll again guides her through the forest. Along the way, the fire from the skull begins to blaze. Vasalisa is tempted to throw it away, but the skull speaks and tells her that it is safe. When she arrives home the stepmother and sisters tell her that while she was away they could not light the fire, no matter how many times they tried. The skull on the stick watches every move of the stepmother and stepsisters and burns into them. By morning it has burnt the wicked trio to cinders.

When working with a myth, it is understood that all its component parts represent a single person's psyche. The way a person responds to the figures, archetypes and symbols in the myth helps the therapist to understand the emotional needs of the client and to explore ways of resolving emotional conflict. In the description that follows, it is important for the reader to be aware that we used no props. When I make reference to objects, they are not a physical reality but created through the use of imagination.

After I had told the story, I offered Mair a choice of roles: it is important for the client to be free to choose a part that resonates with her. Mair chose to be Vasalisa and I, as well as retaining my role as story-teller, took the part of the mother. As the mother, I handed Mair the doll. She immediately began thumping the doll very aggressively, saying 'Dead! Dead!' As she did so, she made eye contact with me – which she held throughout the enactment. The eye contact was very important in this situation as it indicated that Mair was connected to me as an outside reality as well as to the unconscious drama she was enacting. In symbolic terms, the doll seemed to represent our symbolic and intuitive side. For us to function socially, it is important that this aspect of the personality is alive. Therefore I felt it was important to bring the doll back to life. I was able to do this, as the story-teller, by bringing in the concept of magic and saying 'although Vasalisa killed the doll, because it was magic it was able to come back to life.' The use of magic in drama is a great asset for healing, so that aspects of the psyche that feel dead can be brought back to life.

Mair glared at me and shouted 'Dead! Dead!', repeating the thumping actions with more intensity. She was clearly experiencing a deep feeling of rage. To support her in these difficult emotions, I responded to what she was doing by incorporating them into the story. I said 'Vasalisa was so upset and hurt at the way the wicked stepmothers had treated her that she thumped and hurt and killed the doll – and again the doll came back to life.' The message I was trying to convey was 'Yes, you have every right to your anger, to be upset by your experiences and to express your feelings in this way – that is, within the safety of the drama.' Mair repeated killing the doll about twenty times, always maintaining eye contact with me. Throughout, I assured her that no matter how many times she killed the doll, the doll would always come back to life and would always love her. In other words, no matter how angry or destructive you feel, you are still a valued and lovable person. Eventually, with encouragement, she put the doll 'safely in her pocket' and we de-roled and the session ended.

In the next session I created a magic pot and invited Mair to take two things out of the magic pot, one for her to keep just for herself and the other to share. Mair took something out of the pot, made a punching action and said 'Baby dead' ('baby' was how Mair referred to the doll throughout the sessions that followed). She then went on to put the 'baby' in her pocket. I asked her not to put the baby in her pocket unless it was safe. In retrospect, I would not ask Mair to keep something which was just for herself. It was clear from the last session that Mair had been feeling angry and destructive and that she needed support to manage these feelings. To invite her to take something just for herself was giving her responsibility for managing feelings which, at this point in the process, she was demonstrating that she was unable to do. Although she had chosen to share her experience with me, I felt somewhat intrusive to then take hold of the situation. I also felt it was important to do this in order to support her.

Mair then took an imaginary box of crisps out of the pot. She took out a number of packets, one at a time, asking if she could eat them. Each time she asked, I asked her if she was still hungry and she replied that she was. I told her to keep on eating until she was full and she ate several packets. When it was time to end this part of the session I said she had time for one more packet, which she took. After that, when she tried to take further packets, I firmly asked her to put them back – which she did. I felt that wanting to eat so many crisps was her way of displaying her emotional hunger. My asking her if she was still hungry before taking another packet was to encourage her to use her own instinctual side. I was trying to assure her that she could get her emotional needs met. I also felt it was important to set clear boundaries by asking her to return the extra crisps, after it had been agreed that the previous packet was the last. The message overall was that her needs would be met appropriately.

In the next session, working with the same structure, Mair again put the doll in her pocket and ate several packets of crisps. Throughout, I invited her to feed the doll some crisps. Towards the end of the session, she did. This was a very positive outcome. In symbolic terms, she was beginning to nourish herself and this is very healing. The more a person heals, the less room there is for violent and destructive behaviour.

Next time, Mair walked in and said 'Baby, crisps.' She also asked to create a magic pot. We did this and once again she pulled out a box of crisps, but this time she fed the doll throughout the session. After each packet she fed to the doll, she asked if the doll could have some more and I would tell her to ask the doll if she was hungry. Each time she would whisper to the doll and indicate non-verbally that the doll had said 'Yes'. That she was asking me if the doll could have more crisps was an indication that she was relying on me to keep the boundaries for her. This was a new experience for her and she was asking for support. By telling her to ask the doll if she was hungry, I was asking her to trust her own intuition to know what she needed in order to feel nourished. She fed the doll several packets of crisps.

Towards the end of the session I told her there was time for 'the baby' to have one more packet of crisps. She became quite anxious and began feeling the doll frantically. I asked her to feed the doll more slowly, which she did. She was almost pleading with me to let the doll have more crisps. I was assuring her that she could have them next week. After a few minutes of this, she took another packet for the doll. When it was time to de-role she didn't want to let go of the doll and tried to hide it under the chair. I was eventually able to get Mair to de-role by assuring her that she could continue to feed the doll more crisps next week. That Mair did not accept the boundary of the last packet of crisps and did not want to let go of the doll indicated, I believe, that she did not yet fully trust that her emotional needs could be met and that she felt a need to break the boundaries in order for them to be met.

In the next session, Mair again fed the doll. Then she said the doll was crying. Mair had an expression of pain on her face and she made sobbing sounds. She seemed to be demonstrating her own vulnerability and showing that she was in touch with her sadness and pain. I told her to ask the doll what was wrong, but the doll did not know. I suggested that maybe the doll would like to be gently rocked. Mair began gently rocking the doll and this went on for several minutes. It was very moving and seemed to demonstrate the compassion Mair was now able to feel towards her own pain instead of expressing it in violent acts of rage against herself and other people. However, this was a time when she was most at risk of acting out her pain because she was so in touch with it. It was a time in the therapeutic process when demands on Mair needed to be minimal and confrontation avoided if possible. To ensure this, it was very important to have good communication between the dramatherapist and other staff involved in her care, so that our approaches would not conflict and we could work towards a common goal of supporting Mair.

At the end of each of these sessions, Mair would de-role, with my support, all the things which had been created. She would pat and stretch her body from head to toe and massage her face and hands. She would then move around the room and explore the space and copy short movement structures. And she would make eye contact with me.

The work with Mair is still in process as I write and the final outcome of the work cannot be predicted. However, it is my belief that my aims and objectives are being met. Throughout our work I have allowed Mair to set the pace and I have been conscious of her personal space. I have been clear and consistent in setting boundaries regarding inappropriate behaviour: an example was when I stopped the painting after she deliberately painted furniture, which resulted in her refraining from this behaviour. She has used drama, movement and voice work to express emotions: expressing anger by punching and killing the doll, sadness with her sobbing sounds and, eventually, love and compassion by rocking the doll. That she has been able to express herself in this way indicates, in my view, that she feels supported enough to express herself emotionally. There have been many times when she has been co-operative within the drama, becoming very involved and responsive. She has also begun to pat and stretch her body and copy movement structures, which suggests that she is developing body-awareness.

I have been told that Mair's behaviour outside our sessions has changed considerably over the past year. There have been very few outbursts of aggression and she has been more co-operative with staff. I know this has been influenced by a good relationship with her support worker. I also believe that drama and movement therapy has helped this change to come about.

CHAPTER 27

Beginning to Work with the Elderly

Alison Kelly and Chris Daniel

This was our first clinical placement on the Course, working with a group of disabled elderly people in a residential home. Most of the residents were hard of hearing, some with no speech and all with a very limited mobility. How could we begin to work with this group, using the Sesame approach as we had learnt it? Initially it felt as though it would be impossible for us to facilitate in a dignified way, without patronizing. We felt thankful that our tutor was going to lead the first session. With her support, we soon developed a way of working which felt appropriate in this particular setting: telling stories and myths and then enacting them for the group, using props and limited costume.

Then we found ourselves wondering 'Is this really Sesame?' As we had experienced it up to then, Sesame was about participation. What we were offering felt more like performance, with the client group included in ways which felt very marginal. We talked about it among ourselves. We talked about it with Kharis Dekker, our tutor. Eventually Kharis wrote us a letter which approached the subject on another level, helping us to recognize the different psychological aims involved in working with the elderly:

> How can the elderly be helped with their closing moments of life? What are the closing moments of life for? Why are human beings, in old age, experiencing the dissolving of ego concerns with the body's decline? Is there a purpose in this? And if so, should we not be going with this purpose rather than trying, hopelessly, to avert or delay it?

This account of working with the elderly was written during the year immediately after Alison Kelly and Chris Daniel left the Sesame training.

So, what are the aims in working with the elderly – the dying? To me it seems that as long as these dying people are yet living, they have a task they are quietly fulfilling. The crowning years of life seem to set a task, a far more inward task than any previous ones. What is this inward task? It is the slow process of digestion, the quiet, cow-like rumination on all that has been experienced. To a large extent, this massive task must be going on subconsciously, in the psychic rumen, so to speak, where memories, dreams and reflections are being chewed over. Our aim, as clearly as we need to know our aim, must be to assist this task.

Do we know what is being extracted from the chewing of the cud? Some 'house of meaning' must be being made as an 'abode for the soul'. It is a sacred process, don't you feel, when the soul prepares itself for transition, when all that is mortal is left behind? The elderly patients we are all working with have left almost all of their life behind, in the material sense, and they have the task of making something psychologically meaningful or 'spiritual' in the place of this. They are preparing for the biggest change there is...

Having initially thought that working with old people would be limiting, draining, even boring, we now find it is quite the opposite. It is stimulating and energizing. We now work as a pair, feeling that this is beneficial to the groups as it aids concentration, focus and awareness. We position ourselves on either side of the circle. This way one leader is able to reinforce what the other has said, which is helpful to the hard of hearing. Our pattern of working has developed over a year of coming on a regular basis. To begin with, we had to encourage people to move into the circle. Now, the TV is turned off as soon as we are spotted and people struggle forward, eager to begin.

It often surprises us to discover how much people remember of the story and other details of what went on the previous week. We begin the session by recapping. Then we introduce our 'props' for the week – objects which will often have some association with 'their' time and which are relevant to the day's story. Distributing these objects around the group gives us an opportunity for individual conversations with the people taking part. People are often prepared to share personal memories and thoughts, which sometimes leads into a group discussion.

When tea is served this creates a pause. We treat this as a cue to begin telling the story. People listen intently, becoming impatient with anyone who interrupts. Occasionally someone will be unable to resist the temptation to guess the ending. After we have told the story once, people choose roles and play them during the second telling. The pattern we have evolved is for one of us to re-tell the story while the other supports a member of the group in the leading role. This arrangement helps to keep up the flow and momentum of the story. It also helps to compensate for the lack of mobility in the group by giving them something energetic to watch. In this way the thread of the story is kept and members of the group are linked across the circle by the mobile leader acting as a link.

The stories we bring get adapted in novel ways by the group. The Greek hero Theseus ended up with a home help to attend on him. The maiden with the wooden bowl on her head was able to save a packet in perms. Over the year the group became increasingly involved in the action, allowing us to withdraw and do less. It was encouraging to see them evolve and begin choosing stories they wanted to use. One woman who feigned deafness and sleep for a while is now a starring member of the cast and tells us when we are not speaking loudly enough. We have found that even the most frail-looking individuals appreciate us being loud and fierce, rather than gentle and 'nice'. The terrifying, roaring Minotaur was enjoyed. So are the cymbals, which people love to clash loudly together.

We usually end the session with music from their younger days, and sometimes a song. Everyone has an opportunity to dance, either standing in the centre or moving in a more limited way in their wheelchairs.

Through the success of this project, we have been invited to work in two other residential homes. We are no longer in doubt about the value of what goes on in the sessions and hope is that when we are elderly someone will come along and give us a chance to be on the receiving end of drama and movement therapy.

CHAPTER 28

Making the Present Come Alive

Merle Baars

I have been employed as a drama and movement therapist with elderly patients at hospitals in the Guy's Health District in London since completing the Sesame Course in 1984. It seems to me that the best way to show how drama and movement therapy can reach elderly people and help them towards regaining health and confidence is to introduce a few of those I have had the pleasure of working with over the years.

VIOLET, aged 85 (though looking no more than 70), was admitted with an anxiety-related illness, accompanied by a rocking, repetitive movement of her right foot – a stereotype which remained throughout our work together, though it seemed to diminish as she became less anxious. In the first session she attended, she found enough confidence to play a main role, though she felt it was 'a lot to remember.' She got on well with the group and said she had enjoyed the attention she received. After three weeks I went to fetch her for the session and she said 'I'm agitated.' She certainly was: I had some difficulty in containing her agitation during the session, though she initiated some recall work and seemed to enjoy it. At the next session she was still agitated, but laughingly offered to play the part of 'the moaning sister-in-law'. Her agitation gradually slowed in this session, maybe as her confidence increased and maybe in response to some music that I chose with a view to slowing her down. Before her sixth session Violet said she didn't want to attend, but she came nevertheless and entered into her role in an imaginative way. She also showed enthusiasm for other people's contributions. Her grasp was not as forceful as in previous sessions: she held hands in a more relaxed way, an indication that her agitation was subsiding. I felt that there had been a breakthrough.

In the next session Violet made a lively contribution and spoke positively about wanting to go home. She stood up to play her role, entered humorously into the session and asked me 'How do you remember the stories?' – all of this in spite of having pronounced herself 'worried'. Throughout her time in Sesame sessions she would break into spontaneous, enthusiastic applause for other people's performances. I believe that Sesame helped her to recover confidence and faith in herself. Her own performances seemed to be a source of surprise and delight to her: as her confidence developed, she was able to let go of her anxiety. One day she said to me 'You should be very proud of what you get us to do.'

BILL, aged 72, didn't join the group until eighteen months after we first met. He was suffering from a chronic, resistant depression and reacted to our goings-on with bewilderment, saying 'I don't know what it's all about!' He was profoundly lacking in confidence and self-esteem. One day he suddenly elected to join in and took on the main role in the enactment, requiring quite a lot of direction and encouragement to carry it through. That seemed to give him courage and he went on coming, gradually gaining confidence. He was always enthusiastic about the stories we enacted and he began to interact with me, asking me where else I worked. He would often appeal to me to 'help' him in a chosen part. In his fourth session, his acting quite suddenly blossomed: he showed initiative in his chosen role and came out with some lively, spontaneous gestures. He was also willing to 'lead' a mirror dance – a movement sequence with hands which members of the group lead in turn, either with the whole circle or in pairs, copying the leader's movements. His confidence was growing.

Bill came to his seventh session in spite of having fallen and broken his hip. He didn't ask for help, but managed to compensate for his lack of mobility by developing some marvellous facial expressions. His spontaneity seemed to be innate: acting enabled him to use an expressive part of himself, which emerged naturally and easily. His responses often showed a subtle, even an ironic humour. One day, in the role of Somnus the God of Sleep, he had us all laughing with a well-timed aside: 'Maybe *this* will help me to sleep!'

When we had been working together for some months, I arrived at the hospital one day to be told that Bill had attempted suicide. He was rather sheepish about this and expressed a wish to help himself. By coincidence (or was it synchronicity?) I had prepared a session around an old Russian story about a nightingale who is kept in a cage. The owner presumes, because the bird is fed and watered, that it is happy. The owner takes a trip abroad and the nightingale asks him to visit his brothers and sisters in freedom and give them news of him. When the birds hear of their brother's misfortune they fall down as if dead, only recovering when their feathery bodies touch the grass. As soon as the nightingale hears about this he, too, falls down in his cage as if dead. The merchant makes many attempts to revive him: only when he tries laying him outside on the grass does the bird spring to life and soar up into the air, thanking his master for bringing him such good news as he wings away to freedom.

The story was close to Bill's situation. On hearing that we were to enact it, he immediately chose the part of the nightingale. Time and again I notice how people will go for the parts they need to play without any prompting from me – indeed, to prompt in a situation like this would be a presumptuous interference with the way the medium works.

For some weeks after this, Bill was unable to attend the sessions. When he resumed, his confidence appeared to be restored. He didn't seem to remember much about previous sessions. He brought great depth to his portrayal of characters and on several occasions he asked about the books in which I found the stories. His facial expressions and gestures indicated considerable thought and commitment and he appeared to get a lot out of the sessions. At this point he began to show an individuality which had not been evident before, seeming to be developing a new sense of 'self.' Sesame had allowed the creative side of his personality to emerge, supplanting his supposed inadequacy and building up his sense of his own worth. It was a vehicle for self-expression and gave him a sense of achievement which he had not experienced for many years. I often saw his wife when she came to visit him and praised him in her presence – something I wouldn't normally do, but in this instance it felt important to help build up his self-esteem. Our sessions gave Bill a chance to 'shine', away from the constricting atmosphere of the family. I encouraged him to pursue his interest in literature and drama after leaving the hospital.

RUBY was wheeled into my group, about three years ago, draped in a blanket. She is now in her late seventies. To begin with she was subdued and sat with her head down. However, she gradually became animated during the singing. I noticed that she had a beautiful voice and subsequently discovered she had developed it over a number of years. She attended my group for about six weeks before being discharged from the hospital.

The next time I saw Ruby was in another hospital in the district where I work. She was with a group of entertainers of 'a certain age' and, recognizing me, rushed over to greet me. She looked quite different, as one might expect, fully dressed and wearing make-up. It is in the nature of her illness that she fluctuates between being very well and the other extreme. In 1992 she was readmitted to Guy's, again very unwell. In the group, she said 'I used to sing.' Her responses were limited to gesture with no verbal commitment.

Five weeks passed before she attended again. Her face lit up when she spoke about her favourite singer and she stood up to dance, but with averted eyes. As the weeks passed her participation became more animated, she became able to make eye contact and spoke philosophically about going home. There were flashes of humour. Then she had a fall and fractured a hip. After she recovered she returned to the group, she had a sleepwalking quality about her. She always chose a set of bells out of the collection of percussion instruments that we use to create atmosphere for the stories. This went on for about a month.

Then, quite suddenly, Ruby seemed to wake up. She arrived at our session in an exuberant mood – asking after other group members, choosing songs to sing and expressing enthusiasm for the role play. She chose to play a positive role, saying 'It's a nice one.' Her preoccupation with her own symptoms and medication gradually declined after that and she became more aware of other members of the group, becoming able to allow them their space.

She began to choose her roles with care, asking in advance what performing them would entail. Often she would say with a smile 'I suppose it will have to be me!' This happened when we concocted our own Cinderella just before my Christmas break. When I told the group I was going away, Ruby said with a humorous twinkle 'Whatever will we do without you?' She left hospital in the New Year, shortly after I returned from my holiday.

Sesame had given Ruby an opportunity to express herself through singing, a vital part of her being that she had lost connection with through her illness. When she sang to us and with us, she was able to get back in touch with her creative self. She was also helped to move away from preoccupation with her own troubles and to develop an awareness of others, gradually moving towards an independence which seemed new to her.

ALICE was approaching 84 when she was hospitalized for depression and joined the group. She said that she felt unwell, but started tapping her feet to the music at the beginning of the session. During the session she apologized for 'not being any good'. At her second session she said she felt awful: she wanted to go home and die there. Her concentration seemed to be better in this session, though I noticed that her long-term memory was poor. In the following session she had persecutory feelings, felt she was being 'put down' and talked of going to the 'funny farm'. But she seemed to rally when we sang the song 'Apple Blossom Time'. She took on the role of an old lady in the enactment and became very animated playing it. Her memory improved: she began to come out with memories spontaneously. But she was sure we would not meet again.

Alice's awareness developed gradually over the next few weeks, though she remained suspicious of her ward. Her concentration was good. She was able to take part in an enactment, contributing vocal sounds. She remarked how 'fresh' the other patients looked. After a gap of a month, she returned to the group greatly improved. She took the part of a doctor in a story, spontaneously getting out of her wheelchair to go over and 'examine' another patient with a stethoscope. In the same session, she stood up to dance and beamed as she did so.

After this she came frequently to the group. She always responded well to the warm-ups, smiling and taking courage from the music. Her sense of humour emerged and developed and she made clear choices about roles and instruments to accompany them. During a session when I read some familiar poems and one of the group recited a poem during the enactment, Alice came in from time to time with humorous lines that she produced 'ad lib'. She also began to reminisce very accurately at this time, where before she would have said dismissively 'I can't remember'. Her recollections of working life went back over 60 years.

Alice's response to Sesame amazed me. She developed spontaneity and animation in response to the music and stories, enjoyed the transformation element in the myths we worked with and her commitment to the group grew steadily as she learnt how to use the medium.

MAUD, aged 71, has suffered from schizophrenia for many years. Having spent the greater part of 40 years in a 'long-stay' institution, she was discharged into a 'support house' in the district where I work. When she joined my group in this house she was very charming, but the staff warned me that she was mercurial and volatile. She walks rhythmically with a stamping gait and produces rhythmic movements with her mouth, known as tardive dyskinesia (due to the drugs she has taken for her condition over many years.) She also has a pronounced hiatus hernia, of which she is keenly aware.

For the first year she attended my group Maud would sit apart, at the end of the room, with her head in her hands, refusing to take part. When, eventually, she joined us, she was verbally abusive and continually disruptive, seeking attention by these means at every turn – but she did respond to the old songs I sang with the group. Occasionally she would give us glimpses of her condition, telling us that she was very worried or frightened and showing genuine distress. She would touch her body inappropriately and make imaginative but inappropriate suggestions for improvisation.

After 21 months, however, she began to participate in a more spontaneous manner, initiating her own 'warm-ups' to music at the start of the session. She also began to take part in 'touch' work, for the first time making appropriate suggestions. There were still times when she would seek attention and become very trying. She would often tell us 'You're mad!' Around that time, she remarked that she was old. Her participation gradually increased but she declined to take part in the acting, saying that she didn't want to look a fool.

After two years, Maud's humour had improved: she was more integrated with the group and able to initiate more. She began to volunteer for parts in story enactments and to make suggestions for other participants. After 27 months, she stood up to act for the first time, though she remains reluctant to do this. I think she prefers to sit. She can still show flashes of her former behaviour. It took two years to gain her trust and enable her to develop any confidence in her ability. I have written about her because her slow response contrasts sharply with that of the elderly people I wrote about earlier. Throughout the time that Maud spent in an institution, the creative side of her personality seems to have been denied her. She was unused to the experience of making decisions and only felt 'at home' with people she had seen every day over a period, enabling her to develop some trust in them. Attending Sesame sessions enabled her to take her place within a group and not feel she had to be continually the focal point. I am still working with Maud on a weekly basis.

Many of elderly people I work with have difficulties moving about: some will come to sessions in wheelchairs, others walking with the aid of zimmer frames. This does not impede them from acting. I often use a fairy-tale or a mythical story, narrating the tale first and then helping the enactment along with verbal directions and cues. The 'actors' may use words as they play their roles or they may settle for non-verbal sounds made with the voice or the instruments. We all use our voices and the instruments to accompany the story. I always encourage members of the group to play the roles, but will occasionally take on a part myself if there are no takers or if the situation seems to demand it. Sometimes the very elderly amaze me in their response to stimulus, as when the 85-year-old Alice stood up in the role of Doctor to examine a 'patient'.

In many of the stories I work with the theme of death comes in, but the deceased are transformed to become flowers, birds, butterflies and other natural images. These stories, when used with the elderly, acknowledge that they are in the autumn of their lives yet give a measure of comfort through the element of transformation. Fairy-tales often end with 'living happily ever after' and this, too, creates a feeling of hope, which is free from sentimentality because it is in a traditional pattern with which we are all familiar. I am careful, if we perform exercises on themes such as gardening, that we don't leave precious things in the ground and that the plants are allowed to grow. Elderly people can readily associate the image of 'ground' with dying, especially when working the way we do with imagination.

I always look for opportunities for elderly people to authenticate an exercise — for instance, when they know about gardening or fishing — by describing something from their own experience to the group. This helps to rebuild damaged self-esteem and it feels right for me, as a younger therapist, to acknowledge the contribution that they have made in the world. When they take the space which I have been holding in my role as leader, their confidence flows. Here the Sesame Method encourages the emergence and development of a sense of 'self', which may have been profoundly discouraged by the external circumstances of the person's life. Where these feelings of discouragement have remained unvoiced, the way we explore the 'self' through the use of movement, drama and music allows for self-expression and can lead people towards a fuller understanding of who they are.

At the end of a session with the elderly there is often a burst of spontaneous applause. As people are leaving, there are lots of smiles. We have reached out to our clients and they have responded. The unifying and humbling quality in the client/therapist relationship has worked its magic.

CHAPTER 29

The Story of Roundabout
Creation of a Group Practice

Deborah Haythorne and Lynn Cedar

'Roundabout' is the name we chose for the registered charity and group practice for drama and movement therapists which we started over ten years ago after the two of us completed the 1985–86 Sesame Course. In these ten years we have been gathering experience and knowledge not only of the work itself but of the management techniques needed to organize a charity of this size, serving many different client groups, and to administer a group practice working with nine other dramatherapists to do session work on a part-time basis.

The story of Roundabout runs parallel to the development of dramatherapy as a whole and its struggle for recognition, but with special relevance to Sesame and all who share our training base.

Roundabout has grown into quite a large organization. We are now Project Directors working with a part-time Development Co-ordinator and our dedicated Management Committee. We supervise all the work done by therapists working under the name of Roundabout over a wide geographical area including thirteen London boroughs. We set up the placements and engage therapists to work in them, offering weekly team meetings for support, planning, accessing resources, looking at dramatherapy issues and supervision.

Creation of Roundabout

We have come a long way since starting as friends who met on the Sesame training. Looking back, we are both aware how much we gained from working in partnership in those early days when dramatherapy was still relatively new. We had to sell the idea virtually from scratch every time we went into a hospital, school or day centre to look for work. As well as convincing people of our competence, we had to show them that what we were offering was of itself of value for the client group in question. It helped so much that there were two of us to plan, run the sessions together and learn from the experience in discussion afterwards. We also set up supervision for our own work (now a recognized aspect of good professional practice, but at the time very much an optional extra) using it to develop our working partnership as well as our individual skills.

We came into dramatherapy from very different backgrounds, but found we had similar attitudes to the work and the training when we met as students. Deborah came to the training after obtaining an honours degree in English and Drama, having been interested in the field of mental health and learning disabilities for many years. When she heard of dramatherapy she knew it was for her because it combined all her main interests. Lynn felt the same, having studied mime, dancing and acting and obtained an LRAM. She had already worked, using dramatherapy, with the Manpower Services Commission on a project called 'The Ever Expanding Theatre'.

Both the practical and theoretical aspects of the work fascinated us as we discovered more about such subjects as Jung and Laban. We supported our training in these subjects by attending extra lectures and practical workshops. Jung and Laban are tools of the training that we still come back to again and again.

Lynn was surprised at just how effective the training was. Although she already knew much of the theory from working with a Sesame-trained therapist, Bernard Saint, at Manpower Services, she quickly realized one has to experience drama and movement therapy for oneself, to be at the receiving end and know what it feels like, in order to be a useful therapist. Having a whole year of intensive training was both enjoyable and challenging and being able to use the student group as a client group enabled us to do so much hands-on, practical work, in addition to two terms of session work in clinical placements.

We both enjoyed the course and completed it successfully and this encouraged us. It meant that by the time we had finished we were practised as drama and movement therapists and were completely committed to doing it. We had every expectation that we would find the work fulfilling and rewarding. However, we received very little practical help or advice on how to set about doing the work – as many of the tutors in those days were not practising dramatherapists. We were breaking into a new field and needed to access different supportive information about such things as managing accounts, becoming a voluntary organization and informing the general public about dramatherapy.

We realized it would take time to achieve a recognition as dramatherapists and meanwhile we needed to make a living. Lynn was eligible to apply for the Enterprise Allowance Scheme, which she did, and since we were committed to working together we shared a single enterprise allowance payment, receiving £20 a week each! On this we started telephoning around the NHS, social services and schools, systematically following up each call with a letter and a second call. If we were invited for an interview we would both go along and talk about drama and movement therapy and how their clients would benefit from it. It felt rather hit and miss. Eventually we secured some work, first through London Borough Social Services and then with the NHS. We also contacted the ILEA Inspector for Drama and Special Needs who knew a lot about Laban movement work and came to see our work in a school. Her positive endorsement of Roundabout led to further work. In the work itself we adhered to the procedures we had learnt in training, planning our sessions carefully and writing reports. This gave the work a very clear structure, which we needed.

The most common problem we met in our work with adults with a learning disability was a lack of opportunity in people's lives for making disabilities choices. In order to address this we set about creating sessions that would introduce choice. Welcoming people at the start of a session, we would ask 'Do you want to shout? Would you like to whisper? Do you want to wave?' Our greeting, offering each person a choice between a shout, a whisper or a wave, was encouraging to people who were predominantly non-verbal, as they could opt to reply with a wave or a movement. For others it offered the possibility of a shout within the fixed boundaries of the session – enjoyable for anyone who might feel like shouting, but who was generally discouraged from doing so by everyday restrictions. When we first intro-duced this greeting it was received very enthusiastically. The reply would come back from the person addressed and then the whole group would count 'One, two, three and, all together, either shout, whisper or wave, Good afternoon, Anna!'

We would often sing well-known tunes with our own words – a practice that grew out of the work we did with Billy Lindkvist in her placement with people with autism (see Chapter 7). Again we developed this to introduce more choice, leading to a sense of independence. Working with people with complex needs, we would go through different parts of the body with appropriate actions, involving them in the choice of action. For example, to the tune of 'Row, row, row your boat' we would sing:

Stroke, stroke, stroke your leg
Gently as we go
Gently, gently, gently, gently,
Gently as we go.

Songs, as they became familiar, enabled everyone to participate in the session. We might also end with everyone singing a song, addressing each participant around the circle: 'Thank you, Frankie, thank you Frankie, we'll see you again next week!' All this becomes obvious once you think about it, but starting from the base-line of our training, addressing the need of every participant to feel included in the session, we had to think hard and find simple ways of achieving this.

Using rituals of this kind to contain the session, we went on to do all sorts of different things for the 'Main Event'. For example, we worked with movement, story, improvisation and musical instruments.

It was so exhilarating to hear the feedback we received from the centres. Often the staff were amazed by the way their clients reacted. Sometimes we would see members of staff looking in through windows, watching what was going on, surprised at what they saw, the way that people who were generally unable to participate in groups could be drawn in and involved by our way of working as trained therapists. The movement work we introduced created truly profound experiences for people in the group. What they shared in the sessions could be very exciting to watch, both when they were moving alone and when they interacted with other group members. It didn't surprise us so much, because we knew that the material we were bringing in was accessible to the students, but it never failed to move us when we saw their reaction to it.

Case Histories

In January 1986 we began to work with adults with complex needs, including visually and hearing impaired, learning disabilities and physical disabilities, at a large residential unit which is part of a hospital in Surrey. This was the first place where we worked one-to-one with clients, as on Billy Lindkvist's autistic placement on the Sesame training. Movement with Touch came into its own, alongside all we had learnt about the use of music and song and Laban techniques.

The Laban training helped us with the diagnostic part of the work: looking at people's movements very carefully and then, after a session, listing what we felt they did in Laban terms (see Laban 1980). What areas of movement did they participate in? What areas were missing? This would help us reflect on where the individual might be in psychological or emotive terms. Observation of individuals and allowing time and space for each person to develop trust and confidence was vital to the work. On our first day at the hospital unit, in one of the groups, there was a man who was hearing and visually impaired, who also had a learning disability, and was in a wheelchair and very strong: we were told that a lot of departments refused to work with him. Also there was a man who self-harmed and wore a protective helmet, who was very anxious about touch and would scream and hit his head on his chair or hard on the floor. There was also a woman with a history of being aggressive and violent. We were very overwhelmed and worked really hard to connect in a respective and appropriate way with this group. Perhaps we were being tested to see how we would react, whether we would just say 'We're not coming back' and walk out. However, we said that we were coming back and began to plan ways to develop our training to begin to address and meet these challenging needs.

We continued to work with the man in the protective helmet, but week after week we had the same experience with him. At first we left him to sit in his chair for his own safety. He would scream and move away whenever we went near him and self-abuse. This was very distressing and finally we decided that we would have to risk helping him out of his chair or stop working with him, as we both felt we needed to persist in making contact and work with his anxiety. In retrospect, the work we did with him in the chair, having him sit there and be part of the group, was important. He would never have allowed what happened subsequently without that time to get used to us while he was in the chair.

On the day that we took him out of the chair, we sat with him on one the floor mats. We sat around him and became the strength that supported him, helping him to move safely, which was something he hadn't experienced for many years. In the chair he had been restrained with a groin strap. We didn't want to make life more difficult for him by invading his personal space, but we both felt we needed to physically support him through an experience that might enrich the quality of his life.

We listened to his sounds, watching his movements and checking his facial expressions, so that we could respond to how he was feeling and reacting. We worked with him like this week after week, constantly moving him, making sounds, singing and holding him, letting him move off but being with him, staying behind him so that if he tried to self-harm we were there to hold him. It was frightening because he was very strong. It wasn't only a matter of empathizing: it was a very physical experience.

Gradually, he calmed down. After a while he was able to be on the floor without self-harming. Eventually he began to seek us out and move towards us, developing a trusting relationship. There came a time when he didn't need to wear his protective helmet at all. He was more confident and relaxed in the sessions, engaging in activities with little risk of self-harming. The drastic difference it made for him at home was that he no longer had to wear a protective helmet. Other day services started to offer him a service because he was approachable and more responsive to contact and his relationship with his carers really improved. Deborah still works with him and a while ago he gave her a first, truly spontaneous, hug – a celebration of relationship, five years after we began working with him.

An interesting fact about this piece of work is that it took place in the early days of Roundabout. We started the work equipped with our training and professional ability and combined this with our instincts and intuitive responses. The strength of the Sesame training lies in the fact that it equips you with resources to respond to whatever a client chooses to share with you – to 'meet them where they are at'.

At a well-known London psychiatric Hospital School, another of our long-term placements, we worked with a young girl who had been abused. During her sessions she always wanted to hide behind the imaginary furniture in the stories we enacted. She even hid in the oven in the story of the 'Gingerbread Man'. She found it difficult to sustain eye contact and could not concentrate on one thing for very long. We explored the Laban vocabulary with her, working through her light movements and taking her on to firmer movements. This seemed to bring her to a place that felt clearer emotionally and more grounded, from which she was able to progress.

With her light movements, it was like working with a butterfly. Every time one tried to focus her work, she used these movements to move away physically, to move crosswise, to cover up her vulnerability. Each time one faced her, she moved away. Then, as we worked with her, expanding her movement vocabulary, she started to communicate with us through her movements, achieving eye contact and beginning to join in. From that point we were able to develop and engage in other forms of work, but the starting point had been working with her movements, beginning with what she brought in, then gradually extending and developing it. This brought her to a place where others were able to work with her on her underlying issues and difficulties.

At this hospital there was also a boy who had been severely abused. He kept everything to himself, not letting any of it out to anyone. We decided to introduce work with the story of 'Tiddalik the Frog':

> In the dreamtime, Tiddalik gets thirsty and drinks up all the water in the world. The other creatures realise they must do something about it, so they go to the wise old wombat who tells them to try to make Tiddalik laugh. One by one they try and fail, until at last Nabunum the eel dances in front of him, twisting himself into funny shapes until Tiddalik's mouth opens and all the waters gush out, filling the rivers and streams again. (Gersie 1982)

The week after we told the story the boy came to the session with a scarf round his mouth, symbolizing holding it all in, because he knew that he was eventually going to have to tell, to let it all out. It was his way of saying 'I'm not going to do this, I'm holding on.' A process had begun in which he had identified with the story of Tiddalik. Later he took the scarf off, choosing to play the role of Tiddalik, which was unusual for him as he had never chosen a role before. After that session he worked for the rest of the week with the teaching staff at the hospital, drawing and writing out the story. This was the beginning of creative writing for him: he had refused to do any writing before that week. After Tiddalik he started writing other stories, his stories. He had found a place to be free to express himself. This then led him to talk about his life issues.

Stories are an important part of our work, particularly traditional stories and myths, which have a way of touching people in the depths of their being. The results of taking part in drama based on these stories can be moving and sometimes astonishing.

How Roundabout Developed

Having started off in the field of learning disabilities and complex needs we went on to work in a wide variety of settings, adapting our approach to accommodate different needs. At the same time as running our session we went on improving our charity and extending the search for work, following up any interest we encountered. We found ourselves increasingly in demand to a point where we were able to consider employing other therapists. At this time we were successful in a bid to London Boroughs Grants Scheme (LBGS) for the funding of two full-time posts and administrative support. We were approached by people who trained in the years after us, who wanted to come and work for Roundabout after they left the Sesame Course. We recognized that starting up, as we did, with no knowledge of how or where to ask for work, could be quite a struggle. At that time it seemed to take most people starting up alone at least a year before they could earn a reasonable salary. We felt that newly-trained therapists had a great deal to gain from being part of an established network with ongoing supervision and someone else to take responsibility for the business of finding work. It meant that they could concentrate entirely on developing their professional work, leaving the management and administration to us. Consequently Roundabout started to increase in size.

Where We Are Now

We now have eleven qualified and experienced therapists working with Roundabout who have trained in different dramatherapy establishments. We work over a wide area and range of settings: children with learning disabilities, autistic children, disturbed children, abused children, adults and children with physical disabilities, adults with learning disabiliities, complex needs, mental health problems, recovering alcoholics, mentally disordered offenders, adolescents and the elderly, in hospitals, day centres, schools and residential homes. Our work has developed as co-ordinators of a charity to include managerial responsibilities, supervision, funding and ongoing therapy work.

We remain personally involved in all the work we initiate, visiting placements on a supervisory basis. Our Management Committee meets a number of times through the year, receiving regular reports on all aspects of Roundabout. They bear legal responsibility for all of Roundabout's work and therefore need to be carefully and fully informed of what is happening.

Fund-raising is a very important part of our work. When we talk to people about what we do, they will often say 'It sounds wonderful, but we don't have the funds.' Now we have a Development Co-ordinator who is a great asset in helping to run the charity and is extremely competent in the intricate task of finding funding for the work. We have been very successful in raising money from London Boroughs, charities, trusts and fees.

We know there is a need for more dramatherapy provision. We continue to seek out funding to provide an expert professional service. Other therapists can benefit from our experience, while we benefit by learning from the other members of the team and being able to share our workload. As we celebrate our tenth year, we look forward to the future and the continuing development of Roundabout.

References

Laban, R. (1980) *The Mastery of Movement.* Fourth edition, revised by Lisa Ullman. London: Macdonald and Evans.

Gersie, A. (1982) 'In the Dreamtime Lived Tiddalik the Frog.' *Earthtales: Storytelling in Time of Change.* London: Green Print.

CHAPTER 30

Smoke and Mirrors

Priscilla Newman[1]

A full moon popped up behind the dense, towering mass of the rainforest, dimly lighting an endless sky that snuggled against distant misty mountains. The path led steeply upwards to the Mayan temple of Palenque and there, out of the silver-streaked blackness, the pyramid loomed. I was alone, only the sound of my footsteps, the sleepy rustle of jungle green and the smell of ochre earth to mingle this unfamiliar world with my inner being. I began to climb, easing my way up the side of the crenellated cocoon that protected the ancient burial chambers. The ascent was slow and perilous, but finally I reached the top with my legs shaking and breath coming in short gasps that echoed in the stillness. Mournfully beautiful carvings of serpents and contorted human bodies stood out against the white stone of the royal tomb. Here, primitive people had made sacrifices to Itzana, chief of the gods – a people obsessed by the passage of time, who believed their ancestors came from the depths of the earth and must return to her in proper style. The words of Fuentes (1986) ran through my mind: 'One does not explain Mexico, one believes in Mexico with a fury, a passion, and in alienation.'

As I stood there suspended between heaven and earth, an insubstantial speck in time, my sense of alienation was profound. I watched a distant plume of smoke curling into the pre-dawn sky: it could have been the dawn of time, but for that smoke, a symbol of civilization that plunders the rain forest for gain. How meaningless my life seemed.

---

1 Abridged from an essay written while training on the Sesame Course.

Faced with the paradox that makes human beings responsible for what we do while denying us full control of our lives, I felt I had no choice but to close my mind to betrayal, to loss, to an empty marriage, and struggle on. I looked down and the sense of alienation turned to anxiety. I could not return the way I had come: the steps were too narrow, the angle too steep, my balance too uncertain. The dark side of the pyramid offered the only means of descent with the branches and suckers of the rain forest providing a hand-hold. The ground below was hidden by thick undergrowth and looked dangerous. Clambering down through creepers, clutching at sticky, reptilian tendrils, I stumbled and slithered down into the darkness which closed around me like the forest itself. Suddenly I was nowhere. I had lost my sense of direction and was trapped in a prehistoric tangle with nothing but dense jungle surrounding me and no landmarks. The ground began to shudder and I heard movement in the undergrowth, coming closer. A Lacondones Indian appeared, wearing a loincloth and archaic Mayan sandals on his feet, carrying a leather water bag over one shoulder and a wooden spear. He stared down at me for several long seconds and then ran off, disappearing into the dark. I was very frightened, but I got up and followed the Indian. I found myself going deeper and deeper into the jungle until I tripped and fell sprawling across a large slab of stone. In the darkness I could just see the outline of an ancient temple, almost completely overgrown, and carved into the stone that had caused my fall, a hideous, daimonic mask. Everything I had always feared was actually happening to me: I was lost and alone in a dark, alien world, disorientated in space and time. As I lay face down, I began to scratch at the ground and rubbed the loosened earth into my face. And then a cry came from deep inside me that was not mine – a primordial cry of fear and despair. I was, truly, archaic man.

I knew nothing then of Jung, or his concept of a collective unconscious, or his theory that the psyche is self-regulating in its quest for wholeness. I had been drawn to Palenque by a longing for peace, driven by some inner compulsion to climb out of the darkness of my life into that dawn. And now my impulsiveness had landed me in a dangerous situation: I felt I was going mad with fear. Language makes what happened next incomprehensible. I had no rational thought process, no thoughts at all. I just surrendered physically and spiritually to the Earth. What I can only describe as a kaleidoscopic image filled my mind and, quite suddenly, I felt at peace. It was as though an elemental force, an umbilical cord, attached its dark powers to my soul and the rhythm of its life-force ebbed and flowed with my own. I began to laugh, to laugh at myself, at this situation, at this cruel, strange, beautiful, unpredictable world, at human life itself. I knew with all my being

ndividual existence is momentary, unimportant; that when we are dead,
re dead for a very, very long time; that life is as inevitable as death and
only meaning is whatever we bring to it. Abandoning any illusion that
I had control over my destiny, I rolled on to my back. Through a break in
the forest ceiling I saw the moon, my laughing reflection mirrored in her
round, full face, and a wispy trail of smoke. Then I knew the way to go.
Guided by the smoke and the mirror, I found my way back to safety. Both
ancient and modern symbols of change were essential: one, a reality of the
twentieth century that I cannot ignore simply because I don't like it; the
other, the archetypal symbol of myself, my womanhood. I needed my reason
and my intuition, a psychic balance of masculine and feminine principles,
for light to come out of darkness, a clear direction in which to go.

Laurens van der Post sums up the experience perfectly:

> In peace and war I have found that frequently, naked and unashamed,
> one has to go down into what one most fears and in that process, from
> somewhere beyond all conscious expectation, comes a saving flicker
> of light and energy that even if it does not produce the courage of a
> hero, at any rate enables a trembling mortal to take one step further.
> (van der Post 1962, p.171)

From my experience at Palenque and everything that followed, I have come
to believe that the unconscious forces of the psyche are always one step ahead
of the ego. Within weeks of returning from Mexico, I went into therapy and
began drama classes. Both allowed me to express myself in ways that would
harm no one close to me, at least until I could make informed choices and
value judgements from a position of psychological balance. My own pain
was proving to be my greatest asset in searching for the underlying causes
of an unhappiness that had for so long been diffuse, unfocused and frequently
projected onto problems which were merely a smokescreen behind which
deeper issues lurked. Very slowly a process was set in motion that will no
doubt continue for many years. I began to look at my fears, to come to terms
with the realities of my life and try to overcome the feelings of inadequacy
and frustration that had overwhelmed me for the fifteen years since my spinal
injury. A sense of renewed personal strength and a deep belief in the dignity
of human life, together with a growing self-confidence, prompted me to
think about ways of helping others confront their personal dilemmas.

Since drama and therapy were having a positive effect on my sense of
self, sense of worth, a therapeutic training that combined the two seemed
the way to go. My choice of Sesame was rather strange. I could have chosen
a course that would pander to my reductive, analytical, rather abstract mode

of thinking and verbal articulacy. But I was driven by instinct to Sesame with its experiential approach and emphasis on imaginative, non-verbal creative expression through movement as well as drama. Nothing could have been more challenging to the patterns of behaviour that I had developed. Words have been a lifelong hiding place, a defence against unwelcome feelings, a means of exercising control and warding off intimacy that may hurt me; movement is both physically and emotionally painful, forcing me to accept what I attempt to deny and confirming a distorted self-image. But in the rather convoluted way my psyche would appear to operate, I chose a training that would be most personally exposing. It was as though I needed the justification of helping others in order to have what, unconsciously, I wanted for myself: personal growth and the opportunity to find my authentic Self.

I do not know whether I fully understand the Jungian concepts on which the Sesame approach is based. I have no empirical proof that my experience at Palenque is evidence of the 'self-regulating' dynamics of the psyche, but my experience is that the psyche does function in this manner. Moreover, I believe that unconscious contents can be accessed and that the Sesame methodology stimulates the psyche and brings to consciousness those insights we need to make our lives more fulfilling. Since beginning the Sesame Course, many things have come to light that have helped me to experience myself, others and the world in general more creatively. Insight and awareness have given me greater personal choice and a greater sense of who I, a priori, am, in contrast to what I have become. The process has been slow and cumulative, occasionally cathartic, always shifting, often painful but always, ultimately, rewarding. This experience is what I now have to offer others who will have their own dilemmas to confront and who will act upon them in their own way.

In the early weeks of the Sesame training we explored Erikson's 'Eight Stages of Life' (1977). At the time I experienced little by way of releasing repressed or blocked feelings that would give any insight into my childhood and subsequent personality development. Later, an image of myself as a baby appeared out of nowhere in a Laban movement session. I was lying curled up on the floor and suddenly felt deeply sad. With the image and the sadness came a thought that there must have been a time when I was too young to feel 'inadequate' and too young to be punished. I thought of my own sons as babies and remembered how curious they were about themselves and how they would persevere with any new skill, falling down again and again when learning to walk, beginning again and again if a tower of bricks they were building fell down. If we didn't learn to walk when we were so young and had to wait until our twenties, I don't believe we would ever learn: the risks would seem too great. I have often felt that human beings are born too early (because our brains have grown so big that for a woman to give birth at all, we have to be) and that many of our dilemmas and inner conflicts are the result of the dependency on our mothers that this 'prematurity' makes inevitable. To survive, we learn to please those upon whom we depend, to develop attitudes and modes of behaviour that will please them and to control those that are unacceptable. We struggle, on the one hand for a sense of independence, on the other to belong and be acceptable.

When I first attempted to record my experience of drama sessions in a diary that would be assessed, I was thrown into confusion. What was expected of me? What was wanted? What were the rules? There must be a 'right' way if only I knew it, if only I could find the right formula and, by so doing, BE SOMEONE in the eyes of those who counted, the authority figures.

Jung describes the *persona* as a 'mask for the collective psyche' (Jung 1966) that feigns an individual identity. In other words, we try to pretend to ourselves and to others that we are individuals when in fact we are simply playing a part. Fundamentally, the *persona* is an inauthentic compromise between society's expectations of who or what we should be and our own expectations. At some point in childhood, probably when I went to school, I must have decided which role, or mask, fitted best with the social category that I identified with, and adapted my personality and behaviour to fit it. I believe I had several quite different masks: one that I wore for my parents; another, rather mischievous one (my favourite) for my brothers and sister; and a brightly coloured clown mask (that I hated) for school. As I grew older the selection increased: sportswoman, intellectual, flirt, virgin, tragedy queen, young bride, mother, martyr, victim... Always there would be a double illusion, the mask fitting the role and the role fitting the mask. That was the reality I expected people to communicate with. Eventually and inevitably I had an identity crisis: none of the masks fitted and I didn't recognize the person who stared back at me from the mirror. Two of the masks, wife and mother, had gone up in smoke anyway. All the time I had been hiding what was going on behind the multiple façades in my attempts to respond to what I perceived as the demands of the people upon whom I depended for any sense of value and worth.

I have found the Sesame approach to drama and movement a non-intrusive vehicle for slipping a variety of disguises on and off as well as looking at the attitudes that lay behind them. The liberating thing has been the acceptance of others and my freedom of choice. No one has grimaced with horror, roared with laughter or frozen with shock and it has become

increasingly possible to modify some of the masks, develop others and even
– deep breath – not wear one at all. The writing of diaries for the course has
helped me to reflect on these experiences. Over time, my fears, motives and
attitudes have filtered into consciousness and I have been able to look
through the smoke and directly at the mirror. I have seen my prejudices,
intolerance, arrogance, self-pity, manipulation, dishonesty, anger, cruelty, and
much more. I have also seen good things about myself and what I am innately
capable of being. By looking at what seems to be real I have discovered at
least part of what is unreal and hope, therefore, that I now have a less
distorted sense of reality. And while I must take the consequences of my
newly discovered freedom of choice not to conform, I no longer feel trapped
by the conventions and restraints of my upbringing. And I am human: in
recognizing a mask for what it is, I find a human being who is just as good,
just as bad, just as special and just as ordinary as all the other billions of
people on this planet.

I found it difficult to get in touch with my feelings in the early part of
the course. When I did succeed in unlocking my head, unresolved emotional
problems were revealed. The non-verbal emphasis of Sesame facilitated this,
as did the spontaneity required in improvisation, whether in drama, movement or enactment of myths, which goes to show that Jung was probably
right when he said that 'The growth of personality comes out of the
unconscious' (Jung 1969, p.390). Being able to identify one's personality
'type' opens up the possibility of enlarging that personality to fill the gaps.
The value of the Sesame approach is that it gives each individual the
opportunity to express feelings, thoughts, perceptions and intuitions according to his/her own intrinsic nature without the risk of 'getting it wrong' and
being 'punished'. With fifteen people on the course, we have worked closely
together and had to communicate and negotiate with a wide variety of
personality types. As the year has progressed, the nature and material of the
course have taught me to recognize the wealth of creative ideas that free
expression releases. Seeing the various ways in which people have responded
to any given material or circumstance has enlarged my own potential for a
variety of responses. I now try to see what other people see as well as what
I see because, clearly, none of us has a monopoly on reality. It is so easy and
so tempting to make generalizations about other people's motives and
intentions but, as Jung maintained, if a characteristic quality is observable in
a person, then somewhere in him/her you can be sure that the opposite is
also true. This has been my experience of myself, but as soon as it is
observable in the group I find myself in a hall of mirrors.

Jill is a distorting mirror to herself.

Jill has to distort herself to appear undistorted to herself.

To undistort herself, she finds Jack to distort her distorting image in his distorting mirror.

She hopes that his distortion of her may undistort her image without her having to distort herself. (Laing 1972, p.31)

Perhaps the greatest gift of Jung's philosophy is that it opens up the possibility for each of us to find our own path. Ultimately, although we do not live in isolation, we can never overcome our personal shortcomings by looking for substitutes outside ourselves. This would seem to be the central concept of Jung's philosophy: he called the process of self-knowledge and personal growth 'Individuation'. He conceived of the unconscious dynamics at work in the psyche as a growth process whose implicit goal is the union of opposites and the propagation of the 'whole' self. Which brings me back, full circle, to Palenque.

My experience at Palenque was a Gothic terror in which my emotions were opened directly to Nature with its ghostly flood of archaic night. The genie slunk out of the bottle and I couldn't put it back. No rational thinking could have argued away Nature's power. I was subordinate to it, essentially passive. Things happen in the course of our lives in complex patterns of apparent coincidences that Jung called 'synchronicity' and my experience forces me to subscribe to his theory. In the broad light of day, my experience could easily have been dismissed as an hysterical reaction to an over-active imagination. I tried to tell myself this and even found my way back to the hidden remains of the temple the following day with some friends. But attempting an explanation is not the same as understanding: one cannot reason one's way to knowledge and it doesn't diminish the experience. What matters is not why I had the experience, but what it revealed to me and where it led me.

The last three years, and particularly the months since starting the Sesame course, have been a time of unlearning. Subjective processes and 'objective' relationships have muddled along together, accumulating and consolidating an awareness of myself and 'other than self'. Individuation is not individualism, in fact it is the opposite of any 'cult of the individual'. It is an ongoing process of striving to see things in the light of the 'given' factors of our personalities, those present at birth, as well as the qualities of personality we acquire during our lifetime. Individuation is concerned with connecting us to our environment, not severing us from it, and with trying to live in an active relationship with our unconscious, aware of the opposing forces at work in the psyche.

I believe that life's journey meanders between good intentions, the hope of redemption, the ideals of Rousseau and the blatant cruelty of de Sade. Life is a paradox. The psyche is a paradox. The biologists speak of our 'reptilian brain', the most inaccessible, most mysterious layer of our psyche that holds the images, the base emotions, the killer-survivor instincts of our archaic ancestry. Every now and then, like smouldering embers, they burst into flames, but our potential for evil is a gift as well as a burden. We can honour Nature: we can also refuse to yield to her.

Much of life is governed by the illogical, the arbitrary, and it is the non-rational that often seems to motivate behaviour – even though it may hide behind a rational mask. No doubt every thought would reveal a secret meaning, but to attend to each and every one would leave us paralysed and exhausted. Nevertheless, I shall strive to look through the smoke and at the mirror of my neuroses, complexes, masks, repressions, projections and imagination. I am convinced that they are signposts that point the direction to change, to greater happiness and to fulfilment.

References

Erikson, E. (1977) *Childhood and Society.* London: Paladin.

Fuentes, C. (1986) *Where the Air is Clear.* London: Deutsch.

Jung, C.G. (1966) 'Two essays in analytical psychology.' *Collected Works 7.* London: Routledge.

Jung, C.G. (1969) 'Psychology and religion: west and east.' *Collected Works 11.* London: Routledge.

Laing, R.D. (1972) *Knots.* London: Penguin.

van der Post, L. (1962) *The Lost World of the Kalahari.* London: Penguin.

The Contributors

'Alan' is not the real name of the man in a Regional Secure Unit who wrote about his experiences of Sesame session work while he was there. His name has been changed, as have the names of clients described in the sessions, but we do acknowledge and thank him for his very perceptive contribution.

Frankie Armstrong is a singer and voice teacher whose singing was influenced by A.L.Lloyd and the Scottish ballad singers before she evolved a style all her own. Her famous Voice Workshops developed from studying and experimenting with the open-throated style of singing used in the songs and work chants of cultures that still sing as naturally as they speak. Her skill in helping people to find and enjoy their singing voices leans partly on her experience of over 20 years as a social worker and group work trainer. Frankie's voice work is a strong influence in the Sesame training, both through tutors who have worked with her and through her annual visits to work with the student group.

Merle Baars is a Sesame drama and movement therapist and a clinical placement tutor on the Sesame Course. She does regular work in mental health, and with physically disabled people, and has worked for many years with the elderly.

Lynn Cedar was the co-founder, with Deborah Haythorne, of Roundabout – a charitable trust established in 1985 to promote drama and movement therapy which also functions as a group practice for the two partners and nine other dramatherapists. Before training on the Sesame Course in 1984–85, she studied mime, dancing and acting and supervised a dramatherapy project run by the Manpower Services Commission. She has worked with drama and movement therapy in a very wide range of settings.

'Colin' is not the real name of the man in the annexe of Wormwood Scrubs who talked about his experiences of Sesame while he was there. His name has been changed, as have the names of clients in session work, but we do acknowledge and thank him for his very perceptive contribution.

Di Cooper is a former Sesame Course Leader at the Central School of Speech and Drama where she was movement co-ordinator and a full-time movement tutor. She trained at Chelsea College of Physical Education, the Laban Art of Movement Studios and The Central School of Speech and Drama. Her varied work experience in education and therapy spans 30 years as a performer, director, teacher and facilitator both in the USA and the United Kingdom. Most recently she has been working with teachers and therapists in India as a guest of the British Council and the Spastics Society and is an advisor to a newly-established Creative Movement Education Diploma course in Madras. As co-director of the Sesame Institute, she continues to promote the use of Creative Movement and Drama for Mental Health by giving workshops and classes nationally and internationally.

Chris Daniel works as a drama and play therapist in Warrington, Cheshire. After the Sesame training she worked in a wide variety of client groups and trained as a play therapist at Roehampton. Her current work is as a drama and play therapist in child and adolescent psychiatry. She also lectures at the Roehampton Play Therapy Course in London and is working at establishing a new course in the North West. Her piece about work with the elderly was written with Alison Kelly immediately after training on the Sesame Course.

Kharis Dekker is a Sesame drama and movement therapist and recently retired Tutor in Clinical Practice on the Sesame Course. Her knowledge of, and insight into, the work of C.G.Jung has been a major influence on the development of the course. Her practice took her into a variety of clinical settings, including a Psychiatric Day Centre where she did session work for many years.

Morag Deane is a Gaelic-speaking Scot and a violinist from the West Highlands who found her way to Sesame through music and a wish to work with music in a therapeutic way. She studied music for a degree at Edinburgh University and did research in early music, for which she was awarded a fellowship by Trinity College, London. Before and after Sesame training (1980–81), Morag worked in a centre for adults and adolescents with severe learning disabilities. After training she introduced Sesame in a school for children with learning disabilities and worked in a psychiatric hospital, at the same time studying for a second degree in Psychology and Anthropology in order to understand more deeply certain aspects of Sesame. Recently she has been training in chiropractic.

Elizabeth Gall is a Sesame drama and movement therapist. Before Sesame she studied Humanities at the Polytechnic of Wales and did care work with people with learning disabilities. After training she worked in London for a year in a variety of settings – including sexually abused young women, school non-attenders and disturbed children – before taking a full-time post with Gwynedd Social Services working with people with learning disabilities.

Barbara Goossens is a Sesame drama and movement therapist who trained as an actor at East 15 and works on the staff of a psychiatric clinic in Zurich. Immediately after training with Sesame she joined a group of volunteers to work with severely deprived and disabled children in Romania, work in which she was supervised by Marian Lindkvist. Since returning to her home city of Zurich and taking up her work in the psychiatric clinic, she has proceeded to further training for an M.A. in expressive arts therapy.

Deborah Haythorne was the co-founder, with Lynn Cedar, of Roundabout. Before training on the Sesame Course in 1984–85, she worked as a volunteer for children with physical disabilities and learning disabilities, the elderly and the long-term unemployed and took an honours degree in English and Drama at the University of East Anglia. She has worked with drama and movement therapy in a very wide range of settings.

Jocelyne James is an Integrative Arts Psychotherapist (The United Kingdom Conference for Pschotherapy Registered) and Sesame drama and movement therapist. She has worked within the National Health Service, Social Services and the private sector with a diverse range of clients, both adults and children, individually and in groups. She is the current Course Leader of the Sesame Course at the Central School of Speech and Drama and played a key part in achieving its validation as a Postgraduate Diploma Course by the Open University. She is also a tutor at the Institute for Arts in Therapy and Education and works in private practice as a therapist and supervisor inspired by, and committed to, the therapeutic application of the arts.

Alison Kelly is a Sesame drama and movement therapist and recently Tutor in Myth on the Sesame Course. She is facilitator of drama on the Champernown Trust's 'Creative Arts' week at Cumberland Lodge. Her clinical work has been in a wide variety of settings, predominantly with children, and she is a supervisor for the British Association for Dramatherapy.

Marian Lindkvist, the founder of Sesame and originator of the way of working she has called 'Movement with Touch', has an honorary place in this list of authors because her name appears so often in the book. She is at work on another book about the origins and early history of Sesame and her own clinical research – both in the United Kingdom and on a series of working visits to South Africa. Her work as a dramatherapist has been across a wide range of settings and she is a Registered Dramatherapist in the United States where she has worked and lectured extensively.

Mitch Mitchelson is a freelance performer, director, drama teacher, Sesame drama and movement therapist, and a regular tutor and director at Rose Bruford Drama College. He is a practising clown, juggler and unicyclist as well as teaching these skills in community theatre. With Jean Hart he wrote the play *The Lazarus Stone* and is director of the Original Mixture Theatre Company.

Priscilla Newman is a Sesame drama and movement therapist working with emotionally and behaviourally disturbed children and adolescents, and with adults in a variety of mental health settings. She is a clinical placement tutor on the Sesame Course, a supervisor, and Chair of the Sesame Institute.

Jenny Pearson is a Psychodynamic Counsellor (Institute of Psychotherapy and Counselling) in private practice and a Sesame drama and movement therapist – mainly with disturbed children. She is a tutor on the Sesame Course, teaching Human Development, and is also a traditional story-teller and writer of books. Her first profession was as a journalist with *The Times*. Her books include *Adventure Playgrounds*, co-written with Jack Lambert and published by Cape and Penguin in 1974. She is a member of the Bleddfa Trust and is actively involved in arts-based events at their Barn Centre in mid-Wales.

James Roose-Evans is a theatre director, author, priest, teacher and founding director of the Bleddfa Trust in Wales. He began working with Ritual at the Julliard School of Music in New York over 40 years ago when he taught an experimental class seeking the roots of drama in the personal. His theatrical successes include the award winning *84 Charing Cross Road* and Hugh Whitmore's *Best of Friends*. He has written about Ritual in two books: *Inner Journey, Outer Journey* (Rider 1987) and *Passages of the Soul: Ritual Today* (Element 1994). He is a Vice-President of the Sesame Institute.

Mary Smail is a Sesame drama and movement therapist with experience of many settings – including long-term work with the elderly, disturbed children and assertion training with adults. Her speciality is working with voice – having sung, played guitar and recorded cassettes before training with Sesame. She is Tutor in Clinical Practice and a clinical placement supervisor on the Sesame Course and, with Di Cooper, co-director of the Sesame Institute.

Bernie Spivack is a Sesame drama and movement therapist with a theatre background. She went to the Stage School Italia Conti as a child and was there for eight years before working, briefly, in the theatre. Later work, prior to Sesame training, included being a trainee Social Worker for the Jewish Welfare Board and Assistant Voluntary Services Co-ordinator at Tooting Bec Psychiatric Hospital. She has done clinical work in a variety of settings – specializing in mental health – and was a clinical placement tutor on the Sesame Course for many years. For eight years she worked as a drama and movement therapist at Wormwood Scrubs doing regular sessions in the therapeutic annexe and directing the annual play with a cast consisting of prisoners serving life sentences.

Anthony Stevens is a distinguished Jungian analyst, psychiatrist and writer on psychology. He graduated from Oxford and in addition to a doctorate in medicine he has two degrees in psychology. He taught psychopathology on the Sesame course in its early days. His books include *Archetype: A Natural History of the Self* (1982), *The Roots of War* (1989), *On Jung* (1990), *The Two Million-Year-Old Self* (1993) and *Private Myths, Dreams and Dreaming* (1995).

Graham Suter is a professional actor who played a key role in the experimental work which preceded the foundation of Sesame. He directed training sessions and short courses around the country and drew up the basic programme for the first full-time Sesame training with the founder, Marian Lindkvist. He was the first Course Tutor when the full-time Sesame Course was established in 1976, a post he held until 1986.

Jo Syz is a Sesame drama and movement therapist, story-teller and writer who trained on the Sesame Course 1994–95. He has a keen interest in Celtic mythology, traditional stories and ritual within society. Before training, he worked in Theatre in Education, Greenpeace and the Wilderness Society in Australia.

Sam Thornton is a life-long teacher of Laban Art of Movement. Director of the Laban International Summer School, attended by around a hundred people each summer. He trained at the Laban Art of Movement Studios in London, where he was senior lecturer under Lisa Ulmann, he is the author of *A Movement Perspective of Rudolf Laban* (1971), London, Macdonald and Evans. Teaches on Sesame Short courses.

Susi Thornton is a life-long teacher of Laban Art of Movement and Laban tutor on the full time Sesame Course for many years. She is Assistant Director of the Laban International Summer School. She trained at the Laban Art of Movement Studio at Addlestone and took further training in action profiling. She is also a humanistic creative arts therapist in private practice, a counsellor and a trainer of counsellors.

Molly Tuby is a Jungian analyst and studied at the Jung Institute in Zurich when Jung was alive there. She finished her training with Gerhardt Adler and became an individual member of the International Association for Analytical Psychology. She is a founder member of the Independent Group of Analytical Psychologists in London, a past Chairman of the C.G.Jung Analytical Psychology Club – editing their journal *Harvest* for nine years – and a Fellow and past Chairman of the Guild of Pastoral Psychology. She played an active part in setting up the Sesame Training, teaching on the course and creating a Jungian therapeutic group for the students in its early days.

Pat Watts, a psychotherapist and dramatherapist, worked for many years on the Sesame Course at the Central School of Speech and Drama and led the course for four years. She has worked with experimental drama and taught drama in schools – combining these skills with her Jungian understanding of the therapeutic process in her pioneering myth workshops, some of which she ran with Frankie Armstrong. Also, for many years she contributed to 'enactment' weekends, mainly of Shakespeare's plays, at Hawkwood College, Stroud, Gloucestershire, in partnership with David Holt – a Jungian psychologist. She has regularly led the drama sessions on the 'Creative Arts' week at Cumberland Lodge.

Rodger Winn is a Sesame drama and movement therapist with experience in a wide range of settings and a special interest in mental health and learning disabilities. He worked for four years in a Regional Secure Unit doing drama therapy with offenders with mental health problems. He is a member of the Sesame team working with disturbed children at Beech Lodge and is a clinical placement supervisor on the Sesame Course.

Subject Index

Author Index